Open Access: Key Strategic, Technical and Economic Aspects

CHANDOS
INFORMATION PROFESSIONAL SERIES

Series Editor: Ruth Rikowski
(email: Rikowskigr@aol.com)

Chandos' new series of books are aimed at the busy information professional. They have been specially commissioned to provide the reader with an authoritative view of current thinking. They are designed to provide easy-to-read and (most importantly) practical coverage of topics that are of interest to librarians and other information professionals. If you would like a full listing of current and forthcoming titles, please visit our web site **www.chandospublishing.com** or contact Hannah Grace-Williams on email info@chandospublishing.com or telephone number +44 (0) 1865 884447.

New authors: we are always pleased to receive ideas for new titles; if you would like to write a book for Chandos, please contact Dr Glyn Jones on email gjones@chandospublishing.com or telephone number +44 (0) 1865 884447.

Bulk orders: some organisations buy a number of copies of our books. If you are interested in doing this, we would be pleased to discuss a discount. Please contact Hannah Grace-Williams on email info@chandospublishing.com or telephone number +44 (0) 1865 884447.

Open Access:
Key Strategic, Technical and Economic Aspects

EDITED BY
NEIL JACOBS

Chandos Publishing

Oxford · England

Chandos Publishing (Oxford) Limited
Chandos House
5 & 6 Steadys Lane
Stanton Harcourt
Oxford OX29 5RL
UK
Tel: +44 (0) 1865 884447 Fax: +44 (0) 1865 884448
Email: info@chandospublishing.com
www.chandospublishing.com

First published in Great Britain in 2006

ISBN:
1 84334 203 0 (paperback)
1 84334 204 9 (hardback)
978 1 84334 203 8 (paperback)
978 1 84334 204 5 (hardback)

Typeset by Domex e-Data Pvt. Ltd.
Printed in the UK and USA.

Contents

List of figures

List of tables

Foreword

The era of open access is dawning and it could not come a moment too soon. The rapid development of the Internet and its increased use across the globe has meant that there is a wide and growing audience that is hungry and in some cases, desperately in need of information that traditionally few have been able to access.

The idea of open access is highly controversial and divisive. If one were to politely mumble the phrase at a dull gathering of academics, publishers and policy makers, one would be sure to instantly divide the room and instigate a heated debate. This book is therefore an important introduction for those who know nothing of a debate that has been raging in academic circles for a long time. And for those with seemingly entrenched positions, this book will most certainly change some minds.

In science, my own area of expertise, the issue of open access has been making troublesome waves in the last few years. The 2004 House of Commons Science and Technology Committee inquiry 'Scientific Publications: free for all?' which I chaired, looked into a number of issues, such as whether the market for scientific publications was working well, the trends in journal pricing, the impact of new publishing trends on the scientific process, the integrity of journals and so on. What we found was not pleasant.

The commercial publishing world has an increasingly harmful monopoly on a number of prestige journals which are essential to disseminating new ideas and research. This monopoly over knowledge has been one factor underlying an increase in the price of subscriptions, leaving some academic libraries with no choice but to cancel subscriptions as they can no longer afford to pay for a full range of journals.

I believe the current situation is highly unethical. As vast amounts of public money is used to fund research, it should follow that such research should be freely available to the public to boost their knowledge and appreciation of science, instead of increasing the profit margins of a few publishing houses. One would therefore be hard pressed to deny the ethical case for open access. Indeed one only has to think of the need to make new research readily available to developing countries which do not have the resources to purchase such information and yet face some of the world's most devastating problems.

However, better ethical conduct is only one of the many objectives of the open access project as this excellent collection of essays will show. I do not deny that there are legitimate fears about the implications of open access. It is one thing to make information readily available for the public, who through taxation fund such research, and developing countries that need access to life-saving ideas; but it is quite another matter to make knowledge available for those who will free-ride their way through improved access to profit themselves. But these are problems I believe can be overcome with a bit of creativity as some of the authors in this collection show. Turn the page and start reading.

Ian Gibson MP

About the contributors

Chris Awre is Integration Architect within the e-Services Integration Group at the University of Hull, with a remit to examine, advise on and facilitate the integration of existing and future university systems and processes, including the University's institutional repository.

Charles W. Bailey, Jr. is the Assistant Dean for Digital Library Planning and Development at the University of Houston Libraries. He has been publishing scholarly electronic information on the Internet since 1989, including e-books, e-journals, and weblogs. He is the author of *The Open Access Bibliography: Liberating Scholarly Literature with E-Prints and Open Access Journals* and *The Scholarly Electronic Publishing Bibliography*.

Tim Brody is a PhD candidate in the Intelligence, Agents, Multimedia group at the University of Southampton, UK. His PhD research is on evaluating research impact through open access to scholarly communication. He has produced a citation service for arXiv (a repository of physics and maths papers), Citebase Search, and has also developed the Registry of Open Access Repositories.

Leslie Carr is Senior Lecturer in Distributed Information Systems at the University of Southampton, UK. He is technical director of the Eprints software platform and manages the *eprints.ecs.soton.ac.uk* repository. He also runs a number of JISC projects that are investigating practical repository approaches to preservation, scientific data handling, research assessment and impact measurement.

Matthew Cockerill is Publisher at BioMed Central, which he co-founded with Vitek Tracz in late 1999. Prior to BioMed Central, he helped to develop BioMedNet, a pioneering website for biologists and medical researchers. Before that he was a molecular biologist, obtaining his PhD under the guidance of Tim Hunt at the Imperial Cancer Research Fund.

Frederick Friend worked in several UK university libraries before being appointed Librarian of the University of Essex and then Librarian of University College London. He now works for JISC as Scholarly Communication Consultant as well as holding the position of Honorary Director Scholarly Communication at UCL.

Jean-Claude Guédon is Professor of Comparative Literature at the University of Montreal, member of the Sub-Board (Information Programme) of the Open Society Institute, and Vice-President (research dissemination) of the Canadian Federation of the Humanities and Social Sciences.

Stevan Harnad is Canada Research Chair in Cognitive Science at Université du Québec à Montréal and Professor in Electronics and Computer Science at Southampton University, UK. He is Founder and Editor of *Behavioral and Brain Sciences*, *Psycoloquy*, and the CogPrints Electronic Preprint Archive in the Cognitive Sciences.

Robert Kiley is Head of E-strategy at the Wellcome Library. In this role he is responsible for developing and implementing a strategy to deliver electronic services to the Library's users – both in person and remote – and is currently taking a leading role in the implementation of the Trust's open access policy.

Michael Kurtz is an Astronomer and Computer Scientist at the Harvard-Smithsonian Center for Astrophysics in Cambridge, Massachusetts. He has authored papers on subjects ranging from cosmology to data and information science. In 1988 he conceived what has now become the NASA Astrophysics Data System, the core of the digital library in astronomy.

Clifford Lynch has been the Director of the Coalition for Networked Information since July 1997. Previously he spent 18 years at the University of California Office of the President, the last ten as Director of Library Automation.

Andrew Odlyzko is the ADC Professor and Director of the interdisciplinary Digital Technology Center at the University of Minnesota. He has written on a variety of subject, from pure mathematics to economics of e-commerce.

Ramesh Parmar is a Consulting Paediatric Cardiologist with special interest in interventional paediatric cardiology. He has a special interest in the use of information technology in the biomedical publishing. As an independent consultant he has helped manage many journals.

D. K. Sahu is a Consultant Paediatrician. He is currently working as the Editor of the *Indian Journal of Medical Sciences*, Executive Editor of *Neurology India* and Managing Editor of the *Journal of Postgraduate Medicine*. He is on the editorial boards of several other professional journals. He is the CEO of Medknow Publications, which has pioneered in 'fee-less-immediate-free' model of scholarly publishing and helped several journals from the developing world to improve the visibility and the impact.

Arthur Sale is Professor of Computing (Research) at the University of Tasmania. Previously he held positions as Pro Vice-Chancellor and National Vice-President of the Australian Computer Society. He was awarded the ANCCAC Medal in 2001 for best research article in Australia, and a Lifetime Achievement Award at the 2004 Tasmanian ICT Industry Awards.

Nigel Shadbolt is Professor of Artificial Intelligence in the School of Electronics and Computer Science at the University of Southampton. He is the Director of the EPSRC Interdisciplinary Research Collaboration in Advanced Knowledge Technologies and is a Fellow and the Deputy President of the British Computer Society.

John Shipp is currently Librarian at the University of Sydney. He is also Project Director of the Australian Research Information Infrastructure Committee.

Colin Steele is Emeritus Fellow at The Australian National University. He was University Librarian at ANU (1980–2002) and Director Scholarly Information Strategies (2002–2003). He has been an invited keynote speaker at library and information conferences on scholarly communication and open access and has published/edited seven books, and over 300 articles and reviews.

Peter Suber is the Open Access Project Director at Public Knowledge, Senior Researcher at SPARC, and Research Professor of Philosophy at Earlham College.

Alma Swan was a Research Biologist who moved into science publishing and is now a Consultant with Key Perspectives Ltd, a company that carries out market research and business development consultancy work in the field of scholarly communications.

Robert Terry works as a Senior Policy Adviser for the Wellcome Trust, where he has drafted policies on a number of areas including intellectual property, good research practice, access to bioinformatic resources, and open access initiatives. He was previously the Head of International Exchanges at the Royal Society.

Leo Waaijers studied mathematics and theoretical physics at Leiden University. He had an almost lifelong career at the Delft University of Technology, consecutively as Researcher and Teacher, Faculty Manager, Member of the Executive University Board and finally as the University Librarian. In 2001 he accepted a post as University Librarian at Wageningen University and Research Centre and in 2003 he joined SURF, the national ICT-partnership organisation for higher education and research, as the manager of the SURF Platform ICT and Research, which oversees the DARE Programme.

Mary Waltham has been a publishing consultant since 1999 when she resigned as President and Publisher of *Nature* and the *Nature* family of journals in New York. She was previously Managing Director and Publisher of *The Lancet* in London and has worked at a senior level in science and medical publishing companies across a range of media, which include textbooks, magazines, newsletters, journals, and open learning materials.

The contributors may be contacted care of the Editor:

E-mail: *n.jacobs@jisc.ac.uk*

A note to readers

A list of Web-based items – both sites and resources – has been included at the back of this book. The list contains items mentioned in the text, which although not appropriate for inclusion in the bibliography, are still of potential interest to the reader. Resources of particular note have also been highlighted in the text.

Part 1
Open access – history, definitions and rationale

What is open access? Where did it come from? What are the arguments in favour of it? Why does it provoke controversy? In the following six chapters, these questions are explored by some of the most erudite and accomplished thinkers in this area. Open access is contextualised (by Alma Swan) and defined (by Charles W. Bailey, Jr). Its history so far, and likely future, is charted (by Jean-Claude Guédon). The economic and research benefits of it are presented (by Andrew Odlyzko, and Michael Kurtz and Tim Brody respectively), and its technology is outlined (by Chris Awre). These chapters form the foundation of the book.

In Chapter 1, Alma Swan describes open access as emerging from a long history of scholarly communication, which has always been closely tied to changes in technology and economics. She describes how journal articles, books and monographs, and data have all been implicated in recent changes, but it is perhaps the recent developments in the dissemination of journal articles that have most exercised the minds of researchers, librarians, publishers and funders.

In Chapter 2, Charles Bailey follows Alma Swan's introduction of open access as a response to an increasingly strained system of scholarly communication, by guiding us through the maze of definitions and declarations, and describes in detail the two principal approaches to open access, coloured green and gold.

Having armed us with definitions of open access and a clear understanding of the green and gold paths, the next chapter traces a history of the open access movement, and predicts a future. Jean-Claude Guédon shows how early concerns over the strained system of scholarly communication have led to the spawning of a movement for change. Like any system change, this one faces an 'energy barrier' in order to get from where we are now, to a much better future.

Throughout the first three chapters of this book, there have been two strands of argument underpinning the rationale for open access. One of these strands is that open access is good for researchers because it improves what they can access (and therefore the research that they can do), and means that more researchers can access their work (and therefore build on it and cite it). Evidence to support this strand of argument is presented in Chapter 3 by Michael Kurtz and Tim Brody.

Chapter 4, by Andrew Odlyzko, addresses the second strand of argument, that open access has the potential to release considerable economic benefits for the research and education sector. Addressing the 'serials crisis' is only one part of this case (albeit an important one); it turns out that a subscription-based system imposes a wide range of costs on research and education.

If Chapter 4 has shown that the economic case for open access is clear, and should appeal to all those (including the general public) who fund any aspect of research or scholarly communication, then the following chapter demonstrates that researchers themselves have much to gain from open access. Both Alma Swan and Jean-Claude Guédon have noted that researchers publish in order to have their work read and built on by others, and thereby achieve recognition for their efforts. This recognition is often in the form of citations to their published papers. Citation counting (in various forms) plays a large part in the assessment of research, which in turn plays a large part in researchers' careers, their success when applying for research grants, and so on. Chapter 5, by Michael Kurtz and Tim Brody, is perhaps the closest to a research paper in this book. It lays out clearly the sometimes complex evidence and argument which shows that researchers stand to gain a considerable amount by making their research papers open access (for more on this, see Hitchcock, 2005).

With open access defined and its rationale established, the question is then how to do it. As ever, the technology is not the point, although it does continue to play a crucial enabling role for the open access movement. Without the Internet, there would be no open access movement. In Chapter 6, Chris Awre outlines the technology of open access, centred undoubtedly on the OAI-PMH, but with a varied and promising hinterland.

Overview of scholarly communication

Alma Swan

It is almost 350 years since the first scholarly journals entered publication, the year 1665 being a propitious one in this respect with both the *Journal de Sçavans* and *Philosophical Transactions of the Royal Society (of London)* launching within a few weeks of one another. The use of the printed word became thereafter the primary, formal, means by which scholars have communicated the results of their work. It became the means, also, by which scholars established their right to the intellectual property reported in their articles, by which they claimed to be the first to conduct such work and present its findings, and by which some system of quality control was imposed upon the reporting of the results of scholarly endeavours through peer review of articles before their acceptance for publication.

A driver for change: digital technology

And so things continued, almost without change, until well into the twentieth century when new developments in the field of electronics first placed computing power at the fingertips of scientists. Initially, this was limited to standalone computers but networking brought a profound change and opened up an unlimited array of possibilities. By the 1970s, computer scientists at Bell Laboratories were filing their results on electronic archives that could be accessed by their colleagues using FTP protocols. At this point the stage was set for the most significant revolution in human communication since the development of language itself. Gutenberg's printing press, developed in the mid-fifteenth century, had opened the door to mass communication of a sort, but the printed word as a communication mechanism has always been limited in practice, if not in theoretical terms, by economics and the logistics of distribution. Now it became possible for scientists to communicate by permitting access to their own files from remote computers and by accessing those of others in turn. The age of digital communication was born and, necessarily, the rest of this chapter focuses largely upon scholarly communication in the digital age.

The advent of the World Wide Web in the late 1980s supplied the most recent major advance in technological capabilities and a set of protocols for computer-to-computer communication. The development of graphical web browsers in the early-to-mid 1990s brought the Internet out of the computer-science closet and onto the streets. Anyone with a computer and an online link could communicate with anyone else with a computer. A new communication age was born.

Now, bound only by the technological limits of bandwidth and computer power, scholars, wherever they may be in the world, have ways of communicating that mean that scholarship as a whole can progress in different forms, forms that we are starting to see take shape. No longer constrained to the letter, the monograph, the journal article or the telephone, scholars can send a one-line e-mail message or transmit a terabyte of data *within seconds* to another scholar on the other side of the globe. Their communication methods, moreover, are becoming more diverse in form, with systematic, formal mechanisms such as the journal article or the academic monograph being supplemented and complemented by new, informal, self-regulated or community-regulated methods such as online discussion groups, weblogs, webcasts, wikis and podcasts, of which more later. Indeed, the Web now really does seem to be facilitating what Tim Berners-Lee, its founder, originally envisaged as its functions – the real-time (or near-to) collaborative interaction of peer-group scholars and the use of hypertext linking systems to minimise data loss or decay (Berners-Lee, 1989).

There is the implication of informality in that concept and indeed informality in scholarly communication is on the rise, with huge potential repercussions for the progress of scholarship and for the scholarly publishing industry as a by-product. That is something to watch for the future. For now, though, the tried-and-tested 'traditional' methods of communication between scholars predominate.

Journals, books and monographs

The most formal and systematic subset within the array of scholarly communication mechanisms encompasses the peer-reviewed journals and conference proceedings, the contents of which form the official information of record in most disciplines. Until the 1990s scholarly journals were published almost exclusively in printed form. Pioneering journals appeared in electronic form as a supplement to the hardcopy form through the 1990s and, as resistance to electronic publishing dissipated, electronic-only journals were launched. Initially, the resistance – or perhaps informed wariness is a better expression – was based upon concerns both of librarians, who questioned whether these digital publications would be permanently and accessibly archived, and of the research community which debated whether electronic-only journals represented legitimate avenues for publication and whether they would be taken into account in career and tenure decisions.

The lure of electronic journals was strong, though, and their successful adoption was user-driven. They provide inestimable advantages in being accessible from a computer at any time of day or night, in a convenient way, saving busy scholars the time and effort spent physically visiting the library. What is more, they include additional functionality that is now considered essential to scholars' workflow – links from references to the original article, links from the text to supporting data or additional graphics, and powerful searchability.

The concerns about electronic journals waned as the light of the advantages to the user of digital publishing grew and, although in some disciplines print-only journals still persist, in most areas – and certainly throughout the sciences – digital publishing dominates. Even in the arts and humanities, the disciplines that have moved most slowly towards electronic journals, there are now large numbers of digital titles. Project Muse, for example, covers some 250 journals from around 40 different publishers. This is not to say the print format is dead: many librarians consider it is important to hold a print subscription alongside the electronic one for archival reasons.

Following on the heels of journals into the digital age came books and monographs, which remain the main vehicles for scholarly publication in the disciplines of arts and humanities. Acceptance of digital books ('e-books') was slow at first, but in the last few years the rate of e-book publishing has gathered pace, driven particularly by the appropriateness of the medium for text books and learning materials in general, and by demand from younger scholars for texts in digital format. The digital age has also provided publishers with new tools for marketing their books, though it really took Google's digitising programme (Google Books Library Project), which exposes parts of a book's contents to interested searchers, to demonstrate the sales advantage that placing content under the noses of would-be buyers electronically can bring. E-book sales are rising across all sectors, including scholarly disciplines.

Peer review

Behind this type of publication-of-record stands peer review. No journal of repute permits a manuscript to go into publication without it passing a more or less rigorous examination by two or more members of the author's peer group, traditionally remaining anonymous. There are already some new forms of peer review being tried, such as non-anonymous review, where the reviewers' names are made known to the author. The digital age offers yet more variations on the theme (Harnad, 1996). Some journals have already started experimenting with open peer review, where articles are posted on the Web for open discussion between peer group and author, are modified in the light of this and are then formally peer-reviewed by selected reviewers in the traditional way. The Web also facilitates post-publication peer review and open commentary and, additionally and importantly in the light of new communication channels, simplifies the objective measurement of the impact of articles in the form of citation analysis (Hitchcock et al., 2003), which in itself constitutes a form of peer judgment. We can expect further and far-reaching developments in the peer-review system over time.

Data

Alongside the development of electronic publications has come the means for the public provision of types of data that were not possible to disseminate in the print-on-paper world. The early adopters of this facility were mainly scientists, but the humanities scholars and social scientists have not been far behind. In any discipline where large datasets are generated during research work – such as remote sensing, epidemiology, astrophysics, social science and education research – researchers can now easily make these available to their peers around the world by depositing them in a digital repository or on sites provided by publishers so that supporting data may accompany journal articles.

As web technologies advance, moreover, new methods of accessing and manipulating data are being developed. For example, web services, interfaces that simplify access to both data and software, can enable scientists to access multiple existing interoperable databases and mesh together relevant data from each to create a new, richer, data collection. The limitation on the potential of such services is not technological but cultural – they can work successfully only with real-time access to the source databases and, of course, can work only on publicly-available content.

On this latter point, the notion of making publicly available data that support conclusions in published articles is one that is not only popular but may actually be enforced in some cases. The journal *Nature*, for example, has a clause in its conditions of publishing that stipulates that authors must make supporting data available for others to see and use. Many funding agencies now stipulate the same thing, and OECD ministers have recently adopted the Declaration on Access to Research Data from Public Funding (OECD 2004).

As computer technologies are increasingly employed in academic research across all disciplines, the opportunities they bring for sharing data, mining data, simulation and visualisation will profoundly change the way scholars communicate their findings, make their work known and get it built upon.

Ownership and intellectual property

Traditionally, scholars submitting their work to a learned journal have signed over copyright (actually a bundle of rights) to the publisher. Included in this bundle of rights is the right to publish the work, and getting the work published is an outcome which is, of course, exactly what the scholar seeks to achieve. While some publisher agreements are very generous to the author and leave the author with a variety of rights and options over how the work may be used, at the other end of the spectrum there are publishing agreements that impose rather severe restrictions on the use of the work, in some cases affecting even the author's own teaching and research use.

The academic community is beginning to respond to this. It is possible to unpick the bundle of rights, so that the scholar retains most of them while still handing to the publisher a licence to publish. In other creative areas this is the norm, with the creator retaining ownership of the work. Individual universities, such as the University of California at Berkeley, are actively encouraging faculty to retain intellectual property rights altogether or to use only publishers that 'maintain reasonable business practices' (University of California, 2005a).

Additionally, the Creative Commons organisation (and its protégé, Science Commons), has developed a set of licences that content creators, including scholarly authors, can use to retain some control over their ownership of their work while permitting the sort of public use to which they hope their work will be put, such as copying and distributing for teaching or research. This is a facet of scholarly communication that is likely to see much more change over the next few years.

Research assessment

The past three decades have seen profound changes in the way scholars are assessed for their research performance. Previously, peer opinion formed the subjective measure of a scholar's research ability and the number of reputable books or journal articles they published formed the best objective measure. Things began to change when the Institute for Scientific Information (ISI) developed a system for measuring the number of citations to journal articles, thus providing a form of comparative, empirically-based measure of the worth of a scholar's output, worth expressed in terms of whether the work had been built upon after its publication. ISI packaged together the citation figures for the articles from a specific journal, developed a formula for retrospectively calculating the influence of that journal in any given year and called the metric the 'Journal Impact Factor'. Many words have been written about the impact factor over the years and space here does not permit a revisiting of all the arguments for and against it, save to say that as a measure of the impact of individual scholars it has only ever been a proxy. Nonetheless, it has been adopted by employers and funders of researchers worldwide as a metric that gives at least some idea of how influential a scholar's research is proving. Now, ISI has made available the 'times cited' metric for each article, showing how many times that particular article has been cited in the literature up to the time the user searches it out. Not a proxy, but a real measure of the influence of a scholar's piece of work, this is just one of a tranche of new bibliometric factors being developed by researchers and information scientists, all made possible by digitisation and enhanced by the interoperability of repositories of research results.

With a large database of digital articles to work with, it is possible to develop ways to measure not just citations but lots of other metrics too. It has already been demonstrated that download counts predict future citations (Brody and Harnad 2004, Adams 2005, Bollen et al. 2005). New bibliometric measures will tell us much more about impact, influence and interaction in the scholarly literature, measures such as co-citations, time-series analyses of downloads and citations, citation hubs and citation authorities, peaks, decay patterns and trends (Hajjem, Harnad and Gingras, 2005; Harnad, 2005a; and Kurtz and Brody, this volume). But all this awaits the database to work on – the database that will be available for analysis once all published articles reside in a worldwide network of interoperable repositories.

The 'serials crisis'

An overview of scholarly communication would not be complete without a brief review of the so-called 'serials crisis' that has taken place in scholarly libraries throughout the world over the last 20 years. In recent times it has not been possible for a university or research institute library to purchase subscriptions to every journal and book that would form the ideal collection for users of that institution. Articles required from publications not subscribed to have been sourced through interlibrary loan or document delivery services where available. The situation has been exacerbated over the last 20 years or so by ongoing annual price increases for journals that have exceeded inflation, sometimes by many times. The Library and Information Statistics Unit (LISU) at Loughborough University in the UK monitors journal prices: it found that from 2000 to 2004 the increase in median price of journals from a group of 12 scholarly publishers increased between 27 per cent (Cambridge University Press) and 94 per cent (Sage). Inflation through that period has been on average 2.5 per cent per annum in the UK (LISU, 2004). Similar studies by the Association of Research Libraries (ARL) in the USA have revealed much the same story (ARL, 2003). Learned society journals are not immune to this, either: Allen Press reports that in the period 1988–2004 inflation in the USA averaged 3.1 per cent per annum, while the average increase in the subscription price of learned society journals was 7.5 per cent each year (Kean, 2005).

Clearly this could not continue indefinitely. The problem this brings for libraries has been compounded by a concomitant increase in the amount of research being published, resulting in more journals and journals with more content (indeed, the increasing content of journals is one explanation from publishers for their increases in prices). Libraries have adopted various strategies for coping: switching money from their book budgets to serials purchase; cancelling journal subscriptions; signing up to 'Big Deals'; or entering into other kinds of licensing solutions. These are demand-side solutions to a global problem. Unsurprisingly, as the digital age brings the wherewithal, supply-side solutions have also begun to emerge.

New developments in scholarly communication

Early in this chapter the new, informal mechanisms whereby scholars are now communicating about their work were mentioned. Although still a minority activity, with the technologies in their infancy, they should not be underestimated as communication channels for the future. Already, scientific publishers are taking steps to embed such technologies in their operations (see, for example, Hammond, Hannay and Lund, 2004). True, they present citation and assessment problems, but they now form a part of the spectrum of legitimate, accepted and trusted communication mechanisms that ranges from the formal publication-of-record mechanisms at one end to blogs at the other. Web 2.0 (O'Reilly, 2005) is a social being, a concept rooted in interactivity and cooperation, and its emerging models of interaction are dynamic and real-time (or near to it). In some areas of scientific research, blogs and wikis are already proving to be popular and influential ways of communication between scientists. We can expect to see these and other technologies on the rise over the next few years.

At the same time, in the mainstream, the academy and its supporters including, not least, its funders are changing the thinking on scholarly communication. Two library-led meetings in the USA around the turn of the century saw the development of sets of principles relating to the whole process of academic research, academic values, and the communication of these within the academic community and beyond it into the general public domain. Alongside this, they espoused the twin aims of containing the costs of published research and of using digital capabilities to widen access to its results (Keystone Principles, 1999; Tempe Principles, 2000).

The latter issue gelled with already-existing initiatives from the research community itself where efforts to capitalise upon the opportunities offered by the Web had given birth to the open access movement, dedicated to freeing up research output from the constraints imposed on its dissemination by publisher restrictions and the non-affordability of journals. The Web had arrived, and with it the means, finally, for access to the scholarly literature to be truly available to all. Although there have been other initiatives that have significantly widened access to the scholarly literature, such as the collaboration between the University of Stanford Library and scholarly publishers that resulted in Highwire Press,[1] none of them have satisfactorily addressed, nor certainly solved, the access problem.

Open access does address the access problem, though the arguments in its favour work equally well when the whole issue is turned on its head and regarded as a dissemination problem. Formal definitions of open access are contained in the Budapest Open Access Initiative (Open Society Institute, 2002), the Bethesda Statement on Open Access Publishing and, comprehensively, in the Berlin Declaration on Open Access to Knowledge in the Sciences and the Humanities (see Bailey, this volume). Essentially, it means the provision of free, immediate (upon publication), permanent access to research results for anyone to use, download, copy and distribute. Moreover, the definition stipulates that articles are placed in an organised repository (rather than simply on author websites) which is interoperable according to a specific set of standards, the Open Archives Initiative Protocol for Metadata Harvesting (OAI-PMH, see Awre, this volume). Search engines, such as OAIster and, now, Google Scholar, harvest the content of these interoperable repositories, constructing a database of worldwide, freely-available research available to allcomers at no charge.

Articles enter such a repository in one of two ways. They may be published in an open access journal (or are open access articles within an otherwise closed-access journal) in which case the publisher ensures they are correctly deposited in an OAI-compliant open access repository. Alternatively, they are copies of articles published in closed-access journals that are 'self-archived' by their authors, that is, deposited by the author in an open access repository. Such articles then form a constituent of the virtual global database, their text and citations available for capture and analysis and their metadata exposed for search engines or service providers to access and present to searchers around the globe.

The philosophical arguments for open access are rehearsed elsewhere in this book, along with accounts of its technological base, the business models associated with it and its advantages in terms of increasing the visibility and impact of research. This overview is not the place to pursue those topics further. There *is* one other issue that needs to be laid out here, though, as it is of critical importance to the progress of open access and does belong in an overview of scholarly communication. It is the issue of making it happen. Further into this book there is a chapter (Swan) on author responses to open access in which the speed of take-up of the concept – which has been slow – is discussed in the light of author attitudes and habits. If left to authors, achieving full open access will take a very long while. More is needed than that. And more is coming along in the form of institutional or funder requirements for researchers to provide open access to their work. So far, moves in this direction have been instituted by a small number of universities and research centres. Research funders, in the form of government-funded bodies in the USA and UK and private funders such as charities and trusts, have also already made moves to ensure that the results from the research they support are available on an open access basis. There are signs from all around the world that such moves will be followed by similar ones elsewhere. This is significant in scholarly communication terms, for it represents a digital-age counterpart to the 'publish or perish' imperative – implicitly or explicitly applied – that scholars have always acknowledged from their employers or funders. The unchaining of scholarly research is on its way.

Note

1. Highwire Press provides a repository of full-text articles from some 900-plus journals, of which approximately 80 per cent are available via pay-per-view access, approximately 20 per cent offer free back issues after variable periods of time, most commonly 12 months after publication, and approximately 3 per cent are true open access, i.e. immediately available upon publication.

2

What is open access?
Charles W. Bailey, Jr.

Introduction

To further the development of knowledge, scholars require access to relevant scholarly literature. Increasingly, this literature is interdisciplinary, global, expensive, digital and hidden behind technical walls to comply with licence restrictions. It is also burgeoning. Little wonder that even scholars at the richest universities in the world have difficulty accessing the specialised literature that they need, while those at the poorest barely have any access at all. What can be done? The open access movement believes it has an answer to this critical question. Many of its prominent figures have little or no interest in reforming the existing scholarly communication system. Rather, they are interested in transforming it so that it can function effectively in the rapidly changing technological environment (Suber, 2006a).

'Open access' defined

There are a variety of definitions of 'open access', and the concept is still evolving; however, several key documents, which build upon each other, collectively comprise the best current definition of this term.

The Budapest Open Access Initiative

In December 2001, the Open Society Institute convened a meeting of prominent scholarly communication change agents in Budapest that strongly influenced the nascent open access movement. The result of this meeting was the Budapest Open Access Initiative (BOAI). Its definition of open access, while refined by subsequent documents, remains the most influential one to this day:

> The literature that should be freely accessible online is that which scholars give to the world without expectation of payment. Primarily, this category encompasses their peer-reviewed journal articles, but it also includes any unreviewed preprints that they might wish to put online for comment or to alert colleagues to important research findings. There are many degrees and kinds of wider and easier access to this literature. By 'open access' to this literature, we mean its free availability on the public Internet, permitting any users to read, download, copy, distribute, print, search, or link to the full texts of these articles, crawl them for indexing, pass them as data to software, or use them for any other lawful purpose, without financial, legal, or technical barriers other than those inseparable from gaining access to the Internet itself. The only constraint on reproduction and distribution, and the only role for copyright in this domain, should be to give authors control over the integrity of their work and the right to be properly acknowledged and cited...
>
> To achieve open access to scholarly journal literature, we recommend two complementary strategies.
>
> I. Self-Archiving: First, scholars need the tools and assistance to deposit their refereed journal articles in open electronic archives, a practice commonly called self-archiving. When these archives conform to standards created by the Open Archives Initiative, then search engines and other tools can treat the separate archives as one. Users then need not know which archives exist or where they are located in order to find and make use of their contents.
>
> II. Open-access Journals: Second, scholars need the means to launch a new generation of journals committed to open access, and to help existing journals that elect to make the transition to open access. Because journal articles should be disseminated as widely as possible, these new journals will no longer invoke copyright to restrict access to and use of the material they publish. Instead they will use copyright and other tools to ensure permanent open access to all the articles they publish. Because

price is a barrier to access, these new journals will not charge subscription or access fees, and will turn to other methods for covering their expenses. (Open Society Institute, 2002)

Examining this definition, we note several key points. First, open access works are freely available. Second, they are 'online', which would typically mean that they are digital documents available on the Internet. Third, they are scholarly works – romance novels, popular magazines, self-help books, and the like are excluded. Fourth, the authors of these works are not paid for their efforts. Fifth, as most (but not all) authors of peer-reviewed journal articles are not paid and such works are scholarly, these articles are identified as the primary type of open access material. Sixth, there are an extraordinary number of permitted uses for open access materials. Aside from the requirements of proper attribution of the author and the assurance of the integrity of the work, users can copy and distribute open access works without constraint. Seventh, there are two key open access strategies: self-archiving and open access journals (these will be discussed in detail later).

Peter Suber (2006a) characterises the core concept of open access this way: open access removes 'price barriers' (e.g. subscription fees) and 'permission barriers' (such as copyright and licensing restrictions) to 'royalty-free literature' (that is, scholarly works created for free by authors), making them available with 'minimal use restrictions' (e.g. author attribution).

Why are open access works only digital? After the creation of the first digital copy of a work, the cost of creating additional copies and distributing them on the Internet is marginal. This contrasts with paper-based publishing, which not only entails meaningful paper-copy production costs, but also physical storage and distribution costs.

Are all free digital documents 'open access' documents? Just because a digital document is freely available, does not mean that the copyright owner has given consent for the types of permissive uses envisioned in the BOAI. Nor does the absence of a copyright statement necessarily mean that a digital document is in the public domain, and the user should assume that the document is under full copyright until a full investigation of the copyright status of the work is conducted. If a free digital document does not have a licence or special copyright statement that specifically grants additional rights, the user's rights are limited by standard copyright provisions, the most relevant right being fair use (or fair dealing in the UK).

However, it should be noted that some influential open access proponents, such as Stevan Harnad (2003a), assert that free access alone is sufficient to constitute open access.

The Bethesda Statement on Open Access Publishing

Another landmark meeting was held in April 2003 at the Howard Hughes Medical Institute in Chevy Chase, Maryland. It resulted in the 'Bethesda Statement on Open Access Publishing' (Bethesda Statement, 2003), which extended the definition of open access. The key section of the Bethesda Statement says:

1. The author(s) and copyright holder(s) grant(s) to all users a free, irrevocable, worldwide, perpetual right of access to, and a license to copy, use, distribute, transmit and display the work publicly and to make and distribute derivative works, in any digital medium for any responsible purpose, subject to proper attribution of authorship, as well as the right to make small numbers of printed copies for their personal use.

2. A complete version of the work and all supplemental materials, including a copy of the permission as stated above, in a suitable standard electronic format is deposited immediately upon initial publication in at least one online repository that is supported by an academic institution, scholarly society, government agency, or other well-established organisation that seeks to enable open access, unrestricted distribution, interoperability, and long-term archiving (for the biomedical sciences, PubMed Central is such a repository).

The Bethesda Statement builds upon the BOAI, but how does it differ from it? The BOAI does not indicate how copyright owners will operationalise the open access concept. Aside from being able to access it freely, how will users know that a specific work is an 'open access' work? By contrast, the Bethesda Statement specifies that copyright owners will grant users certain rights under licences, and these rights shall be 'free, irrevocable, worldwide, perpetual'. A licence is a contract, with terms and conditions that describe permitted uses. As such, it supersedes users' copyright rights if it specifies terms and conditions that negate them.

One such right under the Bethesda Statement, which the BOAI does not specify, is the right to make derivative works. For example, a work could be translated into another language without requiring permission.

Certain Creative Commons licences can be used to grant open access rights. For example, the Creative Commons Attribution Licence gives users a 'worldwide, royalty-free, non-exclusive, perpetual' licence to reproduce and distribute works and to create derivative works from them in all existing and future media, subject to certain conditions, such as author attribution, retention of the original copyright statement, and provision of the licence or a link to it (the licence also grants other rights). The licence states that: 'Nothing in this license is intended to reduce, limit, or restrict any rights arising from fair use, first sale or other limitations on the exclusive rights of the copyright owner under copyright law or other applicable laws'. A variety of other 'open content' licences also exist (Liang, 2004).

The Bethesda Statement also introduces the requirement that open access documents be deposited in digital repositories in 'well-established' organisations, as opposed to author homepages or digital archives where the long-term prospects are in doubt. These repositories will engage in 'long-term archiving'. In other words, they will digitally preserve open access documents.

Again, some open access advocates assert that these two broad requirements are not necessary for open access (Harnad, 2003a).

The Berlin Declaration on Open Access to Knowledge in the Sciences and Humanities

In October 2003, the Conference on Open Access to Knowledge in the Sciences and Humanities issued the 'Berlin Declaration on Open Access to Knowledge in the Sciences and Humanities' (Berlin Declaration, 2003). Although there are minor differences between the Bethesda Statement and the Berlin Declaration, they essentially say the same thing. The reader is urged to read the original text for details.

A follow-up meeting, Berlin 3 Open Access: Progress in Implementing the Berlin Declaration on Open Access to Knowledge in the Sciences and Humanities, issued the following statement in March 2005 (Berlin 3 Open Access, 2005):

In order to implement the Berlin Declaration institutions should implement a policy to:

1. *require* their researchers to deposit a copy of all their published articles in an open access repository

and

2. *encourage* their researchers to publish their research articles in open access journals where a suitable journal exists (and provide the support to enable that to happen).

The BBB definition of open access

Peter Suber refers to the collective BOAI, Bethesda Statement, and Berlin Declaration open access definitions as the 'BBB definition of open access', (Suber, 2004a) and he notes that this definition 'removes both price and permission barriers'. However, Suber asserts elsewhere that: 'Removing price barriers alone will give most open access proponents most of what they want and need' (Suber, 2006a).

It should be noted that open access is rooted in existing copyright law: copyright owners permit users to freely access their works and grant them additional rights that remove permission barriers. Open access does not require that copyright laws change in order for it to exist (Suber, 2006a).

Other views of open access

There have been numerous additional open access declarations and statements by various groups that further contribute to our understanding of open access, including the:

- 'Access to Research Publications: Universities UK Position Statement', (Universities UK, 2005);
- 'Australian Research Information Infrastructure Committee Open Access Statement', (Australian Research Information Infrastructure Committee, 2004)
- Group of Eight's 'Statement on Open Access to Scholarly Information' (Group of Eight, 2004)

- 'IFLA Statement on Open Access to Scholarly Literature and Research Documentation' (International Federation of Library Associations, 2004)

- 'Messina Declaration' (Messina, 2004)

- 'Scottish Declaration of Open Access' (Scottish Science Information Strategy Working Group, 2004)

- 'Washington DC Principles for Free Access to Science' (Washington DC, 2004); and

- World Summit on the Information Society's 'Declaration of Principles' and 'Plan of Action' (World Summit on the Information Society, 2003a,b)

Peter Suber's Timeline of the Open Access Movement details others.[1]

Peter Suber (2004b) has speculated that open access will extend its scope of coverage in three phases, with 'royalty-producing literature' being included in phase two and copyright reform that expands the public domain occurring in phase three.

In practice, a wide range of scholarly works beyond preprints and postprints (such as books, conference presentations, electronic theses and dissertations, and technical reports) are currently freely available on the Internet, some of which are under Creative Commons or similar licences.

Self-archiving

Self-archiving is the first open access strategy identified by the BOAI. Stevan Harnad (2005b) refers to it as the 'green road' to open access, and this term has come into common usage.

'Self-archiving' defined

When authors make their articles freely available in digital form on the Internet, they are said to be 'self-archiving' them.[2] These articles can be either 'preprints' or 'postprints'.

Preprints are draft versions of articles that have not undergone peer review or editorial review and modification. Most preprints are intended for submission to journals, but some are not. The exchange of preprints among authors, especially scientific authors, has a long history and, prior to the Web, was done by postal service mail, fax, e-mail, FTP servers, Gopher servers, and other means (Bailey Jr, 2005: xvii).

Postprints are the final published versions of articles. They can either be the publisher's version of the article or an updated preprint that the author creates to reflect any changes made during the peer review and editorial processes.

Authors can make digital postprints available because either:

- they have retained copyright and only granted certain non-exclusive rights to publishers;

- they have transferred all rights to publishers, but publishers' policies permit authors to distribute postprints under specified terms and conditions (most publishers now have such self-archiving policies); or

- they have modified the preprint using errata/corrigenda (other less common variations are also possible).

Publisher self-archiving policies are quite diverse. Stevan Harnad groups and codes them as follows: 'gold (provides open access to its research articles, without delay), green (permits postprint archiving by authors), pale green (permits, i.e. doesn't oppose, preprint archiving by authors), gray (none of the above)' (Suber, 2006a). The SHERPA Project maintains a public database of publishers' self-archiving policies, the Sherpa/RoMEO list.

Both digital preprints and postprints are called 'e-prints'.

Although the open access movement focuses on peer-reviewed literature, the term 'e-print' is also widely used to refer to digital versions of articles that will be or have been published in scholarly, but non-peer-reviewed journals and magazines. Moreover, other types of scholarly digital materials, such as conference presentations (e.g. PowerPoint presentations), may be said to be 'self-archived' by their authors.

Self-archiving strategies

The most common ways that e-prints are made available on the Internet are: (1) authors' personal websites, (2) disciplinary archives, (3) institutional-unit archives, or (4) institutional repositories (Bailey Jr, 2005: xvii–xviii).

These self-archiving strategies are not mutually exclusive. An author may self-archive the same e-print in a personal author website, a disciplinary archive, an institutional-unit archive, and an institutional repository. Doing so increases the likelihood that it will be found by interested users. With the exception of the personal website, this act of self-archiving is referred to as 'depositing' the e-print.

While helpful, the following classification of self-archiving strategies is not intended to be comprehensive or definitive. Given the increasingly powerful capabilities of archiving and repository systems and the fecund imaginations their users, self-archiving strategies are constantly evolving.

Let's look briefly at the main self-archiving strategies:

- *Author's personal websites*: These websites are often as simple as a few linked web pages, with associated e-print files in HTML, PDF, Word or other formats; however, they can be much more elaborate. E-print links are typically in a separate publications list or integrated into a vita. Website files are usually indexed in major search engines, which is useful if the searcher has specific information about the desired e-print, such as its title. As the life circumstances of authors change (e.g. they change jobs) and they die, the stability of these e-prints is variable and their permanence is not assured. For an example, see Stevan Harnad's 'Online research communication and open access': *http://www.ecs.soton.ac.uk/%7Eharnad/intpub.html*.

- *Disciplinary archives*: Disciplinary archives include e-prints (or e-prints plus other types of digital works) by authors from around the world covering one or more subjects. They are typically full-featured systems that support author deposit and metadata creation, deposit screening by archive moderators, fielded and keyword searching, browsing, and export of metadata to specialised search engines using a protocol called OAI-PMH (see Awre, this volume). The stability and permanence of these archives is usually determined by their formal affiliation with institutions or professional organisations; informal individual or small group efforts may be subject to the same issues outlined for personal websites, plus the ongoing level of interest of participants. Disciplinary archives are often implemented using free open source software, such as Eprints. For an example of a disciplinary archive, see arXiv (a major disciplinary archive for computer science, mathematics, nonlinear sciences, physics, and quantitative biology): *http://arxiv.org/*.

- *Institutional-unit archives*: Institutional-unit archives include e-prints (or e-prints plus other types of digital works) by authors in a single academic unit, such as a department or school, in an institution. While departmental (or smaller unit) archives can be simple and resemble personal author websites, they can also use the same free open source software and have the same functional capabilities as disciplinary archives. As they are associated with institutional units, the stability and permanence of these archives is generally high, although archives in smaller units may depend on informal individual or small group effort. For an example, see Duke Law Faculty Scholarship Repository: *http://eprints.law.duke.edu/*.

- *Institutional repositories*: Institutional repositories include diverse types of digital works (such as electronic theses and dissertations, e-prints, learning objects, presentations and technical reports) by authors at one institution or, less frequently, at multiple institutions. They are often established and maintained by libraries or libraries working in partnership with other major institutional entities, such as the institution's information technology unit. As they are formal institutional functions, institutional repositories are permanent and stable. There is often a commitment to use digital preservation techniques to ensure the continued availability and usefulness of the digital materials that they contain. Institutional repository systems share the capabilities described previously for disciplinary and institutional-unit archives, but may be further optimised to more fully support a wide range of digital materials, the autonomous operation of institutional units, and digital preservation. They may include electronic document publishing functions, such as e-journal management or conference paper management systems. They typically utilise free open source software, such as DSpace, Eprints or Fedora, but may be externally hosted by vendors for designed fees. Institutional repository staff may offer a range of services, such as document deposit, metadata creation, repository promotion, training, and user support. (Although less common, there are also institutional e-print archives that only contain e-prints.) For an example, see DSpace at MIT: *https://dspace.mit.edu/index.jsp*.

Some universities, such as Queensland University of Technology (2004) and the Universidade do Minho (2004) have mandated self-archiving by their scholars. The Registry of Open Access Repository Material Archiving Policies provides access to university self-archiving policies.[3]

Self-archiving copyright practices

Although e-prints are freely available, their authors do not follow consistent copyright notice or licence practices, and, consequently, they may have: '(1) no copyright statement (under US law they are under copyright by default); (2) a conventional copyright statement; (3) a copyright statement that is modified by specific use provisions (e.g. liberal use permitted for non-commercial purposes); (4) a Creative Commons or other licence, which may or may not permit commercial use or derivative works; or (5) another variation' (Bailey Jr, 2006).

Open access journals

Open access journals are the second open access strategy identified by the BOAI. Stevan Harnad (2005b) refers to open access journals as the 'gold road' to open access.

'Open access journals' defined

Open access journals have the following characteristics: (1) they are scholarly; (2) they utilise quality control mechanisms like those of conventional journals (such as editorial oversight and copy editing); (3) they are digital; (4) they are freely available; (5) they may allow authors to retain their copyrights; and (6) they may use Creative Commons or similar licences (Bailey Jr, 2005: xviii–xix).

There is some dispute as to whether open access journals must utilise peer review as a quality control mechanism. Most do, but there are also some high-quality journals that do not, yet meet all other criteria, and have great impact on their fields of study. *D-Lib Magazine* is an example of such a journal.

Likewise, the question of whether the journal must use a Creative Commons or similar licence is another area of dispute. This dispute reflects the deeper, fundamental question of whether 'open access' is just free access or free access plus a set of specified use rights that go significantly beyond normal copyright rights.

The Directory of Open Access Journals,[4] which is published by Lund University Libraries, provides access to about 2,000 digital journals that have been classified as open access journals based on stated criteria. Open access journals may also be included in conventional index and abstract databases.

Types of open access journal publishers

The major types of open access journal publishers are: (1) born open access publishers, (2) conventional publishers, and (3) non-traditional publishers (Bailey Jr, 2006). The same disclaimers apply to this taxonomy as were indicated for the self-archiving one.

Let's examine these types of open access journal publishers in more detail:

- *Born open access publishers*: With the establishment of the open access journal publisher BioMed Central in 2000, a new type of journal publishing venture was created – what I call the 'born open access' publisher. These digital commercial or non-profit publishers were established for the sole purpose of publishing open access journals, and they typically utilise the Creative Commons Attribution Licence (or a similar licence) for their publications. Authors usually retain their copyrights. Different funding strategies are employed by these publishers, including advertising, author fees (these fees may be paid by authors' grant funds or waived by the publisher in cases of financial hardship), grants to the publishers, library membership fees (these fees entitle authors at the library's institution to publish articles without paying all or part of the publisher's author fees), and supplemental products such as print copies. For an example, see The Public Library of Science: *http://www.plos.org/*.

- *Conventional publishers*: As the open access movement has gained momentum, conventional commercial and non-profit journal publishers have begun to experiment with open access publishing programmes or to establish permanent open access programmes. For example, the Springer Open Choice Program currently allows authors to publish their articles as open access works for a fee of US$3,000. The articles are published in both print and digital form. A licence is used that is similar to the Creative Commons Attribution Non-commercial Licence. The author can self-archive the digital article, and it is freely available on SpringerLink. Once a year, Springer adjusts the library subscription price for journals in the programmme in accordance with the number of open access journal articles published (so that if more were published than in the prior 12 months, the cost is reduced). You'll note that, unless all authors choose the open access option, this programme results in journal issues having a mix of open access and restricted access articles. For an example, see Hindawi Publishing Corporation: *http://www .hindawi.com/oa/*.

- *Non-traditional publishers*: During the late 1980s and early 1990s, the Internet had developed to the point that scholars began to publish free digital journals utilising existing institutional infrastructure and volunteer labour. Examples included *Ejournal*

(Jennings, 1991), *PostModern Culture* (Amiran and Unsworth, 1991), and *The Public-Access Computer Systems Review* (Bailey Jr, 1991; Ensor and Wilson, 1997). These journals were not intended to generate income; they were 'no-profit' journals. Although many of these journals allowed authors to retain their copyrights and they had liberal copyright statements regarding non-commercial use, they preceded by a decade or more the Creative Commons, and, consequently, did not embody that kind of copyright stance. While some of these journals ceased publication and others were transformed into non-profit ventures, they provided a model that others followed, especially after the popularisation of the Internet began in the mid-1990s, following the introduction of web browsers. In recent years, the availability of free open source journal management and publishing systems, such as the Open Journal Systems, further simplified and streamlined digital journal publishing, fuelling additional growth in this area. Now, a wide variety of academic departments or schools, institutes and research centres, libraries, professional associations, scholars and others publish digital journals, a subset of which comply with the strictest definition of an open access journal and a larger subset of which comply with the looser definition of an open access journal as a free journal. As these diverse 'publishers' would have been unlikely to be engaged in this activity without facilitating digital technologies and tools, I refer to them as 'non-traditional publishers'. Many of them are also 'no-profit' publishers as well. For example, see *SCRIPT-ed: A Journal of Law and Technology*: *http://www.law.ed.ac.uk/ahrb/script%2Ded/index.asp*.

Open access journals' copyright practices

Although the ideal is for open access journals to use a Creative Commons or similar licence for their articles, the reality is that they can use a variety of copyright strategies that mirror those described earlier for self-archived e-prints.

Learning more about open access

An annotated listing of a wide range of resources about open access (e.g. bibliographies, directories, e-journals, FAQs, mailing lists, organisations, overviews, specialised search engines, projects, programmes for developing countries, and weblogs) can be found in the open access Webliography (Ho and Bailey Jr, 2005).

Notes

1. See *http://www.earlham.edu/~peters/fos/timeline.htm*.
2. See the BOAI Self-Archiving FAQ, available at: *http://www.eprints.org/self-faq/*.
3. See *http://www.eprints.org/openaccess/policysignup/*.
4. See *http://www.doaj.org/*.

Open access: a symptom and a promise

Jean-Claude Guédon

Open access and scientific communication

Alexandre Koyré, the great historian of science, was fond of defining science as *iter mentis ad veritatem*.[1] The vision was lofty, inspiring, but lacked a bit in concreteness and materiality. It was in keeping with Koyré's characterisation of another great historian, Henry Guerlac, as '*un petit peu marxiste*' – Guerlac's 'sin' was that material conditions could not be entirely neglected. Koyré in short could not be expected to anchor the doing of science in anything more concrete than ideas.

While scientists are acutely aware of the material conditions of their work – filling out application forms for research grants is an extremely good, if annoying, reminder of the less ethereal sides of science – they tend to behave a little like Koyré. In particular, they tend to overlook the material dimensions of scientific communication: it is simply something that has to be done with journals that practise peer review and that are as prestigious as possible. The rest of what normally constitutes 'publishing' is of little or no concern to them. Debating with an editor whether a comma is more appropriate than a semi-colon is considered normal; on the other hand, perusing the copyright transfer contract with some care is a bore. Scientists may lightly brush against the economics of the communication process when they come across page charges or discover that the subscription price of a journal has risen to such an extent as to dissuade them from acquiring their own personal copy. However, with desktop access made possible by digitisation, this is less and less a problem. *In toto* the economics of scientific publishing simply does not appear on the radar screens of most scientists. They are happy to continue travelling on the *iter mentis ad veritatem*. Meanwhile, librarians, despite enormous financial difficulties, have managed to keep the system sufficiently well lubricated to shield scientists from most of the bumps on the same '*iter mentis...*' – but they know that the system is broken.

Open access has emerged in reaction to the unsustainable nature of the present economic model of scientific publishers, but countless debates and arguments have helped redefine its aims, claims and means away from this point of origin. In particular, open access has gradually focused on the issue of scholarly communication *per se* and it has tried to imagine what the world could be like with total open access. Two conclusions have emerged from this long series of efforts:

- Scientists publish to be read and cited, exactly as peacocks spread their tail to be seen and courted. Toll-gating one's publications behind high subscription fees runs counter to the scientist's quest for 'impact', that is, the number of citations garnered from legitimate scientific publications. Without open access, loss of impact occurs – a situation that various studies are beginning to document (see Kurtz and Brody, this volume).

- Symmetrically, in the absence of open access, scientists miss access to potentially important information if their institution does not subscribe to the relevant publication. The access situation is simply a function of the wealth of the institution. The distance from comprehensive access can vary from negligible in very wealthy institutions to dramatic in poor institutions. This means that many good ideas are not circulating as they should, and that many good brains miss these ideas and, therefore, cannot exploit them. This means that the ability to do scientific work and enjoy impact from it depends, among other factors, on the economic ability to access the relevant scientific literature. In a knowledge economy, pricing access to research results at a level which only the wealthiest can afford ensures an important comparative advantage for the rich fraction of humanity.

In short, if we envision the world communities of scientists as a complex network of distributed intelligence, open access now appears as one of the essential means to make it work in a fuller, more efficient, fashion. It also appears as a tool to move toward an even playing field in scientific research and education. But it also undermines established practices and threatens existing power centres, and hence encounters various forms of resistance.

Issues and concerns

It was Pieter Bolman, a former CEO of Pergamon Science, and until recently an employee of Reed-Elsevier, who framed an interesting metaphor in the course of one of the countless meetings where our paths crossed. In effect, he said, open access may well be a better system, but the energy barrier that prevents moving to this state is such that it is much easier to improve the existing system. The admission that open access may well be a better system, at least in the abstract, should not be forgotten, coming as it did from one of the most ardent defenders of commercial scientific publishing. Whether the 'energy barrier' is really as high as claimed has been the object of many discussions between supporters and critics of open access. Within the open access movement itself, the same issue has emerged in relation to the issue of the optimal path – if there is any – to open access.

When open access began to acquire the trappings of a broad-based social movement after the Budapest Open Access Initiative in February 2002 – it came armed with a dual strategy that has accompanied it until now (see Bailey Jr, this volume):

- creating open access journals, or transforming existing journals into open-access publications: the 'gold' road to open access;
- self-archiving articles into suitable repositories to make them universally available: the 'green' road to open access.

Initially, back in 2002, the so-called 'gold' road to open access was easier to conceive than the 'green' road. The latter seemed to be fatally handicapped by copyright restrictions and Web dispersion. However, two distinct sets of events have contributed to making the 'green' road far more credible nowadays, to the point that it is viewed in several quarters as the most promising (or threatening, if seen from some publishers' perspective) of the two roads.

The first important change has been the designing of a metadata exchange standard that allows the systematic harvesting of the contents found in repositories: this is OAI-PMH, the brain-child of Carl Lagoze, Herbert van de Sompel and several others. It emerged at about the same time as the first attempts to promote self-archiving, around 1999–2000.

Once perfected, it allowed the creation of search engines that increase the value of collections of articles that, otherwise, would probably remain hopelessly scattered (see Awre, this volume).

The second important step was the (reluctant) acceptance of self-archiving by a number of publishing houses. The terms granting the right to self-archive vary a good deal from one publisher to the next, but this – so it has been argued – is but the consequence of healthy competition among publishers. Of course, it also contributes to creating a fuzzy landscape that tends to confuse scientists to the point that many will not concern themselves. Yet, despite all the ambiguities, the emergence of so-called 'green' publishers has allowed the development of institutional repositories, generally under the leadership of librarians, in a large number of universities and research centres. They now number in the hundreds.

In parallel, the 'gold' road has also grown to the point that a list such as the Directory of Open Access Journals now tops 2,000 titles and various countries or groups of countries have begun to promote open access publishing of their national scientific journals. SciELO, initially based in Brazil, now covers several Latin American countries as well as Spain, and contains over 300 journals in open access. Similar open access projects are being contemplated or studied in a number of countries worldwide. This said, the 'energy barrier' on the 'gold' road has turned out to be higher than had been initially envisioned with the result that, while 'gold' remains a credible strategy on the way to open access, it is no longer 'the' approach that some may have dreamed about back in 2002.

Supporters of both approaches have begun to test the 'energy barriers' predicted by Pieter Bolman, and it may be useful to review some of their main characteristics.

Barriers to 'gold' open access

On the 'gold' road, the main problem rests with designing viable business plans. The discussion has been made more difficult by the fact that many scientific associations finance a great many of their admittedly valuable activities with profits accruing from the subscription model applied to their publications (see Waltham, this volume). On the whole, these associations, although not-for-profit organisations, remain strongly committed to the traditional subscription-based business plan. In fact, some of the most vociferous critics of open access belong to this quarter.

The American Chemical Society is famous in this regard, but it is far from being the only society resisting the trend to open access. At the same time, the tradition of independent scientific associations is often linked with a degree of distrust in governmental intervention, even though the same governments are regularly petitioned to generate more research funds.

However, in a number of countries, governmental agencies that support public research have begun to re-evaluate the subscription model and are beginning to perceive that the level of subsidies already present in the publishing system is probably sufficient to maintain an open access publication system, especially if it coincides with a general transition to electronic publishing. Going electronic and open access are separate issues, but it turns out that many scientific publications maintain a paper version, the functions of which do not seem to justify the expense.

In parallel, transition business plans have been floated, generally including author-proxy-pays schemes coupled or not with an 'open choice' strategy, to re-use a slogan initially emanating from Springer in its new incarnation. 'Open choice' here refers to the possibility of an author to choose between submitting an article in the traditional manner, and having someone pay money upstream (US$3,000 per article in the case of the Springer Open Choice Program) to allow for free access to it. At present, the situation is very fluid.

Barriers to 'green' open access

As mentioned previously, the 'green' road has seen two of its initial handicaps addressed at least partially to the point that it now looks like a credible partner in the efforts to reach open access. However, despite irrefutable success stories – arXiv, the physics disciplinary archive, remains both the oldest and most brilliant result in this regard – self-archiving has encountered its own 'energy barriers'. The most glaring has been the inability to convince 100 per cent of authors to self-archive 100 per cent of their articles. Various factors have been mentioned to explain why no more than about 10–20 per cent of articles are being self-archived (see chapters by Swan and Harnad, this volume), most notably the novelty of institutional repositories and their relative invisibility in the majority of institutions. In addition, scientists poorly understand their value. The fact that institutional repositories are often called upon to play a number of disconnected roles, such as that of a show-window for the local institution, has also blunted the functional edge of the device.

To increase the filling of the repositories, two main and complementary approaches have been proposed by various supporters of institutional repositories.

■ Make it mandatory for scientists who receive certain kinds of funding (public, or some private) to deposit their papers in a suitable repository. This approach has been favourably greeted by a number of granting agencies, be they private charities like the Wellcome Trust, or public organisations like the National Institutes of Health (NIH) in the USA. The main reason is that it gives a concrete and full picture of the research results to which they have contributed financially. However, the move has been fiercely resisted by scientific publishers who, thereby, have demonstrated the limits of their self-archiving 'generosity': so long as it is not too successful, self-archiving can be tolerated ... or perhaps even used to demonstrate how utopian open access really is. The noise of the lobbying battles waged around the NIH's proposal in favour of self-archiving, even though it was conceived in a constrained fashion, still resonates in the affected quarters (see Suber, this volume). Britain has lived through similar events (see Friend, this volume).

Although more arduous than initially imagined, and although it includes an authoritarian dimension that may irk some, mandating self-archiving in a suitable open access repository remains a commendable objective. In the institutions – alas too few – that have implemented it, most notably CERN in Geneva, impressive results have rapidly been achieved. Were it not for the political difficulties associated with mandating in any given institution, it would be the most effective way of ensuring rapid and full open access repositories everywhere. Political difficulties associated with implementing mandatory self-archiving, however real and complex, should not deter efforts in this direction.

■ In parallel to the mandating strategy, which can be characterised as a kind of frontal approach to the whole issue of open access, other, more indirect strategies have been suggested. They tend to emphasise incentives rather than coercion. Incentives, in the case of scientists, are necessarily related to impact because it translates into visibility, prestige, authority, and so on. In other words, to return to the peacock metaphor, the point here is not to train the bird to spread its tail in unfamiliar, and therefore, potentially misunderstood circumstances; it is to make it realise that the new setting is full of rewards, however unexpected they may be at first.

More concretely, the idea is to endow the repositories with various mechanisms to generate 'symbolic value' – this is Pierre Bourdieu's term for branding – for the archived papers and thus gain the capacity to 'brand' authors in a different way. The list of such mechanisms is about as large as the imagination of their designers, but some ideas have been implemented or, at least, debated. For example, the Cream of Science project uses repositories to project the works of 207 Dutch scientists into full light (see Waaijers, this volume). Presumably, this is going to attract the attention of other Dutch scientists and even trigger some clamouring, particularly on the part of those claiming to be 208th or 209th, to be part of the privileged lot. In the same vein, creating evaluation teams similar to prize juries or editorial boards to create the equivalent of a 'Michelin Guide' to repositories (with a rating scheme involving, perhaps, one brain, two brains, three brains, etc.) would start enriching repositories with an ability to brand, exactly as journals do.

Whether 'gold' or 'green', the strategies used, like all strategies aiming at changing existing situations rather than adapting to them, are meeting important difficulties. This was to be expected. Recent progress also leads us to believe that most of these 'energy barriers' will be superseded in the near future. Open access is here to stay, and most publishers are learning to live with this situation in one way or another. Their attitude may range from fierce resistance to total acceptance with anything possible in between, such as sly adaptation, but one simple point remains: open access will not disappear.

Case studies

Because there are many uncertainties, many doubts as to how best to proceed, case studies have come to take on a particularly important role for open access. The present volume contains some good examples of such studies. Exploring the realities of scientific publishing, the problems of access, the institutions behind the institutional repositories, the motivations behind the push for open access, the arguments being proposed in favour or against open access reveal a variegated landscape. The point to keep in mind is that open access is best defined in terms of immediate access to the validated results of research and that the means to achieve this goal may vary greatly from country to country, as well as from discipline to discipline.

Let us take up a few examples: much has been said about institutional repositories, relatively little about disciplinary repositories, and nothing has been said about how they should relate to one another. Other issues remain, such as publishing formats, preservation, networking of repositories. While these issues are secondary compared with the primary aim of total, immediate access to validated research results, they may adversely affect the future. For example, some kinds of file formats presently widely used – for example, various generations of PDF or Word (DOC) files – will not allow the kind of indexing or the kind of preservation we may need in a few years. Pushing this issue to the background on the basis that open access has more pressing problems to solve first assumes a competition between these concerns, and then further assumes that these problems can be just as easily solved at any stage of open access implementation. Some open access supporters obviously exaggerate when they write about the loss of impact in breathless fashion; they equally exaggerate when they write as if the resources were so rare that any effort diverted from their favourite approach can only slow down the whole movement, given that their pet tactic is the only good one. The reality, luckily, is richer and more nuanced. Some energy can and should be diverted to thinking about mid- and long-term issues.

Case studies must be multiplied, analysed and re-analysed until the right lessons begin clearly to emerge in the form of a widely shared consensus. Far from being a handicap, alternative approaches should be seen as a wealth of opportunities; at the very least, they will allow a kind of institutional selection to take place and, with any luck at all, this weeding out will bring us closer to better solutions. Most likely, they will help uncover dimensions of scholarly communication that only empirical studies could have brought to light.

The future(s)

However arrogant this may sound, the future of open access is not so very difficult to predict, provided no one asks for precise dates or a precise sequence of events. A number of trends are already sufficiently obvious to ensure further expansion. Let us review some examples:

- Institutional repositories will multiply and their roles will become better defined. One may predict that peer-reviewed material will tend to be ever more clearly separated from other materials. At the same time, the organisational basis for peer review stands a good chance of extending beyond journals. Repositories may include research results that have been validated by means other than scientific journals. This may involve the networking of institutional repositories in a variety of ways. Whether this is seen as a 'publishing reform', as some insist it is, or whether this is seen simply as an incentive to stimulate the intake of articles by repositories is ultimately of little importance: what counts is making validated research results universally available, not preserving present validation schemes.

- Disciplinary repositories will also develop and, actually may build on top of, and across, institutional repositories. The beauty of open access is that it allows endless possibilities in the ways in which information is packaged and presented to the reader. But these possibilities may not be so open if poorly chosen file formats introduce unwanted constraints or limitations.

- The political battles for mandating will continue for a while. How long is anybody's guess, but a clear hope is that there exists a 'tipping point' in the process. This is a hope, not a certainty. Yet, it is a reasonable hope for the following reason: institutions, even more than human beings, act very much like sheep and thus tend to imitate each other. Once a movement begins to take form in one country, most institutions in that country will follow. Mandating will take hold within one country. Then, a number of countries will follow and the movement will accelerate. At that point, victory will be at hand. No one knows how long it will take before the movement becomes perceptible, but the moment it does, the successful end will be near. For the moment, we have four institutions spread across as many countries. This is encouraging, but it does not yet bring us to the tipping point. Meanwhile, every attempt to implement mandating from the top has met with fierce resistance on the part of publishers. Their deep pockets seem to yield some real, if temporary, success. Interestingly, publishers do not spare any efforts to stop mandatory archiving, despite assurances by various open access advocates that open access has nothing to do with publishing reform: obviously, publishers think otherwise.

- Open access journals will also continue to develop, particularly in countries where governmental support is central to local scientific publishing. For example, one may expect SciELO to expand greatly in the next couple of years, as well as act as a model for similar developments in countries such as India and China. It may even turn out that SciELO, China and India will join forces, or at least coordinate efforts, to create a powerful collection of open access journals that will quickly gain in reputation and credibility on their own, and thus challenge the traditional fortresses of branding that are largely concentrated in the rich, industrialised, countries. Meanwhile, journals developed along the lines of the Public Library of Science will continue to demonstrate that they can successfully compete with traditional journals on the front of impact factors – a form of competition bound to be deeply affected by the advent of new citation indices beside the venerable (and not entirely reliable) Science Citation Index. Ultimately, we may expect open access journals to win this battle. Once the financing issues are solved with the help of the granting agencies, the very open nature of open access journals will give them a natural advantage over toll-gated journals. Gradually squeezed between ever larger collections of open access journals supported by governments and top branding open access journals in the world of societies, traditional commercial and society journals will have to move closer to open access. Springer's decision to support 'open choice', despite all of its ambiguities and strategic possibilities in terms of counter-attack, can be interpreted in this fashion. Derk Haank, Springer's new CEO, is obviously sufficiently strategic in his thinking to try to anticipate what must soon become obvious to all.

- Publishers will be mandated to move to open access. Mandating publishers to do anything is impossible if they are financially autonomous. However, when publications are supported by public money, as is the case for a large number of scholarly and scientific publications in many countries (France, Italy, Finland, most of Latin America, etc.), mandating open access publishing for these journals becomes possible. In many parts of the world, scientific publishing is not patterned after the Anglo-American economic model and strategies that will miss their target in one particular cultural and/or economic context may well succeed in another. Flexibility in open access approaches, in other words, is of the essence.

Open access, obviously, is still evolving, and so are all the other communities involved in scientific communication in one way or another. Imagining the future(s) of open access requires taking all of these viewpoints into account, as well as trying to understand how they interact with each other. If history is cunning, as Hegel argued, it is first and foremost because it is complex.

Conclusion

Open access is often approached conceptually. While this is useful, particularly in sharpening concepts and focusing issues, it also tends to exclude crucial historical dimensions. The transformations presently affecting scientific communication may have been triggered by a pricing crisis, as librarians often (and rightfully) claim, but this crisis is itself the product of deeper mechanisms. Within the print world, Robert Maxwell and Pergamon Science explored how to make scientific publishing global. As a result, prices began to explode. However significant this phenomenon was, it was quickly dwarfed by the paradigm shift induced by digitisation and the Internet. Without the latter, neither the licensing framework that now presides over scholarly communication, nor open access would have emerged. Self-archiving would simply be impossible without computer networks; so would the objective of making science publicly available. Objections to the effect that Africa is poorly connected, while all too real, do not change the fact that, without digitisation, Africa could not even hope to gain access to the scientific literature of the world at some time in the not too distant future.

Open access is more than just a tactical innovation in scientific publishing; it is more than just a clever plug-in added to the existing publishing system. These characterisations are not without validity, but they fail to capture the essence of what is going on. More to the point are discussions focusing on the opening up of raw data in open archives, as pioneered in particular by genomics, or the discussions around community-wide peer review, or the questions raised by processes of scientific communication that may emerge soon around devices that are entirely different from the present journal model: perhaps science communication, since the seventeenth century, has been nothing but an enormous (and enormously successful) prototype of a future scientific kind of Wikipedia.

In the end, we must approach open access as a symptom and a promise. The symptom points to deep shifts in the tectonic plates supporting scientific communication, and these shifts will not go to completion without redistributing elements of power in profound ways; the promise is for a system where the world of distributed intelligence will be accompanied by a far more efficient communication system. Far more efficient because it is more open and more equitable.

Note

1. 'The journey of the mind to truth'.

Economic costs of toll access
Andrew Odlyzko

Introduction

Many of the early discussions of scholarly electronic publishing, including precursors to what we now call open access, originated among librarians, and were stimulated by the 'serials crisis'. With prices of serials escalating far faster than inflation, libraries were forced into subscription cancellations and drastic cutbacks in book acquisitions. The hope was that something like open access would displace expensive publishers, or at least pressure them to moderate price increases. In practice, though, the revenues of the publishing industry have continued growing, and there are many cases of continuing high profit margins.

Historical precedents suggest that this should not be surprising, and can be expected to continue. Information is becoming ever more important in the economy, so total spending on it can be expected to grow. The invention of printing lowered the costs of information dissemination, and largely eliminated the job of scribes. But it also led to growth in total spending on books.

In recent times, library spending has kept growing, although not as rapidly as journal prices, and in most cases not as rapidly as university budgets. But something else has been happening as well, namely the rise of a large communication infrastructure. Its costs are higher than those of libraries, and it enables new types of scholarly communication (as well as improved access to library resources). It already provides essentially all the resources needed for open access.

The goal of this note is to sketch the monetary costs of toll access, and how they compare with other costs in a typical university setting. This note does not discuss the opportunity cost of toll access, namely the benefits to society of making scholarly information available through open access – this is covered by other chapters in the present work (see Terry and Kiley, Harnad, Harnad and Shadbolt, and Lynch). Suffice to note that these include the benefits to society that would have accrued as a result of more effective research due to researchers' access to and building on relevant research, rather than research their institution can afford; better information discovery tools for researchers, and new research methods (e.g. based on text and data mining), that become possible when research texts and data are not hidden behind access control systems; and better research management, built on reliable data about which research is being used, by whom, when, and so on.

Toll access costs and other costs

We do not have precise statistics on scholarly publishing. Still, it is estimated that the peer-reviewed literature grows by about 2.5 million papers a year, published in approximately 25,000 serials. Of these 2.5 million papers, somewhere on the order of 15 per cent are open access (Hajjem et al., 2005).

The total revenues of scholarly publishers are estimated at around US$10 billion per year. This is a huge sum, but the world's annual spending on research and development (R&D) amounts to about US$1,000 billion per year (National Science Foundation, 2006). As the R&D enterprise relies heavily on the published literature, it is easy to see why there would be a reluctance to make drastic changes in something that costs just 1 per cent of the total.

On the other hand, subscription fees collected by publishers are just one part of scholarly communication costs. Some rough estimates (see Odlyzko, 1995; Odlyzko, 1997a) suggest that the unpaid work of editors and referees costs society about as much as publisher revenues. On the other hand, internal library costs (at least in high-wage industrialised countries) are at least twice as high, while the costs of authors' time (which are not captured explicitly in any accounting) spent writing the papers are at least five times as high. Higher still are the costs (also not accounted for in any formal budgets) of the time of readers of the papers. The frequently heard claims that only a handful of people read the typical paper are disproved by studies by Don King and others. It appears that there are usually several hundred readers per paper (see for example Tenopir and King, 2000). Therefore the total time readers devote to a typical paper is substantial. Hence, in a global sense, one could justify even a very high cost of peer review if it led to higher-quality publications that were easier to locate and absorb. One could even argue for increased support for the kind of extensive editing and proofreading that some publishers used to provide. However, global optimisation is not something one can hope to achieve.

In scholarly publishing, optimisation is done on a local scale in a system with complicated feedbacks and indirect money flows. This system, in which most of the costs are borne by libraries, while the scholars (who are the users as well as the creators of the material) have only an indirect say in what happens, is similar to the US medical industry (see for example Odlyzko, 1997a). As a result, there are many clear inefficiencies. However, as in the medical system, these inefficiencies are not easy to remove.

Partially as a result of the complicated scholarly publishing system, but even more as a result of the extreme inertia among scholars, change is extremely slow. Just about the only way to quickly alter established habits is through mandates (see Odlyzko, 1997b; and chapters by Swan, Harnad and Sale, this volume). A sense of the glacial rates of evolution that are typical of academia is given by the report 'ARL Statistics 2003–04' (Kyrillidou and Young, 2005). Graph 1 in that publication shows that, for the large research libraries of North America that are members of ARL, the following changes took place:

- interlibrary borrowing: +148 per cent
- student population: +18 per cent
- circulation: −1 per cent
- reference transactions: −34 per cent

These are noticeable changes, but they occurred over the 13-year period from 1991 to 2004. Interlibrary loans, which are a small part of the typical research library budget, grew the fastest, to compensate for local library collections not being able to keep up with the growth of literature. But even there, the annual growth rate was only 7.2 per cent.

An institutional perspective

Let us next consider a real example, that of the University of Minnesota. It is a large state university with the full range of undergraduate and professional schools, and several campuses. It has approximately 65,000 students, some part-time, most full-time. During the 2003–04 academic year, total spending came to US$2,100 million, of which US$422 million was sponsored research, funded by outside sources. ARL statistics (Kyrillidou and Young, 2005) show that in that year, library expenditures were US$31.6 million. However, that figure applies only to the Minneapolis and St. Paul campus (although that is the largest campus, by far). In addition, this figure, because of the ARL methodology, does not include some significant accounts, especially employee benefits. If we include all those other items, we find total library budget for the entire University of Minnesota of US$40.8 million, of which US$13.6 million was for acquisitions of serials, books and (the most rapidly increasing part) electronic databases. Thus we find that libraries spent two-thirds of their funds on internal costs (primarily pay for their staff) and absorbed just about 2 per cent of the total university budget. If we had proper accounting for all expenses, we would obtain a somewhat higher figure, as the libraries are not charged for depreciation or maintenance of their buildings, nor for usage of the common communications infrastructure. A decade earlier, the libraries' share of the total budget had been closer to 2.5 per cent although the nominal library budget was far lower than in 2003–04.

Libraries are just one part of scholarly communication. At the University of Minnesota, total spending on information and communication technology (ICT) during the 2003–04 academic year came to about US$150 million, or just about 7 per cent of the entire university budget. This includes about US$4 million of the libraries' spending. Most of that spending, again over two-thirds, is on people, all those systems and network administrators and webmasters (the vast majority employed by departments and other small units) who are required to keep the infrastructure operating.

ICT enables a multitude of activities, from high-performance computing, through telephone services and Internet access, and on to payroll and facilities for students to sign up for classes.

Although ICT spending in Minnesota has been stable at just about 7 per cent of the total university budget for the last few years (a figure similar to that of many other large research universities in the USA), it has surely grown substantially compared with two decades ago, say. (Precise historical data are not available, unfortunately, as spending is decentralised and was not tracked until recently.) And much of that growth of ICT spending has been driven by the demands of scholars for better communication, some related to teaching and departmental affairs, but much for their research. This has enabled the rapid growth of new types of scholarly communication such as described in Odlyzko (2002), in which researchers download papers from online archives and search using Google instead of asking librarians for help. (Note the substantial decline in reference transactions in the ARL data previously described.) With the increasing volume of information available on the Web, ease of access is paramount, especially as satisfactory substitutes are often available even for the most esoteric results.

The real value of discussing a specific institution is the ready availability of data for its ICT spending. In this instance, we find that this spending is far larger than the library budget, and over ten times as large as the book and serial acquisition costs of the library. So costs of supporting open access, which even under the most conservative assumptions are far lower than the costs of the library, are a very small fraction of ICT costs. Almost the entire required infrastructure is already in place, and it requires relatively small steps to make open access a reality, either by mandating self-archiving, or by funding publication charges made by open access publishers.

Conclusions

It is the explicit costs of toll access, namely the costs of journals and books that attract most attention. But these costs are only a small piece of the intricate jigsaw of expenditures that support scholarly communication in its various forms. Internal library costs in large research institutions in industrialised countries are about twice as high as the costs of serials and books. Furthermore, total library costs are dwarfed by the costs of the information and communication technology infrastructures. Many of these expenditures have multiple purposes, and all have their constituencies. Given the slow pace of change among scholars, we should not expect any major changes in funding flows. Although open access does not require much new funding, the 'gold' route might require a 'level playing field' to be established in terms of public funding, as between open access and subscription models. The basic infrastructure for it is already in place, built for other purposes, and with enough capacity to handle the extra load that open access would impose.

5

The impact loss to authors and research

Michael Kurtz and Tim Brody

Introduction

The history of scientific communication is one of increasing access. The Gutenberg press allowed rapid and relatively inexpensive reproduction of the printed word. The advent of postal services allowed for the distribution of papers across countries and around the world by airmail. Peer-reviewed journals created consistent collections of quality-controlled papers, distributed to a wider audience of subscribers. And, as the volume of journals increased, research libraries created collections of journals, catalogued, and made them accessible to patrons from the shelves. The Web – and open access – will allow anyone with an Internet connection to access all the peer-reviewed literature anywhere, anytime. Increased accessibility of peer-reviewed literature should allow that literature to have a greater impact on future research, which will improve the quality of that research. Those who invest in and benefit from primary research, including the general public, have an interest in improvements to the quality of that research. The authors of the peer-reviewed literature also have an interest in increasing its impact, as that impact, as traditionally measured using citation counts, is a major element in the way their work is evaluated.

Without debating the merits of evaluation by citation counting, this does provide a measurable (potential) benefit for authors who provide open access to their research papers. If open access increases citation impact – due to a greater number of scientists being able to access the paper – that presents a strong self-interest argument to encourage authors to go open access. It also hints at the extent to which restrictive access policies negatively affect research and its potential impact on future work.

Open access articles have higher citation impact

Evidence for the greater citation impact of open access articles – compared with similar articles available only through subscription-based journals – has been shown by a number of studies. This greater citation impact of open access articles, as compared with similar subscription articles, is known as the citation advantage of open access. Lawrence (2001a) found a citation advantage for computer science articles freely available on the Web, compared with articles available only through printed conference proceedings. A study performed jointly between the University of Southampton and the Université de Quebec used the Thomson ISI Science Citation Index on CD-ROM to compare papers published in online peer-reviewed journals that were or were not available as e-prints in arXiv.[1] Papers in arXiv are 'self-archived' by their authors – a version of the article, often a preprint, is deposited by the author. arXiv has become an indispensable tool for physics researchers, as it has grown to include almost all published literature in certain sub-fields, and provides early-day access to the published literature. The Science Citation Index contains references to papers published in some 5,000 journals over 20 years, although this study is only relevant to an 11-year subset of that data (1992–2003 inclusive). Those papers found to be both in arXiv and the Science Citation Index received over double the number of citations compared with articles in the same ISI subject area, but not also available from arXiv. Figure 5.1 shows the proportion of papers in arXiv (OAP), the citation advantage (OAA), and the total papers broken down by the year an article was published. The citation advantage is considerable, and increases noticeably in more recent years, probably because an increasing number of papers cite preprints that are only available via arXiv.

Hajjem 2005 has performed a similar study on other disciplines, using a web crawler to determine whether an article is 'open access'. Hajjem found an advantage between 25–250 per cent, depending on field and year.

Figure 5.1 Open access advantage for arXiv papers (based on ISI citation data)

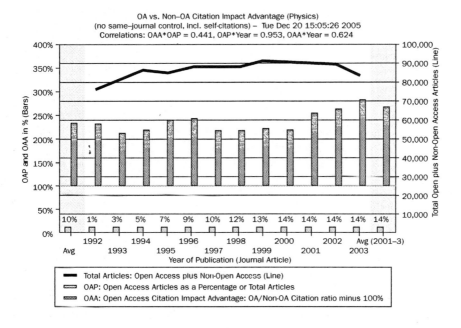

OA vs. Non–OA Citation Impact Advantage (Physics)
(no same–journal control, incl. self-citations) – Tue Dec 20 15:05:26 2005
Correlations: OAA*OAP = 0.441, OAP*Year = 0.953, OAA*Year = 0.624

- ▬ Total Articles: Open Access plus Non-Open Access (Line)
- ▭ OAP: Open Access Articles as a Percentage or Total Articles
- ▨ OAA: Open Access Citation Impact Advantage: OA/Non-OA Citation ratio minus 100%

The NASA Astrophysics Data Service (ADS) allows a comparison to be made between the number of citations to a journal, and the proportion of articles in that journal that have also been posted to arXiv. Querying for articles published in the *Astrophysical Journal* in 2003 finds 2,592 articles cited 48,388 times. Of those articles, 1,935 were found to have an equivalent in arXiv (75 per cent), and accounted for 43,411 of the 48,388 total citations (90 per cent). The 657 'non-arXived' articles received on average 7.58 citations each (4,977/657). The other 1,935 articles received on average 22.43 citations each (43,411/1,935). arXiv articles published in the *Astrophysical Journal* in 2003 received nearly three times the number of citations than non-arXiv articles published in the same journal (or a 196 per cent open access citation advantage). Similar queries were performed for three other journals, and the results are given in Table 5.1.

It is important to note that the open access advantage reported in Table 5.1 compares articles within a journal, rather than between journals. It is a competitive advantage for open access articles within a

| Table 5.1 | Open access advantage for four journals, based on data from the NASA Astrophysics Data Service |

	Nuclear Physics A	Physica	Astrophysical Journal	Physical Review D
Total articles in 2003 (citations)	1,134 (2,878)	3,920 (3,204)	2,592 (48,388)	1,990 (24,441)
Percentage in arXiv	32	11	75	95
Citations	2,590	1,314	43,411	23,952
Open access advantage (%)	667	548	196	181

% open access advantage = no advantage

journal, compared with non-open access articles within the same journal. Comparing journals with each other, Pringle (2004) looked at the relative standing of open access journals in the total ISI journals index, and found little evidence for a citation advantage for them. Any difference that might be found would be more attributable to the editorial standards of quality, than the mode of access, and this underlines the limitations of comparing between journals, rather than between articles within a journal. However, that open access journals compare favourably with established, subscription-based journals is still quite surprising, given that the reputation – hence impact – of a journal takes time to build in a community.

Kurtz et al. (2005), studying astronomy, did not find any evidence that changing from subscription to free access increases the number of citations. First, this confirms astronomy as a special case; it implies that:

> there is no significant population of astronomers who are both authors of major journal articles and who do not have 'sufficient' access to the core research literature. This also implies that increasing access above a 'sufficient' level has no influence on citation frequency. (Kurtz et al., 2005)

Second, it suggests that the wholesale shift to open access within the core literature of a discipline does not result in increased citation impact for that core. However, other advantages accrue to those disciplines that are wholly open access (see Lynch; Shadbolt et al., this volume).

What causes the open access citation advantage?

Given that the open access advantage is at the article level, rather than at the journal level, what are its causes? It is clear that papers available through arXiv receive more citations on average than papers available only through subscription journals. Kurtz et al. (2005), in a study based on seven leading astronomy journals, outline three possible factors that could cause increased citation impact:

- the advantage due to the article being openly (that is, freely) accessible (the 'open access advantage');
- the advantage due to the article being accessible before its potential competitors, for example, as a preprint on arXiv (the 'early access advantage');
- possible bias in the open access sample of papers owing to authors tending to put on the Web (e.g. arXiv) more of what they consider to be their better papers ('self-selection bias').

A fourth possible factor is that inclusion in arXiv itself confers an advantage to a paper, because arXiv is indexed in various alerting and search services, and so raises the profile of the papers it contains (the 'arXiv advantage'). These four factors are discussed below.

The 'open access advantage' is the most difficult factor to test independently, as it demands comparisons between samples of articles that are similar in all other aspects – that is, articles that are provided by the same service(s) (to remove the 'arXiv advantage'), on a comparable topic and at a comparable 'quality' level (to remove the 'self-selection bias'). One approach would be to conduct longitudinal analysis of citations to papers in a particular journal, as the proportion of open access papers increases.

The 'early access advantage' occurs because the preprint establishes priority and 'presence' in the literature, while the journal peer-review process provides the stamp of quality associated with a journal (and the associated impact the journal version affords). Henneken et al. (2006) found that the 'early access advantage' is a permanent benefit – the higher the number of citations to an article, the more 'pointers' there are to that article, hence the more likely researchers will find, read, and cite it. Evidence showing that authors are increasingly citing articles in arXiv *before* those articles are published in a journal is discussed in the citation latency analysis that follows.

Kurtz et al. (2005) provide strong evidence that author 'self-selection bias' explains some of the strength of the citation advantage for articles in astronomy, where there is no open access effect (because the discipline operates as if it had open access, see above), and where the 'early access advantage' can be discounted. An author cannot know what the eventual citation impact of an article will be, but they may have a sense of its quality (hence likelihood to get cited), and opt not to put poorer work in arXiv. The obvious motivation would seem to be that authors are unwilling to place articles in the highly used arXiv service, but are still pressured to publish as much material in journals (as journal publication is recognised in formal research evaluation, and 'grey' literature – like arXiv – is not).

The 'arXiv advantage' occurs because arXiv is an invaluable resource for physicists: as well as providing full texts, it provides alerting services that allow physics researchers to be e-mailed listings of new papers, simplifying discovery of new research. arXiv is also indexed by Google, as well as many research-specific search tools such as Elsevier's Scopus, OAIster, and the new ISI Web of Knowledge. Another tool, Citebase Search (developed by the University of Southampton), provides citation navigation and search tools. The ADS indexes arXiv as part of a wider collection and back-catalogue of physics, astrophysics and astronomy papers. ADS provides e-mail alerting services, similar to arXiv. All of these services increase the exposure – hence impact – of authors who place their papers in arXiv. This 'arXiv advantage', combined with 'early access advantage', provides a citation impact advantage to papers deposited in arXiv.

Citation latency

'Citation latency' is the time between a paper being published and it being cited. In the example in Figure 5.2, a paper 'A' is published on 5th April 2002. A subsequent paper 'B' is published on 14th February 2003 and cites paper 'A'. The time difference between these two dates is ten months, hence the citation latency for these pair of papers is 315 days. Because arXiv date stamps articles to the nearest day (and – being the Web – articles are instantly accessible) it is possible to use an accuracy of days; something not possible in the on-paper era.

Citation latency is a measure of the efficiency of research communication. While research may be citable for a very long time – especially in natural

Figure 5.2 Definition of citation latency

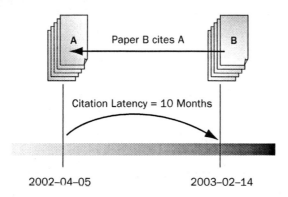

fields, such as chemistry, where the properties and rules of the natural world don't change – most activity, and hence citations, tends towards more recent research. However, it has long been recognised that considerable differences exist between disciplines in this respect (Price, 1970).

As the volume and pace of research inexorably increases, so research publication must follow suit. It is no longer tenable to have research papers languishing in the publication cycle for years when scientific understanding can change dramatically in months. The Web – and preprinting in particular – has a profound effect on the speed with which research results can be made public. The Web allows the instantaneous transmission of information around the world, to any user with an Internet connection, and yet few researchers are taking advantage of this to rapidly distribute (and establish priority on) the results of their research. Rapid preprinting in arXiv demonstrates the effect that instant access to research results can have. Using arXiv as a case study, it is possible to see this effect in action over the 15 years of arXiv's existence.

Open access decreases citation latency

To analyse the effect that arXiv has had on physics communication the citation latency has been plotted for each year (Figure 5.3). All of the citations for each year are plotted according to the number of days between the citing and cited article being posted to the arXiv (see Brody, Harnad and Carr, 2006). As the number of papers held in arXiv has been growing linearly since its inception, the number of citing papers (and hence citations) has grown linearly year on year. This is reflected in older

Figure 5.3   **Citation latency measured across time**

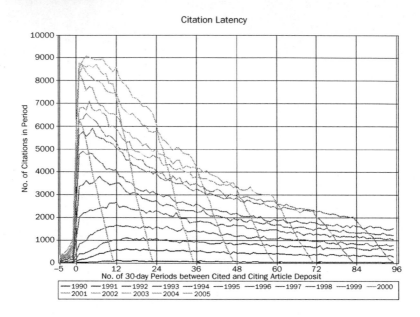

years having a lower line. The oldest (hence lowest) years show a steady increase in the number of citations to a peak at around 12 months, then decreasing over time. This peak-point of citations has decreased each year until the most recent years where there is no apparent delay. This suggests that, as more physicists have deposited their papers in arXiv, so they have also increasingly cited arXiv papers and, with the near instant distribution nature of arXiv, so the peak-point of citation latency has reduced. As these data are based on Citebase (Brody, 2003) they only include citations to arXiv articles, and bias those citations that include an arXiv identifier. That is, it doesn't necessarily follow that the cited 'half-life' has got shorter for articles in arXiv (the amount of time it takes for an article to receive 50 per cent of the total citations it will ever receive).

Restrictive access policies restrict users

Kurtz (2004) compares the number of full-text accesses to a widely accessible journal in astronomy, the *Astrophysical Journal*, against publishers with fewer subscriptions and more restrictive access policies. Kurtz estimates the fraction of ADS users who do not have access to the *Astrophysical Journal* to be 'a few per cent or less'. Hence it provides a 'virtual' open access baseline to test how many would-be users of other journals are denied due to toll barriers. For the *Astrophysical Journal,* the fraction of total visits that included a request for the full text was 63 per cent (presumably the abstract was sufficient information for the 37 per cent remainder). This was taken as a baseline, that is, it was assumed that 63 per cent of visitors to other journals also wanted access to the full text. On this assumption, the *Astrophysical Journal* was compared with a number of other groups of journals (grouped by discipline/publisher) and, in the case of the group of journals with the most restrictive access policies, over half of all would-be users of the full text were denied access to it.

Correlation between use and citation impact

As journals have moved from print to the online medium, analysis of the *usage* of research articles has been made much easier. Web download analysis consists of counting the number of times users request the full text of an article (sometimes augmented with an analysis of the number of requests for pages about the article, such as an 'abstract' page). Similar to counting citations, the Web download impact may be used as an indicator for the importance of that work. This argument is supported by the relationship between the number of times an article is cited (its citation impact) and the number of times it is downloaded (its download impact). Web downloads may even provide a better indication than citations for the usefulness of articles to a research community (Bollen et al., 2005).

A number of studies have calculated the correlation between the numbers of citations and downloads to individual articles. Perneger (2004) found a correlation (Pearson's *r*) of 0.54 for the *British Medical Journal* between downloads from the journal site and citations from the ISI Web of Science. Moed (2005b) found a correlation (Spearman rank) of 0.35 for *Tetrahedron Letters.* Moed attempted to separate the mutual effects of citations on downloads and downloads on citations. Moed found a correlation of 0.11 between initial downloads and later citations, suggesting there is little predictive power in usage data. However, using Citebase Search (Brody, 2003) we have found the correlation between citations (from Citebase) and downloads (from the UK arXiv mirror) of *r* = 0.44 (for the high energy physics sub-field, excluding first seven days of downloads). Restricting the period of downloads to three months (90 days) reduces the correlation to *r* = 0.35, which appears to disagree with Moed's findings.

As has been shown by Kurtz (2004), restrictive access policies can result in a significant reduction in the number of accesses by users. Given the (at least partial) relationship between the number of accesses to full texts and citation impact, reduced download impact may result in reduced citation impact.

Conclusions

Peer-reviewed journal articles also available as open access receive – on average – double the number of citations. This effect is easiest to measure early in the life of a journal article, as the preprint generates citations in addition to the journal article. The advantage is, however, sustained throughout the life of the article, as the more citations that point to an article, the higher the likelihood a researcher will navigate to it by following citation links (hence more reads, more impact and more citations).

We have outlined a number of potential causes for the advantage conferred by open access: through rapid preprinting (which also leads to decreased citation latency), removing toll barriers to authors (and researchers) without the journal subscription, depositing in high-profile open access services and a systematic effect of authors self-selecting higher quality material for author self-archiving.

The 'open access advantage' is a promising author-incentive to promote free access to the scholarly literature (with all the public benefit that comes with that), but establishing clear evidence that free access increases citation impact is beset with technical difficulties. So far, the evidence points towards greater access resulting in higher citation impact and, while some disciplines – like astronomy – are fortunate enough to already enjoy virtual 'open access' (by near-universal journal subscriptions), most disciplines and most countries will not be able to afford such widespread access. For authors in these fields, providing open access through open access journals and author self-archiving (while publishing through a high-quality journal), is the best way to maximise citation impact.

Note

1. See unpublished study by Brody, T. (2004) 'Citation impact of open access articles vs. articles available only through subscription ('toll-access'); available at: *http://www.citebase.org/isi_study/*.

6

The technology of open access
Chris Awre

Enabling open access

In a presentation to a symposium on 'Free culture & the digital library' in October 2005, Simeon Warner looked back over the 14 years since the beginning of the arXiv, the first major preprint archive (Warner, 2005). This archive initially aimed to facilitate the sharing of preprint articles between scholars in the high-energy theoretical physics community, though it has now grown to encompass a varied spectrum of subjects including mathematics, computer science and quantitative biology, as well as many other branches of physics. E-mail had already been used to distribute preprints of articles between interested scholars and research groups, but arXiv provided a place where these preprints could be deposited, organised and subsequently disclosed to the wider community. Originally both deposit and distribution was also by e-mail, though this was quickly followed by FTP and, not long after, by web interfaces to support this interaction.

E-mail and FTP have been two developments among many that have assisted scholars in communicating with each other and sharing information. Technology has long been harnessed to support this process: the origin of the Internet, ARPANET, was built between four US universities in 1969 to support the work of the Advanced Research Projects Agency (Leiner et al., 2003). The development and wide adoption of the World Wide Web, another initiative originally developed to support scholarly communication within the high-energy physics community (Berners-Lee, 1990), has arguably, though, provided more and greater opportunities to support scholarly communication than any other development since ARPANET was put in place. Journal publishers were quick to take advantage of this, providing web access to the electronic equivalent of printed journals. However, as arXiv had shown, the Internet and the Web can be used to facilitate scholarly communication in other ways as well: the boundaries of the printed journal publication are no longer limits in the networked world.

The advent of the open access movement has been chronicled elsewhere in this book (see chapters by Swan, Bailey Jr. and Guédon). The Budapest Open Access Initiative proposed in 2002 (Open Society Institute, 2002) suggested two complementary strategies through which open access might be achieved, taking full advantage of the networked opportunities that had arisen. These were self-archiving into repositories (BOAI1), as demonstrated by arXiv, and the production of open access journals (BOAI2), titles that facilitated the structured dissemination of research articles in a non-subscription environment. This chapter focuses on the technology that underpins these approaches and the ongoing development of solutions to further the exchange of scholarly communications in a world of networked access.

The Open Archives Initiative

The success of arXiv stimulated similar activity in other subject fields: CogPrints, covering psychology, linguistics, neuroscience and computer science; RePEc focused on economics; and the Networked Digital Library of Theses and Dissertations (NDLTD). As the number grew it became apparent that it would be valuable for open access archives to cooperate to enable easier access across them by researchers and others wishing to access their contents. In October 1999 a meeting in Santa Fe, USA led to the Santa Fe Convention of the Open Archives Initiative (Van de Sompel and Lagoze, 2000), subsequently renamed the Open Archives Initiative (OAI) and its Protocol for Metadata Harvesting (OAI-PMH), now at version 2.0 (Lagoze and Van de Sompel, 2003). The Initiative is a series of organisational principles and technical specifications to facilitate a level of interoperability between e-print archives. The underlying mechanism to enable interoperability is metadata harvesting, where metadata from different e-print archives can be harvested into a central service or services that can then be searched independently. Bowman et al. (1995) had originally described this architecture as part of the Harvest project.

At an early stage, the OAI established two separate roles or participants in the harvesting model: data providers, which make available the data from an e-print archive or collection for harvesting;

and service providers, which carry out the harvesting and provide end-user services based on these harvested collections. Data provision is an integrated part of many repository systems (see later) used to store content and associated metadata, though separate data provider software tools are also available. An early, but now well-established, service provider system is the open source Java-based Arc, developed at Old Dominion University (Liu et al., 2001, 2005), and now used widely by other service providers, notably the ePrints UK initiative (Martin, 2003). The Arc service provider can in turn be harvested by other service providers, and thus act as an aggregator data provider service as well as provide end-user search access. Other open source tools to enable both data providers and service providers are listed on the OAI website. Of note are harvester software tools in Perl and PHP and a tool, DP9, that allows web crawlers such as Google to access metadata exposed for harvesting by OAI data providers. The OAI website also lists a number of existing data and service providers.

Adopting the OAI model is relatively straightforward, but does still require that the data provider be implemented fully, a task better suited to organisations than individuals. Two approaches have emerged to allow individual researchers to provide their outputs on open access. The team behind the Arc harvester developed the Kepler framework (Maly et al., 2001), which makes use of 'archivelets' to enable the publication of outputs and make them available for harvesting rapidly from a local PC rather than an institutional server. The executive managing the OAI itself has also developed a specification for OAI Static Repositories, which allows a locally stored XML file to be made available for harvesting by a remote service.

The OAI-PMH can quickly enable the sharing of metadata in most circumstances, although it is accepted that it cannot meet every need yet. Usage has identified areas where improvements might be made for the future. The protocol is currently limited to XML files, requiring data conversion where relevant, and cannot work with RDF (Resource Description Framework). It also makes specific use of the HTTP protocol, where a more abstract model would allow greater flexibility in the network transport protocol used. The format for metadata to be harvested is, by default, unqualified Dublin Core. The protocol makes this mandatory, though only as a lowest common denominator, and leaves open the possible use of more complex metadata schemas. There is increasing experimentation with more detailed metadata formats (e.g. see Bird and Simons, 2003; Richardson and Powell, 2003), though many OAI-PMH transactions continue to use Dublin Core as their basis.

The OAI does not sit in isolation in enabling open access. When building services the protocol can be combined with a number of other digital library protocols and standards to enable a range of functionality. The IMesh project developed a module that allows OAI records to be delivered using RSS (Duke, 2003), while there are also synergies and complementarities between OAI-PMH and SRW/U (Sanderson et al. 2005). The Ockham project has also described how a number of 'lightweight' protocols can be combined to add value to services for the end-user (Xiang and Lease Morgan, 2005). There is much potential in how the OAI-PMH can be used that remains to be revealed, including the possibility of harvesting content as well as metadata.

Implementing self-archiving

At the heart of the first proposed BOAI strategy is a place to store content that will be made available through open access. By virtue of depositing e-prints or other objects in this place, they can be disclosed for others to view. arXiv is an example of such a place, and researchers voluntarily add their preprints to this in order to foster the sharing and discussion of ideas. As noted earlier, a range of other subject-related and other archives have emerged since arXiv. These have not always limited themselves to preprints of potential journal articles, but encompass a wide range of documents and other resources that those in the community are willing to disclose.

E-print archives have been built on top of many technical platforms. The three main components required are a place to store the materials, a mechanism for depositing them and a mechanism for allowing access to them by others. Additional functionality may be provided alongside this. The terms 'archive' and 'repository' have both been applied to this package of functionality and have also been applied to the software available to support such systems. arXiv has been built on a platform of in-house development and the incorporation of tools as required. Others have made use of dedicated repository software. For example, the E-LIS archive for library and information science is built on top of Eprints software (Medeiros, 2004), developed at the University of Southampton as part of the Open Citation Project, which also examined and developed tools to enable citation linking from e-print archives (Hitchcock et al., 2002).

The establishment of e-print archives for subject communities has been gradual since the origins of arXiv. Since 2002 there has also been a great deal of activity in establishing and promoting institutional e-print archives (often labelled institutional repositories). Early repository initiatives at the Universities of Nottingham and Edinburgh both used the Eprints software (Pinfield et al., 2002). At about the same time, SPARC in the USA commissioned a report to investigate the potential of institutional repositories (Crow, 2002) and Cliff Lynch from the Coalition for Networked Information described the benefits institutions would gain from establishing a repository: enabling alternative scholarly communication paths was prominent among these (Lynch, 2003). The interest in institutional repositories led to the Open Society Institute producing a report on available open source software packages (Crow, 2004). This report offers a good starting point in consideration of open source software packages: it is noteworthy that the majority of e-print repositories use one of these systems, predominantly Eprints or DSpace, a collaborative development between MIT and Hewlett-Packard. Current usage of these systems can be viewed through the Registry of Open Access Repositories (ROAR) or Directory of Open Access Repositories (DOAR). The commercial sector has, though, also developed repository software that can assist open access, for example ProQuest's Digital Commons@, Innovative's Symposia, and BioMed Central's Open Repository service. The latter is notable for providing a hosted service for institutions or organisations that are unable to implement their own system.

There are many aspects to implementation of an institutional repository, including both technical and non-technical aspects (Grieg and Nixon, 2005). Technical planning at an early stage is vital, however, to ensure the repository is capable of supporting its intended needs. Technical architecture and metadata are key to this planning.

Technical architecture

Planning for an institutional repository to allow open access to e-prints requires consideration of wider repository needs. Within the institution different views of the repository may be required: these specific needs could be addressed through alterations to the user interface or separate installations of the repository software, each with their own view of the relevant content. The nature of the content being stored in the repositories will also have an impact. E-print repositories that focus solely on copies of peer-reviewed published papers (providing open access to these) can be set up separately to those for preprints or other materials, or they can all be included in one repository and flagged accordingly.

In an open access environment, it is also important to consider how any one repository will be accessed alongside others. Service providers were discussed earlier. The University of Glasgow investigated the use of a local OAI harvester to provide a single view across their repositories and have also been able to expose their repositories to Google (Nixon et al., 2005). This approach has also been adopted by the OAIster service provider with Yahoo! With the flexibility of being able to move metadata (and potentially content itself) around using OAI-PMH, there is scope for individual repositories to be included in a wider federation through which content can be accessed and delivered in a flexible manner. Work on the aDORe architecture at the Los Alamos National Laboratory has highlighted many of the issues (and requirements) needed to enable this (Van de Sompel et al., 2005).

Metadata

Metadata has been at the core of cataloguing and information discovery systems for many years: catalogues hold metadata about a library's holdings, and bibliographic databases hold metadata about a variety of different materials. This metadata has been used largely to describe physical content, although the metadata schemes employed, often MARC, have been adapted to describe digital content where required, often at a local level. Implementing an institutional repository offers an opportunity to re-visit how digital content should be described, and appropriate metadata scheme(s) put in place. A number of alternatives have been developed to meet the needs of managing digital content (Jeevan and Nair, 2004), and the purpose and role of repository will influence the choice.

For an e-prints repository, Dublin Core metadata provides a means of describing articles to support interoperability between repositories and open access to them through appropriate services, and is, of course, mandated as the minimum requirement for use with the OAI-PMH. Metadata quality is an important part of facilitating management and access and this requires careful attention in the implementation of a self-archiving environment (Barton et al., 2003). The ePrints UK project has proposed some recommendations for how to describe e-prints using Dublin Core to encourage standardisation (Powell et al., 2003).

Implementing open access journals

The second strategy of the BOAI revolves around the production of journal titles that do not charge for subscription or access. A number of models have emerged from this strategy to provide free access to e-prints over the Web. The first port of call in discovering which open access journals exist is the Directory of Open Access Journals, based at Lund University in Sweden: as of February 2006 over 2000 titles are listed in this directory. The technology underpinning these titles varies, as an open access journal can range in complexity from a simple web page to a fully interactive database-driven service. However, two mechanisms have emerged that can help facilitate the generation of open access journals.

E-prints in repositories provide a source of material for an open access journal. Indeed, generating a journal from repository content can be a value-added mechanism of providing more structured access to the repository's contents. The emphasis can come from both directions. The journal can be based on repository contents, such as the *Lund Virtual Medical Journal* which is based on the Lund University institutional repository LU:research; or the repository can hold e-prints submitted for inclusion in the journal from, for example the *Journal of eLiteracy* at the University of Glasgow. Overlay journals, as these titles are sometimes referred to, have also been set up over subject-based repositories: *Advances in Theoretical and Mathematical Physics* is based on submissions to arXiv and additional titles based on arXiv's holdings have also been established.

It has been argued that true overlay journals amalgamate from across more than one repository (Smith, 2003). The American Institute of Physics and American Physical Society offer a series of virtual journals that bring together content from other publications, although these are not open access. However, in a discussion at the 3rd CERN Workshop on Innovations in Scholarly Communications it was considered that more content and greater consistency is required in institutional repositories to fully support this model of overlay journals (Warner, 2004).

The Australian Research Repositories Online to the World (ARROW) project based at Monash University in Australia has, as part of its remit, the development of an e-press, to be built alongside and supported by the repository. This 'overlay' activity doesn't just rely on repository contents, though, but proactively seeks to use the repository as part of the e-publication process. More specific development of systems to support the running of an open access journal has also taken place, for example the development of the DPubS open source publishing system, created as part of Project Euclid, a project assisting with electronic publication in mathematics (Ehling, 2005).

Looking ahead

The technology to enable the establishment of e-print archives and repositories is now relatively mature in its ability to support open access scholarly communication. Much development focuses on the policy framework within which these technologies sit. However, there are also many ongoing technical investigations in areas that will enhance open access scholarly communication still further. Two are briefly mentioned here.

Following on from the Open Citation Project mentioned earlier, citation analysis of open access articles is attracting growing attention. The project itself led to the development of the Citebase Search citation search index based on harvested open access e-prints. A report by ISI in 2004 noted that open access articles were being cited highly alongside those published through toll journals (McVeigh, 2004; see also Kurtz and Brody, this volume); they are now releasing the Web Citation Index, which will cover institutional repositories as well as open access journals. These tools will enable ongoing analysis of the impact of open access publishing.

Harvesting e-prints has largely been limited to metadata about them – the OAI-PMH is about metadata harvesting, after all. However, there is scope to harvest the full content of an e-print and related materials where relevant. One potential path is to allow complex objects to be harvested using OAI-PMH, containing both content and metadata wrapped up in an MPEG-21 DIDL package (Van de Sompel et al., 2004); this has the potential for enabling a step up in the ability to communicate over the network and share research outputs.

In conclusion, technical advances and the underpinning network have opened up the development of new techniques to support scholarly communication. It is likely that such advances will continue and support future scholarly communication and research through open access and collaboration.

Part 2
Open access and researchers

The main participants in open access are researchers. They are both the subject and primary beneficiaries of open access. The following three chapters, by Alma Swan, Stevan Harnad and Arthur Sale, focus on researchers and, in particular, on researchers and 'green' open access (self-archiving). It is significant that two of these three chapters are written by active researchers, for whom open access is a means to an end, and makes sense within the practical demands of their research work. All three chapters take the rationale for open access as read and then ask, in different ways, 'what is to be done?'

In Chapter 7, Alma Swan draws from the surveys undertaken by Key Perspectives Ltd into researchers' attitudes toward open access. She describes the context in which researchers work, and how this leads to them valuing (or not) the potential of open access. Based on this evidence, she outlines a range of practical moves that can be made to configure open access as a solution to researchers' very real needs and concerns.

The evidence collected and presented by Alma Swan has been invaluable in establishing open access as a practical and feasible enterprise. As an academic researcher, Stevan Harnad also has the advantage of being an insider, of knowing from personal experience how researchers work and, therefore, what barriers exist to open access. Stevan has also been at the vanguard of the open access movement for as long as it has existed, maintaining a clear focus on the 'green' road to open access, that is, self-archiving. In Chapter 8 he describes why open access makes sense from a researcher's perspective, outlines a range of objections that are raised by fellow researchers to self-archiving, and counters each in turn.

While Alma Swan focuses on the evidence that researchers find open access, particularly 'green' open access, a practical option, and Stevan Harnad counters some of the objections they sometimes raise against it, Arthur Sale in Chapter 9 takes a very practical approach – what works, in terms of setting up and filling an institutional repository? To do this, he takes the two hats that researchers wear, searcher (reader) and author, and examines how the repository works from these points of view.

7

The culture of open access: researchers' views and responses

Alma Swan

The last couple of years have seen the acceptance of open access as a desirable goal by institutions, research funders, libraries and some publishers, to the point that these parties have taken action towards achieving it. Scholars themselves, however, have proved somewhat harder to prod into action. Once they understand the aims of open access, however, they generally identify with the concept – unsurprisingly, as it is scholars themselves who stand to benefit most from its inception. Nevertheless, in general scholars have been slow to act in ways that bring about open access, a significant retardant to progress for open access as its implementation is largely in the hands of the research community itself. What is behind this?

Before that question can be answered, it is instructive to revisit the primary motivations of researchers with respect to publishing their work. Why do they publish at all? We feel we understand the answer to that one: it is largely because if they do not publish, their work remains obscure and their life's toils are as worthless. On a more mundane note, they publish because it is the overt expression of their effort and because it offers a way of measuring, albeit fairly crudely, their 'worth'. Finally, they publish because it is expected of them, by their employers and by the bodies that fund them.

If their motives are examined more closely, though, scholars provide further clarification on this point. Figure 7.1 shows the proportions of authors in the respondent pool from one of our author surveys who gave a 'very important, classification to various reasons for publishing the results of their work (Swan and Brown, 2005). Several reasons are considered very important, but the one that comes out top is *to communicate my results to my peers*. Researchers consider it a top

Figure 7.1 Researchers' reasons for publishing their work

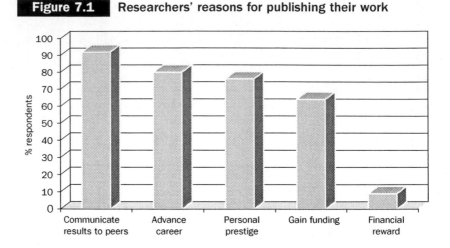

priority to report their results to their peer community so that others can read and build upon them. They wish to make an impact.

Now that we understand the major aspiration of researchers with respect to publishing their work, it comes as a surprise that, given the impact advantage that open access brings (see Kurtz and Brody, this volume), more authors do not see the connection and make providing open access to their work a priority. So far, according to our own data, around a quarter of researchers have placed copies of their articles on their own website (or their department's site), around 20 per cent have self-archived articles in their institutional repository and even fewer have done so in a subject-based centralised repository. Around one-quarter have submitted at least one article to an open access journal, although 49 per cent say they intend to do so over the next three years. These are not figures that support the notion that researchers care most of all about making an impact on their field, so what is the explanation for the discrepancy between intent and practice?

First, there is the issue of awareness. Many researchers simply remain unaware of the concept of open access or, if they have heard of it, they remain largely ignorant of its implications. Our findings show that over one-third of researchers are not familiar in any way with the possibility of self-archiving their work, for example. There is evidence, though, that things are changing and that awareness is growing. In two surveys one year apart, we found that there had been an increase in the percentages of researchers self-archiving their work (Swan and Brown, 2004, 2005); a further study indicated that awareness of open access had grown in the period between it and its predecessor carried out by the same body a year earlier (Rowlands and Nicholas, 2005). Nevertheless, within the academic community there still remains work to be done to raise awareness of open access.

Second, there is a lack of clear understanding and appreciation of the issues concerning open access, even when scholars consider themselves to be familiar with the concept. The arena is a minefield of misconceptions, some arising from incorrect information in the first place, some from simple misunderstandings and some rooted in the nomenclatures and terminologies – and their unfortunate misuse – that pervade the scene.

Third, there is disinterest on the part of some researchers who feel, for one reason or another, that access to the research literature is not a problem. Some such people may be privileged enough to work in well-funded institutions whose libraries can supply all they want. Others fall back on the 'information overload' angle, declaring that they have quite enough information to contend with and do not need access to more, freely-provided or not. Such cases are misguided, for, as I have argued elsewhere, the term open access is a misnomer – though one we are stuck with – for the issue is about enhancing research dissemination and not, primarily, access. Enhanced access (for others) is the outcome of a process that requires active participation on behalf of researchers, who should understand that they are being offered an opportunity to maximise the potential impact of their own work in this way.

Fourth, there are a number of specific, practice-based reasons that researchers give for not providing open access to their work. In the case of open access journals, authors who have already published in such journals say they have done so primarily because they subscribe to the principle of free access for all readers. Conversely, those who have not used such journals say the main reason they have not done so is that they are not familiar enough with such journals in their field to submit their work there.

With respect to self-archiving, the alternative method of providing open access, authors have anxieties about what the process actually entails (see also Harnad, this volume). There are three commonly-expressed worries: that if they self-archive they will be infringing a rights agreement with their publisher, that it will take too much time, and that it will be difficult to do. It is easy to debunk all three of these (though harder to get the message over to researchers).

Regarding copyright, over 90 per cent of journals explicitly permit authors to self-archive their articles, in most cases as postprints (after peer review, in the form of the author's final submitted manuscript) and in a few cases as preprints (before peer review, in the form of the author's final draft before submission to the publisher). The policies for each journal and for each publisher can be consulted at two sites on the Web maintained by the University of Southampton (Eprints Journal Policies) and the SHERPA Project at the University of Nottingham (Sherpa/RoMEO list), both in the UK.[1]

As far as the worry about time pressures, the answer is that it takes a few minutes to deposit an article in a repository. Our own data show that this is true for the majority of researchers (Figure 7.2). Data from the log files of the repository at Southampton University's School of Electronics and Computer science corroborate this finding. The log files show that each article takes about ten minutes to deposit (Carr and Harnad, 2005).

That leaves the issue of difficulty. Once again, we can turn to our own data to see what authors say about this. Most of them say it is very easy; in fact almost three-quarters of them say it is either easy or very easy and only 9 per cent express any degree of difficulty at all with the procedure (Figure 7.3). Any reader doubting this can try a sample deposition themselves using the Eprints software on the Demoprints facility.

Researcher anxieties and objections on these points can therefore be very simply answered, and researchers reassured, but there remains one more factor which is much harder to counter, and that is inertia. Researchers whose institution has a repository and who fully identify with the aims and objectives of open access still grin ruefully if challenged informally as to why they have not deposited their articles, or have done so in a less than systematic fashion – depositing some but not others, perhaps, or omitting the most recent ones – and say they will 'get round to it'. Every reader will recognise this: it is a condition that afflicts us all over one aspect or other of life. But what can be done about it?

Figure 7.2   **Time taken to deposit an article in a repository**

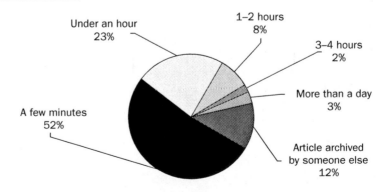

Figure 7.3 Ease of deposition of an article in a repository

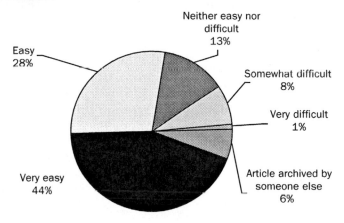

The answer is very simple – *require* researchers to provide open access to their work. This may seem a tough stance, especially when the constituency involved is a body of independent-thinking researchers. Isn't this a somewhat dangerous course of action? It turns out that it is not.

We asked researchers, in two separate surveys, how they would respond to a requirement from their employer or funder to make their work open access by self-archiving their articles in an open access repository. The answer could not have been clearer, with the vast majority (81 per cent) saying they would comply with such a requirement willingly. Fourteen per cent said they would do so reluctantly and only 5 per cent said they would not comply at all (Figure 7.4).

That is what researchers *say* they would do. What happens in practice, though? Well, we can see, because already several institutions around the world have implemented such a mandate, as recorded in the Registry of Open Access Repository Material Archiving Policies. It seems that such a policy works in open access terms while making no waves in terms of researcher reaction. Elsewhere in this volume my colleague Arthur Sale presents the evidence, demonstrating that an institutional mandate is successful in producing open access, by providing the deposition data (the number of articles deposited in institutional repositories) for a number of Australian universities that have differing policies on open access. He contrasts the high proportion of published articles self-archived in a university with a mandatory policy (Queensland University of Technology) with the much lower proportions at other universities, institutions that have only voluntary policies.

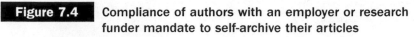

Figure 7.4 Compliance of authors with an employer or research funder mandate to self-archive their articles

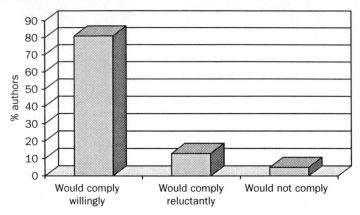

We can look elsewhere, too, to see that this holds up across the world. In Europe the particle physics laboratory, CERN, has a mandatory policy on open access, with the result that approaching 90 per cent of articles published by CERN scientists are now in their repository and available to all. The School of Electronics & Computer Science at the University of Southampton has over 90 per cent of its published articles self-archived in its repository, thanks to its own mandatory policy introduced in 2003. And there are other examples, too.

In contrast, where self-archiving is a voluntary issue, researchers succumb to the aforementioned inertia, unfounded anxieties, or just lack of awareness. The National Institutes of Health in the USA, for example, introduced an open access policy in 2005 (see Suber, this volume). After much deliberation about wording, the final version *requested* NIH-funded researchers to deposit their articles in the PubMed Central repository, rather than *requiring* them to do this, despite all the advice and blandishments from open access experts that this would not be sufficient to produce the open access that the US Congress had intended when it instructed the NIH to act on this matter (US Government House Appropriations Bill, 2004). The open access advocates proved right: in the first few months of the policy's operation, fewer than three of every 100 articles that should have been deposited actually appeared in PubMed Central. The upshot is that the policy and its implementation must now be reviewed and amended in the light of this, costing another year of lost access (as well as more US taxpayers' money into the bargain).

In contrast, the London-based Wellcome Trust implemented its own open access policy in October 2005 (Wellcome Trust, 2005a) with a requirement – rather than a request – to its funded researchers to provide open access to the results of the research it funds (see Terry and Kiley, this volume). In the first few weeks the Trust received a considerable number of responses from its fundees, none of them voicing any objections: the queries were about how to comply with the mandate – either specific questions about self-archiving or questions about how to find out what rights policies their favourite journals espouse (Terry, R., personal communication). Moreover, articles *are* being deposited by Trust researchers.

That is the stick, then. Is there also a carrot somewhere, too, to tempt researchers to provide open access? Yes – several.

First, there is the enhanced visibility that open access brings their work. Downloads lead to citations in a predictable way (Brody, Harnad and Carr, 2006) and so the more an author can maximise the number of downloads to their articles, the more citations should result. Elsewhere in this volume Tim Brody and Michael Kurtz describe their work on the effect of open access on citations.

Some researchers have already made the link between the opportunities of the digital age (new dissemination channels), visibility, and eventual impact, as witnessed by the reasonably high numbers of researchers who have put their articles up on their websites for all to access, along with other information about their professional activities. This is, however, the least satisfactory way to self-archive as from the user point of view, as locating articles placed on websites, even in the age of Google Scholar, can be a haphazard process and from the provider's end there is no systematic provision for long-term access of any individual articles. One challenge, then, is to convert these people to self-archiving not on websites but in formal, organised, OAI-compliant repositories so that they become part of the global open access corpus. There is some reason to think that this might already be happening: our data show that there has been an increase in all three types of self-archiving over the year between our surveys, the biggest increase having been in the use of institutional repositories (Figure 7.5). Part of the explanation for this may be that there has been an increase in repositories themselves over this time as more and more institutions see the benefits of having such a digital archive for providing open access as well as for other reasons. As repositories become established, institutions begin to advocate their use to their research communities. Researchers see their articles being downloaded from their institutional repositories and they know their work is gaining an increased readership.

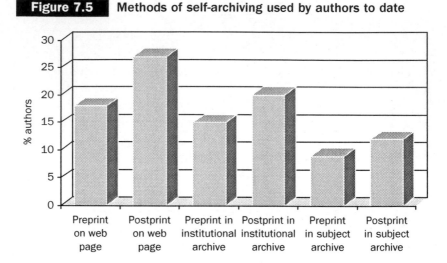

Figure 7.5 Methods of self-archiving used by authors to date

Second, repository managers can help this edification process by providing usage statistics, such as the feature introduced to the University of Tasmania's repository by Arthur Sale, which he describes in this volume.

Third, repository managers can assist in other ways, by providing guidance, advice, encouragement and practical assistance where necessary for researchers willing to self-archive but deterred by some aspect of the process.

Finally, funders and employers can help researchers who wish to publish their work in open access journals. They can do this in two ways: by explicitly permitting funds from research support to be used to pay, at least in part, any publication fees such journals may levy, and by explicitly affirming – as the Wellcome Trust has – the principle that it is the intrinsic merit of the work of the researcher, rather than the journal in which it is published, that will be considered in any career, research assessment or funding decisions.

Note

1. See *http://romeo.eprints.org/* and *http://www.sherpa.ac.uk/romeo.php*.

8

Opening access by overcoming Zeno's paralysis

Stevan Harnad

Optimal and inevitable, but when?

First, the foregone conclusions: open access means free Webwide access, immediately and permanently, to the full texts of all 2.5 million articles published annually in the planet's 24,000 peer-reviewed research journals across all scholarly and scientific disciplines.[1] One hundred per cent open access is optimal for research, researchers, their institutions, their funders, and their funders' funders (the tax-paying public) because it maximises research access and impact (Harnad, 2006). One hundred per cent open access is also 100 per cent feasible, immediately. So it is safe to say that something that is both optimal and immediately feasible is also inevitable (Harnad, 1997). The rest is just about (1) *when* 100 per cent open access will be reached, (2) *how*, and (3) *what has been taking it so long*?

I will be unable to say here precisely when 100 per cent open access will be reached, apart from saying that it is already well overdue historically, and could already have been reached at least a decade ago (Harnad, 1995). It is clear that 100 per cent open access will not be reached via the 'golden road' of first converting all or most of the 24,000 journals to open access publishing; the golden road is too slow and uncertain, and out of the hands of the research community. One hundred per cent open access will be reached via the 'green road', with researchers making their own articles – published in non-open access journals – open access by self-archiving them free for all on the Web (Harnad et al., 2004) – although it is possible that green itself will then lead to gold!

What is taking 100 per cent open access so long to reach has been a series of purely psychological obstacles that I have dubbed 'Zeno's paralysis' (Harnad, 2000). Although each paralytic phobia can be shown to be spurious and based on easily dispelled misunderstandings, a rather relentless history of symptom-transfers, hopping from one phobia to the other, possibly in circles, has by now demonstrated that the only swift and sure way to break free of this paralytic circle is for researchers' own institutions (see the Registry of Open Access Repository Material Archiving Policies, ROARMAP)[2] and funders (such as the UK Research Councils, see RCUK, 2006) to *mandate* open access self-archiving, as some have already begun to do, successfully.

The status quo ante

Worldwide open access today is hovering somewhere between 5–25 per cent (Hajjem et al., 2005). Yet 100 per cent open access has been reachable in principle since the 1980s, with the possibility of immediately depositing all those articles in 'anonymous FTP sites' (Harnad, 1995). Such sites, however, were rather like unmarked common graves if users didn't know what was where; and search and retrieval were awkward, inefficient and indirect. The author just deposited the document and hoped for the best. Anonymous FTP was just being improved upon with tools like Gopher, Archie and Veronica (now all obsolete), when Tim Berners-Lee invented the World Wide Web in the early 1990s. Websites then immediately became the natural place to deposit articles.

Before the advent of FTP and the Web, researchers had been mailing reprints (hard copies) of their articles to would-be users who wrote to request them; now, however, 'eprints' could be e-mailed, or, better still, deposited on an openly accessible FTP or website, so all would-be users could search and retrieve them directly as/when needed. As of 1999, such websites could even be made 'interoperable' by making their metadata (author name, title, date, journal name, etc.) compliant with the OAI-PMH (see Awre, this volume). That means they could all be automatically harvested from the many distributed websites and seamlessly searched and retrieved as if they were all in one global archive reserved only for research articles.

Research impact

It is worthwhile pausing at this point to ask why, in the paper era, researchers would have taken the time, trouble, and expense to mail out paper reprints in the first place: don't authors just want to publish their work and then collect the sales royalties? Not researchers. They publish their findings so that neither they nor their research perishes, but instead progresses ('publish or perish'). They need to publish so as to earn their salaries and research grants, and their research is evaluated and rewarded not just on the basis of its quantity but on the basis of its quality and importance – and its quality and importance depends on its research impact.

What is research impact? A cure for cancer or global warming is what most laymen have in mind when they think of research. In reality, however, research is a slow, collective, cumulative process, with occasional punctuated leaps; and even those leaps are mainly leaps in basic research progress, measured in terms of still more research generated. Only rarely are they direct leaps to applications such as curing cancer.

For research to lead to progress, whether in the form of further basic research or in the form of applications, the research findings first have to be accessed and used by those who might build upon or apply them. And therein lies the reason why no author of a peer-reviewed research journal article ever sought payment from users for the privilege of accessing their article: because whatever restricts research access also restricts research impact and progress, thereby also restricting the researcher's own career progress (Diamond, 1986; Garfield, 1988) as well as the return on his institution's and funder's investment in his research (Harnad et al., 2003; Harnad 2006).

So researchers don't want to be paid for their articles: that would be an access restriction. They just want their articles to be read, used, applied and built upon, in as much further research as possible, without restriction. That is also why researchers are rewarded by their institutions and funders not merely on the basis of the number of articles they publish, but on their uptake, influence and impact on further research – of which one important measure is the number of subsequent articles that use and cite their findings. This is known as their 'citation impact' (Garfield, 1973; Moed, 2005a).

From reprints to eprints

Researchers' quest for maximal research impact is also why, in the paper era, they used to give away free reprints of their articles to all would-be users (rather than trying to collect fees or sales-royalties, as other kinds of authors do). Their publishers *did* have to charge access-tolls to subscribing user-institutions, because there were real costs that had to be recovered in order to pay for the peer-review, editing, printing and distributing the paper edition. The online era reduced some of those costs, but as long as there continues to be a demand for the paper edition, the costs for the double edition, paper and online, remain higher than costs had been in the paper-only era, not lower. And even online-only journals still have real costs to recover.

So, just as providing reprints to would-be users had been a parallel practice in the paper era – supplementing the subscription-based access for users whose institutions could afford the journal with free copies for those who could not – so providing open access by self-archiving eprints on a publicly accessible website is the natural online-era extension of the researcher's perennial effort to maximise the accessibility and impact of their work.

Is open access needed?

If it is natural, feasible, optimal, and inevitable, why is open access still hovering at around 15 per cent instead of immediately fast-forwarding to 100 per cent? One hypothesis might be that open access is no longer necessary: online toll-based access, via institutional subscriptions and licences, already ensures that all users have access to all the articles they need, and all authors have all the users and impact they want. But is this true? There is no doubt that the online medium itself has increased access; but there is considerable evidence that it has not maximised it:

- Librarians continue to report that their institutions cannot afford all the journals they need (the 'serials crisis'), and the Association of Research Library statistics confirm that most institutions can only afford a small fraction of the total number of journals published (ARL Statistics interactive edition)[3]. That all represents lost potential access and impact.

- User surveys suggest that many researchers do not feel they have access to all the journals they need (e.g. Swan and Brown 2005, Question 8; but cf. 'Pretty-sitting', below). A very small number of disciplines do already have 100 per cent open access: astrophysics, because it has a small, closed circle of journals that are open access to virtually all research-active astrophysicists worldwide online via the

Astrophysics Data System, ADS (Kurtz et al., 2004); and high-energy physics, which has been self-archiving nearly 100 per cent of its research for many years now (Harnad and Brody, 2004). But most disciplines are still nowhere near 100 per cent open access.

- Thirty-four thousand biomedical researchers signed the Public Library of Science open letter in 2001, demanding open access from their publishers – which they presumably would not have demanded if they felt they already had.

- When the citation counts for open access and non-open access articles in the same journal and year are compared, open access articles consistently have 25–250 per cent more citation impact in every year and every field tested so far (see Kurtz and Brody, this volume), beginning with computer science (Lawrence, 2001b) and physics (Harnad and Brody, 2004), and ten other fields in biological and social sciences (Hajjem et al., 2005). Many factors contribute to the open access impact advantage, including (1) a selective tendency for better authors' better papers to be self-archived, (2) a competitive advantage of open access over non-open access (which will of course vanish at 100 per cent open access), (3) a permanent added advantage from providing open access earlier, (4) and an early usage advantage (many more downloads) (Kurtz et al., 2005), which is itself correlated with and predictive of a citation advantage 18 months later (Brody et al., 2006; Moed, 2005b). These consistent open access advantages in citation counts also confirm that non-open access articles are not maximising their research impact.

Hence both the accessibility data and the usage/citation data indicate that neither access nor impact is being maximised today, and that substantial benefits still await the 85 per cent of articles that are not yet open access. Even on the most conservative estimate, research is losing 0.25×85 per cent or at least a fifth of its potential impact today. Yet the remedy has been within reach for at least a decade, and entails only a few keystrokes per article (Carr and Harnad, 2005). Why has the research community taken so long to reach for the optimal and inevitable?

Digital dystonia

There are many reasons for the research community's inertia, and virtually all of them unaccountably begin with the letter 'P', which also happens to be the first letter of 'paralysis'. I have therefore dubbed the condition that they induce 'Zeno's paralysis', after the philosopher who worried, 'How can I possibly walk across the room? There isn't enough time! Before I can get across the room I first have to get half way across the room, and that takes time; but before I can get half way across the room, I have to get half of half-way across the room; and so on. So there isn't the time even to get started; hence I can't possibly walk across the room.'

The pragmatic solution to Zeno's paradox is of course to just go ahead and let your legs do the walking anyway. The cure for Zeno's paralysis is the same, except it's your fingers that need to do the walking. Why would anyone ever have thought that they couldn't possibly do the few keystrokes that would get us all to 100 per cent open access?

The Public Library of Science petition to publishers

Before I list all the Ps that have held our fingers back, I begin with another P that merely portends the syndrome: the 34,000 biomedical researchers I mentioned earlier, who signed the October 2000 Public Library of Science (PLoS) open letter to their publishers (threatening to boycott them if by September 2001 they did not agree to make all their contents open access within six months of publication). The 34,000 did all the keystrokes required to sign that petition, but the petition was unsuccessful: publishers failed to comply. So, come the day, September 2001, as there was nowhere else for them to go, the 34,000 signatories did not abide by their boycott threat either, and are, to this day, still waiting for journals to convert to open access. Indeed, so far, fewer than 10 per cent of journals have done so, as reported by the Directory of Open Access Journals. Hence the puzzle that already portends Zeno's paralysis: for if the 34,000 had simply performed a few more keystrokes per paper, they themselves could have provided the very open access they were passively petitioning their publishers for, without having to wait for or count upon the compliance of any other party!

Why did the 34,000 PLoS signatories – and 85 per cent of the rest of the world research community – not do the optimal, inevitable and obvious in order to *provide for themselves* the open access that (the boycott threat would tend to indicate) they so urgently needed and wanted? What has instead been keeping most researchers in a state of Zeno's paralysis for a half-decade as of the PLoS petition (and for more than a decade, if we date the pandemic from the time self-archiving was first formally proposed (Harnad, 1995) – or even longer, if we reckon as of when *de facto* self-archiving had first begun to be practised by the stout-hearted computer scientists who had created the online medium itself and the philanthropic physicists who had been systematically sharing preprints among themselves even back in the paper era)? Here are 19 of the most common causes of Zeno's paralysis,[4] and their antidotes.

- *Permission/piracy: 'How can I possibly self-archive? It's illegal!'* This is the most common worry. First, of the nearly three-quarters of a million self-archived computer science papers harvested in Citeseer or the nearly half-million physics papers self-archived in arXiv across the past decade and a half, fewer than 0.0001 per cent have since been removed citing copyright reasons. That is the sensible strategy: to self-archive all papers immediately, and consider whether or not to remove them only if/when there should ever be a request from the publisher. If the authors of all those articles had simply remained paralysed about whether or not they should self-archive, on the off-chance that publishers might object, computer science and physics would have had 1.25 million fewer articles freely accessed and used across the past 15 years.

  Second, far from requesting removal, the principal journal publishers in physics subsequently became the first to officially endorse author self-archiving. Since then, 93 per cent of the nearly 9,000 journals registered so far (and this includes virtually all the most important ones) have also given author self-archiving their 'green light' (see Eprints Journal Policies statistics).[5]

  Third, the remaining 7 per cent of papers should also be self-archived in any case; if access to their full texts is set as 'restricted' instead of open access, their OAI-PMH metadata (author name, title, journal name, date, etc.) are still visible and searchable to everyone, and the archiving software will allow would-be users to automatically transmit their e-mail addresses with one keystroke to the author, who can in turn automatically e-mail the full eprint to them with one keystroke. So even restricted-access articles are just a few extra keystrokes and a short delay away from being open access – as long as they are all self-archived OAI-compliantly.

  Fourth, and perhaps most important, 'piracy' pertains to consumer *theft* of the producer's product (music, video, software), presumably against the producer's will. Self-archiving, in contrast, is producer *give-away* of his *own* product (to maximise access and impact) (Harnad, 1995).

- *Peer review: 'How can I possibly self-archive? It's not peer-reviewed!'* Open access self-archiving is the self-archiving of peer-reviewed journal articles, before (preprint) and after (postprint) peer review. Open access self-archiving is a *supplement* to – not a *substitute* for – publishing in a peer-reviewed journal.

- *Prestige: 'How can I possibly self-archive? It lacks the prestige of publication!'* Variant of the above: the self-archived version simply provides supplementary access to a published, peer-reviewed journal article. The prestige comes from having met the established quality standards of the journal. Self-archiving merely maximises access and impact.

- *Promotion: 'How can I possibly self-archive? It won't count for performance review!'* Another variant of the above: self-archiving is not self-publishing. It is the peer-reviewed, published journal article that counts for performance review. Supplementary access provided by open access self-archiving merely serves to increase the article's citation impact, which then also counts for performance review (Smith and Eysenck, 2002).

- *Preservation/posterity: 'How can I possibly self-archive? It may not last forever, like paper!'* First, once again: open access self-archiving is a *supplement* to – not a *substitute* for – publishing in a peer-reviewed journal. It is the published journal version, whether paper or digital, that needs to be preserved for prosperity, just as it always was. The purpose of the self-archived supplement is to maximise access and impact.

  Second, the self-archived supplements nevertheless can, and should, and will be preserved too. The older self-archived articles by computer scientists and physicists are still with us, and continuing to be used and cited to this day. If the authors of all those articles had simply remained paralysed about whether or not they should self-archive, because it might not be preserved forever, computer science and physics would have had 1.25 million fewer articles freely accessed and used across the past 15 years.

- *Priority: 'How can I possibly self-archive? I may lose priority for my work!'* Publicly self-archiving a date-stamped preprint online is the best way to establish priority even before publishing.

- *Plagiarism/poaching/property: 'How can I possibly self-archive? My work could get plagiarised!'* All work that is made public can be plagiarised, but plagiarism of online open access text is also easier to detect and document. The only way to make plagiarism impossible is to neither publish nor make it accessible to anyone.

- *Privacy/patents: 'How can I possibly self-archive? My ideas could get stolen!'* Again, the only way to prevent ideas from being stolen is to keep them secret, by neither publishing nor making them public. But open access is for research findings, published to be used and applied, not for secrets, kept private to be patented and sold.

- *Paranoia: 'Why should I self-archive? My institution would then own or control my work!'* A researcher's institution, like its researchers, has vastly more to gain from maximising the impact of its research output by maximising access to it, than it does from trying to collect access tolls. But in any case, authors retain their article's authorship, the journal editors and peer-reviewers control the article's quality, and the institutional archive merely provides supplementary access, to maximise the article's impact. (There is no need, by the way, as a precondition for self-archiving, for authors to retain copyright, or to transfer copyright to their institutions, or to adopt a Creative Commons licence. Although any of these, especially the Creative Commons licence, are welcome and desirable in their own right, it is a great mistake to make self-archiving contingent in any way on first having to successfully re-negotiate rights with one's publisher. Again, if the self-archiving computer scientists and physicists had waited instead for successful copyright retention, their research would have lost the decade and a half of maximised usage and impact that 85 per cent of research still lacks.)

- *Proliferation: 'How can I possibly self-archive? Users won't know which is the authentic version!'* The definitive version of a published article is the publisher's version, accessible to those who can afford it, as it always was. The supplementary author-self-archived version is for those who cannot afford access to the publisher's version, and who would otherwise have to do without access altogether. In addition, authors can and will self-archive pre-peer-review preprint drafts if they wish; but what they should always self-archive is their peer-reviewed, accepted final draft ('postprint') – as well as any subsequent corrections, revisions or updates. Nevertheless, version-tagging and control can and is feasible, and is being implemented in the self-archiving software packages.

- *Paper-glut: 'Why should I self-archive? It's already hard enough to find things and to keep up!'* Open access self-archiving is done in order to maximise the impact of one's own research, by maximising access to it. Online navigation, search and retrieval is incomparably more powerful and efficient than any other means of navigation, search and retrieval, but it also has the virtue of being self-limited: if a user has had too much, they can always quit surfing. But the reverse is not true: if an article has not been made open access online, and a would-be user cannot afford access to it, they cannot access it at all – and that bit of its potential usage and impact is lost. Surely interest and time is a less arbitrary arbiter of what we can access and use than is affordability (to our institutions).

- *Pricing: 'Why should I self-archive? All we need is affordable journals!'* What is needed in order to maximise research impact is to maximise potential-user access. Making journals more affordable (that is, lowering the cost of access) increases access but it does not and cannot maximise it; for even if all 24,000 journals were sold at-cost (zero profit), and their costs were minimised, most institutions worldwide still could not afford all or most of them. Hence articles and authors would continue to lose potential users and impact. Any cost barrier is always an access/impact barrier.

- *Pretty-sitting: 'Why should I self-archive? I already have all the access I need!'* Author and user hats are being mixed up here (see Sale, this volume): authors self-archive their work for impact, not for access – they already have access to their own work! Even if an author is 'sitting pretty' (that is, even if their institution seems to be able to afford access to all the journals they, as a user, feel they want and need) there is still the problem of users at other, less well-endowed institutions, who may wish to access (and use and cite) that author's work. There is an element of golden-rule reciprocal altruism underlying self-archiving, insofar as user-access alone is concerned, but when it comes to author-impact, self-archiving is a matter of pure self-interest. And with 85 per cent of articles not yet open access, and no institution able to afford even 85 per cent of the planet's 24,000 peer-reviewed journals, there just might be a few items out there that even the prettiest-sitter today would find useful, even if they don't realise it, from where they sit.

- *Papyrophilia/print/PDF: 'Why should I self-archive? It's print-on-paper we need!'* The print journal is fine for those who prefer and can afford it. For the rest, either online use, or printing off hard copy have to suffice. For surfing and browsing, online is even better than on paper. For users starved for access, only Marie Antoinette would counsel 'let them read paper!' Furthermore, the knock-on effect is there for authors too, starved for impact.

- *Publishing's future: 'Why should I self-archive? It's open access journals we need!'* To just keep waiting passively for publishers to provide gold open access, instead of going ahead and providing green open access for one's own articles is not only a counsel of despair, but it casts some doubt on the research community's putative need and desire for open access: if we want it so much, why are we not yet providing it for ourselves? If open access is so important, how can we afford to sit waiting for the remaining 22,000 journals to convert, one by one? And why *should* journals convert, at some sacrifice and risk to their revenue streams, if the authors clamouring for open access cannot even be bothered to do some obvious, risk-free self-help, in order to get it, by giving it?

Of course, self-archiving is not without *perceived* risk: that is what gives rise to Zeno's paralysis! But the 93 per cent of journals that are 'green' have already taken the step of eliminating even the perceived risk for 93 per cent of authors, by giving self-archiving their explicit blessing. So waiting passively for gold in particular seems particularly paradoxical (and I suspect it is more often publishing-reform-theory-driven rather than research-access-impact-need-driven...)

- *Publishers' future: 'How can I possibly self-archive? It will put my publisher out of business!'* All the evidence to date is that subscription-based journal publishing and author self-archiving can co-exist peacefully, the latter supplementing the former, to maximise research impact, to the benefit of both. The two foremost publishers in physics (where self-archiving has been extensively practised for 15 years, with some subfields having reached 100 per cent years ago) report that there has been no detectable decline in subscriptions associated with self-archiving across those years (Swan and Brown, 2005).

But if 100 per cent self-archiving ever were to create a decline in subscriptions that made cost-recovery via subscriptions unsustainable, that would not put non-open access publishers out of business; it would merely put them into the open access publishing business (Harnad, 2003b). Each institution's annual windfall savings from cancelling the subscriptions for its incoming journals would be more than enough to cover its annual costs for the open access publishing of its outgoing articles.

All of this is counterfactual speculation (Zeno style), however, for all the actual evidence to date is that self-archiving has highly positive effects on research access and impact and no negative effect on journal subscriptions.

■ *Professional societies' future: 'How can I possibly self-archive? It will ruin my learned society!'* The reply is the same as for publishers in general, except that whereas commercial publishers are presumably only in the business for the revenue, learned society publishers are supposed to be acting in the interests of their memberships, that is, the research community. To the extent that learned societies fund their good works (meetings, scholarships, lobbying, etc.) out of their publishing revenues, an illuminating way to put the question to their member-researchers is whether – if the two were ever in conflict – they would willingly and knowingly choose to continue subsidising their learned society's good works with their own lost research impact? The reply is very likely to be that the good works should find some other way to fund themselves.

But that too is speculation, as all evidence to date is that self-archiving has highly positive effects on research access and impact and no negative effect on journal subscriptions.

■ *Professional future of librarians: 'How can I possibly self-archive? It will put librarians out of work!'* The library community too will find plenty to do in the digital world, including the open access subset of it. As with publishers and learned societies, the status quo cannot be sustained and subsidised by needlessly lost research access and impact.

■ *Priorities/perspiration: 'How can I possibly self-archive? It's too complicated and time-consuming and I already have more to do than I can manage!'* This comes closest to Zeno's original paradox about it being too time-consuming to cross the room. Part of the antidote is to stop sitting on one's hands and simply let one's fingers do a few deposits, to discover for themselves how simple and quick it really is to self-archive (Carr and Harnad, 2005). But for the bigger problem of assigning self-archiving its proper priority in researchers' time-management hierarchy, 95 per cent of researchers surveyed the world over have signalled that if their institutions and/or their research funders mandate self-archiving, they will comply (Swan and Brown, 2005).

The prophylaxis against Zeno's paralysis

It is accordingly time now to put the prophylaxis against Zeno's paralysis into place. The UK Research Councils have proposed mandating self-archiving (RCUK, 2006), and five institutions – the Universities of Minho, Southampton, and Zurich, Queensland University of Technology and CERN – have already done so (see the Registry of Open Access Repository Material Archiving Policies).[6] They are, as a result, well on their way toward 100 per cent open access, exactly as the Swan and Brown (2005) survey predicted. Once the rest of the planet follows suit, the optimal and the inevitable outcome for research, researchers, their institutions, their funders, and their funders' funders – the tax-paying public – will be upon us at long last.

Notes

1. This figure is derived from Ulrich's Periodical Directory, available at: *http://www.ulrichsweb.com/ulrichsweb/*.
2. See *http://www.eprints.org/openaccess/policysignup/*.
3. See *http://fisher.lib.virginia.edu/arl/index.html*.
4. A full treatment of all 32 symptoms identified to date is available at: *http://www.eprints.org/openaccess/self-faq/#32-worries*.
5. See *http://romeo.eprints.org/stats.php*.
6. See *http://www.eprints.org/openaccess/policysignup/*.

9

Researchers and institutional repositories

Arthur Sale

The two hats

In discussing the roles that researchers take relative to open access, it is important to note that they approach it with two different attitudes, depending on which phase of the research they are in. The most familiar is the researcher while conducting research and looking for information about the research topic – the *searcher*. Libraries have long dealt with searchers. The other role is that of researcher as disseminator – the *author*. Libraries infrequently deal with authors, and usually as a special case.

The distinction between these two 'hats' or roles is important: the needs of the researchers are very different, and so is their behaviour. Let's tease out the consequences of this classification.

Researcher as searcher

Client communities

When an institutional repository is proposed, one of the first questions to ask is 'Who are the intended readers?' Unfortunately, the answers are not so simple:

- Every operator of an institutional repository (see Bailey Jr, this volume) would nominate researchers in other institutions as one of the prime client communities. Open access is supposed to open access to local research to researchers globally. Such searchers may be in universities, research institutes, or in business operations. This is, of course, absolutely correct and the first priority, but this group does not comprise all searchers.

- The second obvious group is really a class of meta-clients: the institution's research management entities, the grant-giving authorities, and often government. Because of the power of this group, their needs as searchers for meta-information may be given almost an equally high priority as the genuine researchers. Their influence can often be spotted in otherwise unnecessary metadata and search facilities. Other meta-clients include the researchers into repository usage and impact.

- Third, there is a diverse group which I will call the general public. These may comprise school teachers, school students, and the simply interested individuals. As much research is often of esoteric interest and may be written in highly technical language, members of this group may not be interested in it. However there are classes of research for which this is not so. Personal health, eco-systems and environmental issues, politics, history, culture and art are examples. For instance, a paper I wrote 30 years ago (Sale, 1975) on generating Pythagorean triads (whole-numbered right-angled triangles like [3,4,5] and [5,12,13]) continues to evoke a consistent stream of enquiries from this group, mostly amateur mathematicians or school teachers (145 downloads in a year).

Knowing the target readership can affect the responses to the rest of this discussion. Let's concentrate on the researchers.

Priorities and tolerance

Searchers have clear ideas of their priorities, which are often surprising to the operators of repositories. Their top priorities and expectations are that:

- what they want should be easily discoverable;
- everything provided by the institution should be available online.

These two aspects are not negotiable. Searchers will simply not pursue hard-to-discover resources, and if the second expectation is not met, the resource will not be discovered. A subtle variant of this occurs if the repository contains only a bibliographic record of the resource, and not the 'full text'. Most searchers will ignore such resources as trying to acquire them does not seem worth the effort. Some improvement can be achieved by placing an e-mail link on the metadata display page that creates and formats a request to the author for a copy, thus minimising the work involved (one or two clicks), but this is at best a palliative. Much lower on the priority list is:

- authoritative content.

The evidence suggests that searchers would like to see authoritative content such as actual refereed research papers published in journals but their need for this is low. Their primary need is to read the paper to determine whether it is of interest to them, and even the provenance of the paper is of lesser interest. A pre-publication postprint, a preprint and even a version in plain-text with no formatting and all the diagrams removed may be quite acceptable. If the paper interests them, then they will be prepared to invest more work in finding a more authoritative source, if only to quote the page numbers in a reference of their own. The lowest priority is:

- eye candy.

Searchers couldn't care less about eye candy on the pages they are presented. By eye candy I mean added headers, footers, prettiness, and so on added to the basic scholarly paper they have come to read. At best it just wastes screen space or paper; at worst it irritates the reader. Plain is good.

What are the consequences for the repository operator? They are simple to enumerate: capture 100 per cent content, and make your content discoverable by as many means as possible. Provide an e-mail link on plain bibliographic records, and certainly always provide a link to the authoritative source. Keep the web pages simple and clean, maximising information content.

Journals respond to this analysis too. An institutional repository is not an alternative to a journal for a researcher intending to reference a paper. Rather it is an alternative discovery tool directing researchers to the authoritative article. This is possibly one of the reasons why the open access movement does not seem to have any negative influence on journal subscription rates in research institutions: researchers as searchers still want to have access to as much authoritative content as they can, even if they discover the content otherwise than on paper or at the publisher's website. Although the actual accesses to the publisher's website might drop, there is no pressure from the researchers to cancel subscriptions.

Discoverability

I suggested that making content discoverable by as many means as possible is desirable, and so it is. For example, the metadata for a PhD thesis in several repositories (such as the University of Melbourne) is harvested by the Australasian Digital Thesis Program (ADT) and by the ARROW Discovery Service. ARROW also harvests from the ADT Program, so the thesis metadata appears twice in it. Google, Yahoo, Scirus, OAISter and other search engines harvest from ARROW, ADT Program and the Melbourne repository. Find it whatever the route.

However, since the Google Scholar program was announced in late 2004, it has been increasingly obvious from inspection of the logs on my repository (and from the user statistics) that a high fraction of the hits on the repository come from Google. Even more significantly, these hits were direct to the 'full-text' file. On analysis it was discovered that Google was indexing PDF files, and the searchers were choosing them preferentially over the pages that presented the metadata (title, abstract, etc). An example of a search result with both destinations is shown in Figure 9.1.

The implications are serious. It is totally desirable that people using Google as their search strategy, perhaps their only one, found a resource on our site. However, it meant that all the metadata and all the extra information that we might put on the metadata page (such as links to the authoritative source) was simply not viewed by the searcher. This posed questions for repository management investment.

Our consequent analysis suggests that metadata generation, and especially 'perfect metadata' should take a low priority. Author or automatically-generated metadata may well be satisfactory. The metadata may increasingly have the main role of allowing porting of content to a new repository and similar library and archival functions. Only local searchers use local repository search; few searchers use

Figure 9.1   **Result of a Google search**

federated national gateways either, as they don't know about them. Federated global gateways are the primary discovery tool.

This is not to say that federated national gateways have no use, rather that they address a different group of clients: those I nominated as meta-clients. National gateways are used by in-country librarians (who know about them) and government. They also help slightly in multiplexing the discovery routes. But their search engines and federated metadata repositories should not be seen as major contributors to searcher discovery.

Researcher as author

Let's turn our attention to the quite different behaviours exhibited by researchers when they are acting as authors.

Research impact

Researchers that know about open access practise it for one major reason: to get their research disseminated to as many people as possible. The reward comes in knowing that the research has been used and valued by other people, and that the effort and money in producing it has not been wasted. Secondarily they may receive monetary awards in the form of prestige, tenure, promotion, or more research grants.

One measure of research impact is citations of the work. A citation means that someone, whose research it presumably influenced, thought the article significant enough to include a reference in their own publication. Research-measuring authorities are slowly realising that journal impact factors are just a surrogate for citations, and as they do researchers will become more and more interested in citation counts. Other chapters in this book (principally that by Kurtz and Brody) address the increased citation rate that open access articles generate, compared with subscription-only articles.

There are, however, other forms of research impact. There is increasing literature showing that download statistics predict citations. Some downloads are not related to citations, but may nevertheless affect the behaviour of non-researchers. Examples are government policy changes, changes in teaching practices, and industrial developments. Some self-archiving open access researchers have been known to complain that they get too many e-mails about their articles; my riposte is always 'Would you prefer to be ignored?'

Copyright

Authors seldom have any knowledge of copyright law, and are extremely hazy about what they sign away in a journal–author agreement. Their institutions have historically shown little interest in rights, so authors have (roughly speaking) signed them away for free. Consequently when asked to self-archive, their instinctive response is to be risk-averse: 'I don't know anything about this and I don't want to be sued, so let's play safe and say no'. This is a significant barrier to overcome, even if it is nonsense (see also Harnad, this volume).

University copyright officers and librarians also raise this problem to a much higher level than is necessary. They do know or want to know copyright law, but they often mistakenly conflate music and video piracy with scholarly publishing. The two domains are worlds apart. Scholarly research output is always given away for free; indeed sometimes the author is asked to pay to have their work published, and the publishers make their money out of disseminating this material they get for free.

Their angst is totally unnecessary as over 90 per cent of publishers have no problems with self-archiving at present. Conference organisers are similarly approving. However it is a major barrier to take-up of open access self-archiving, and strategies to attack it must be undertaken by the repository managers. One useful strategy first employed by the Queensland University of Technology is to say to the authors: 'Just deposit your article. We (the library editors) will check your copyright agreement and make it open access if possible, otherwise it will be restricted to *on*-campus use. Of course if you want to, you can specify the article should be open access or restricted.' This works!

An interesting feature of author response to open access is that once a researcher has deposited one or two articles in a repository and seen the value, they cease to become copyright-sensitive. They integrate the issue in their general research practices at the back of their mind, many of which have legal consequences of which they are blissfully unaware or reluctantly aware, and never look back.

Mandatory policies

My colleague Alma Swan has written about her study of research attitudes to policies that require (or imply censure for not) archiving an institution's research publications. Briefly, most authors won't self-archive voluntarily. Only a little work is required especially compared with producing the publication in the first place, but this work is avoidable and will be avoided. Aversion to getting involved with copyright may also play a part. However if required to self-archive, authors will comply willingly as the authorities obviously value the activity and will handle the copyright, and it is only a little work.

Let's look at a graph of how this works out in practice, examining all seven Australian universities that operated a repository in 2004 and are harvested by the ARROW Discovery Service. Figure 9.2 shows the number of items in each repository with a publication date of 2004 or 2005, as a percentage of the officially reported research publication count to the Australian Government (Department of Education, Science and Training, DEST). Three universities are identified as exemplars of the major factors:

- University of Tasmania (low library support, voluntary deposit);
- The University of Queensland (strong library support, voluntary deposit); and
- Queensland University of Technology (strong library support, the only one of these seven having a requirement to deposit all research output, commenced on 1 January 2004).

Clearly, voluntary policies don't work, even with above average effort. On the other hand, requiring researchers to deposit is easily accepted even in a nation of rugged individualists like Australia. Since at the time of writing all 2005 input had not been received, Queensland University of Technology content looked like reaching 60 per cent of available

Figure 9.2 Content of Australian repositories, January 2006

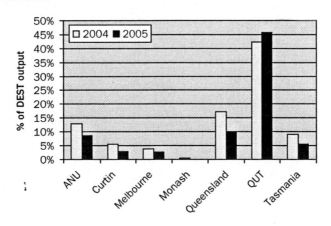

research in its second year of a requirement policy. The implication is clear. Any institution that does not have a compulsory deposit in its kitbag is wasting its money establishing a repository. Twenty per cent success is the most that can be expected otherwise and even that is optimistic (Sale, 2006a,b).

Conversion

There is an interesting phenomenon to be observed with authors. Although they are difficult to convince to self-archive, for the reasons discussed earlier, once they have self-archived one or two articles, they don't look back. It becomes a routine part of their research activity, and a significant number become enthusiastic.

It is almost like St Paul's conversion on the road to Damascus: many researchers become evangelisers and start infecting their own colleagues with their enthusiasm. E-mail feedback from readers, citations, and the evidence of the download statistics, pays off in spades. Some of the consequences are discussed later. However, this is good news for the operators of institutional repositories: initial hard work to provide author support decreases with time, as more and more of them come on board, and fewer and fewer need support.

Research training

If open access is a key activity for researchers of the twenty-first century, are we doing enough to train the researchers of the future, even if they are more Internet-savvy than their elders? Maybe not yet totally integrated, but in my university and school we are doing our best. I run a short generic skill course for PhD candidates in self-archiving. PhD candidates immediately see the benefit of self-archiving their publications (citations, exposure, comment, claim to priority) much faster than faculty, and adopt it very easily. They then have a Trojan horse effect on their supervisors – weak, but it does sometimes work.

We have also incorporated this into our honours programme (fourth year) by making the first class honours theses available online, as well as any publications that these students achieve, thus encouraging transfer into the PhD programme by exposing the students to modern practices. I view this as part of training the candidates and inducting them into the practices of twenty-first century researchers.

Retrospectivity

As noted, some researchers become avid open access supporters. And frequently they will scavenge their old files to find old articles that they can mount. The more enthusiastic will even bring out their paper-only articles and scan them as text images. Generally this behaviour is restricted to those articles that the author feels really proud of, or thinks could stand the test of time. Articles that are somewhat dated may be passed over. To give an example, my institution's own archive has 15 articles with an original publication date prior to 1980.

Some researchers adopt a different approach, which I call the 'just in time' strategy. They don't post all their old articles, but as soon as someone asks for a copy of an old article, they arrange to have it scanned (or scan it themselves) and put it on the repository, sending the URL to the requester. This is equally effective, but driven by the readers rather than the authors. The problem with this, however, is that the article may not be discovered, because even its metadata are not on the open access repository.

Why do authors do this? I believe that the answers are in the next two sections.

Avid dissemination followers

Some authors become interested in their dissemination success, and add this into their research strategy. The benefits are that they see where their work is cited, in broad terms who is interested in their research, and which areas might be most productive for future work. They also learn about citations and their importance and tend to follow some of the meta-literature about research.

This can be encouraged by providing the authors with feedback from the repository in terms they can understand. Conventional web statistics are no good as authors cannot understand the ICT jargon – the statistics must be couched in meaningful language. For example, I wrote a statistics package which is used by my own and other universities. At the bottom of each document metadata page is a statistics link (alternatively available from the homepage) which gives access to counts of metadata views and downloads for the last four weeks, month, year, or all time, broken down by country of access and month. Figures 9.3 and 9.4 show sample statistics for a document in the University of Tasmania repository, for the year 2005.

Figure 9.3 Example of download statistics, first screen

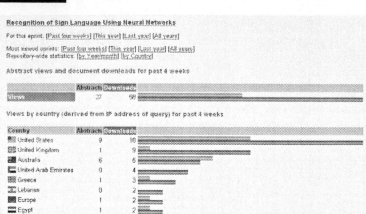

There are several salient things to notice.

- As previously discussed, the number of downloads may exceed metadata views, indicating that some searchers are finding the full-text file without going through the OAI-PMH interface (e.g. via OAIster) or the local search engine.

- This document (a PhD thesis) is downloaded from a variety of countries, but the USA, the UK and Australia predominate (there is a long tail of countries with lesser downloads).

Figure 9.4 shows the time series analysis of the same document. Something happened, probably in July/August 2005, to cause a surge in downloads of this document. The author's interest was piqued, and he

Figure 9.4 Example of downloads by month

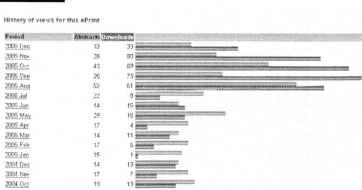

traced the cause down to a citation of another paper of his, which itself cited this document. This resulted in him identifying the research of another person working in his field, half a world away.

CVs and websites

Besides becoming involved in the dissemination process, the open access repository can be a useful tool in reducing work for the researcher, and in making a case for promotion. Let's look at these two cases.

Some researchers realise quite early that if they self-archive their articles they do not need to mount the same articles on their personal or research website. They therefore modify their website so that instead of links to an internal copy of an article they provide a link to the persistent URL of its repository metadata page. This is an easy realisation, and many make it instantly.

Another development may occur to the researcher, or as I have observed, it may spread like a meme. The researcher will delete all the links to articles, and all the papers on his or her website and instead they put a simple link which is a search on the repository for their name, of course with some text like 'Click here to see all my articles since 2003'. With one simple move they have simplified their website maintenance (the article lists never need to be updated) as long as they keep self-archiving. A similar approach may be used on websites devoted to a department's research, or to recruiting new graduate students, with even more saving in effort and better accuracy.

Promotion, improved jobs and grant success are cases dear to every researcher's heart. Citations have been estimated to be worth between $AUS100 to $AUS2000 per annum to a researcher in either direct income prospects or grant success, so the increased citation benefit of open access is obviously a plus. However, evidence from download statistics can also be quoted, especially as evidence accumulates about how they translate into citations. Some researchers have been observed to use download statistics, or download rankings, to mention in a promotion application or a grant application. The relevant committees are generally not yet sophisticated enough to fully realise what they are seeing, but they soon will be. The Internet generation is growing up into influencing decision-making at this level.

It is also possible to extract data (like a list of papers in a consistent format) for insertion in a curriculum vitae, whether that be for a job application or a promotion application. This is simply using the repository as a personal database: convenient, accessible, provided by the institution, and backed-up by professionals.

Plagiarism

One feature of open access repositories that is seldom mentioned is their ability to detect plagiarism, and thereby lower the level of scientific fraud. One author was experimenting with a popular piece of plagiarism software, and tried it out on one of his own papers. He was interested to see that it turned up a substantial direct quotation from his paper by an author in another country, but less pleased to find that the quotation was unattributed. He took legal advice, and the offending author was contacted for redress.

This application worked only because the document was open access on the Internet. Conventional paper publications and toll access journals cannot be searched for plagiarism.

Part 3
Open access and other participants

Three chapters have been devoted to researchers' perspectives on open access, but there are other potential participants in any move to open access. Indeed, some of the most significant moves so far have come from them. The following four chapters turn our attention to the views of, and business implications of open access for, research funders, open access publishers, learned societies and institutions. Whereas the focus of the chapters concerned with researchers was primarily on 'green' open access (self-archiving), the focus of the following four chapters is spread across both 'green' and 'gold' open access, and those concerned with publishers and learned societies are exclusively focused on 'gold' open access. These differences in emphasis represent the understandable interests of the authors of those chapters, but also serve to underline the breadth of the open access debate, and the extent and potential impact of the changes that may be underway. While open access has advantages for all, the picture is varied, and there is work still to be done if all the current participants in scholarly communication are to join the open access movement.

Research funders have a key stake in scholarly communication; it is both evidence with which they can demonstrate the return on their investments, and the foundation for the continued viability of the enterprise they support. There is increasing interest from funders around the world in the potential of open access to further their aims. In Chapter 10, Robert Terry and Robert Kiley, both of the Wellcome Trust, outline the reasons for the Trust's position in favour of open access and the practical steps being taken to support researchers in moving to an open access model.

The Wellcome Trust supports both 'green' and 'gold' open access. In the following two chapters the focus is specifically on open access publishing ('gold'), and illustrates one of the key debates around open access: is there a viable open access business model for those currently publishing journals? In brief, Matthew Cockerill (BioMed Central) argues that yes, there is, whereas Mary Waltham is more circumspect.

Matthew Cockerill, in Chapter 11, draws a parallel between open access and open government, noting that only by making information freely available can we hope to build the kinds of systems and services that are already useful, and that will be essential in the future.

If Matthew Cockerill is clear about the benefits, indeed necessity, of open access, then Mary Waltham is more circumspect. Her chapter is based on an investigation commissioned by the Joint Information Systems Committee (JISC) Scholarly Communications Group in the UK. It reveals that the business models of learned society publishers lead them to question the viability, in their circumstances, of current models of open access publishing. Nevertheless, undeniable strains within the subscription model mean that further experiments and investigation, perhaps on a disciplinary basis, are likely.

If the attraction of open access to learned societies is not unalloyed, its attraction to institutions might be expected to be clearer. And indeed, Colin Steele in the following chapter presents a cogent case for the institutional benefits of open access, if institutions take a broad cost/ benefit approach to scholarly communication. This is only partially because open access is prompting the establishment of institutional repositories, which then bring all kinds of other benefits to the institution besides those directly attributable to open access. There are barriers here too, though, that derive from researcher inertia (see chapters by Swan, Harnad and Sale), and from the separation of library and research funding, with scholarly communication sitting uneasily across both.

10

Open access to the research literature: a funder's perspective

Robert Terry and Robert Kiley

Introduction

In a declaration to commemorate the publication of the first draft of the human genome, UK Prime Minister Tony Blair and US President Bill Clinton commented that, 'unencumbered access to this information will promote discoveries that will reduce the burden of disease, improve health around the world and enhance the quality of life for all human kind' (quoted in BBC, 2000).

One of the major funders of the human genome project was the Wellcome Trust,[1] an independent charity that funds research to improve human and animal health. And, having been at the forefront of the decision to make the genome sequencing data freely available, it was perhaps inevitable that this funding body would lead the way in advocating free access to the research literature. If, as the Trust believes, it makes sense for scientists to have free access to raw, genomic data – to help realise the promise of this research – then it makes equal sense for scientists to be able to access the outputs (journal articles), to enable this research to be built on and developed.

This chapter considers the issues around open access from the perspective of a research funder.

Background

The Wellcome Trust first began to look at issues of access to the research literature following concerns raised by its own Wellcome Library Advisory Committee during 2001. In response, the Trust commissioned two reports from economic consultants SQW in order to understand the structure and economics of scientific journal publishing (SQW, 2003, 2004). These reports highlighted a number of issues.

One was the rising cost of paying to read the research literature. Subscriptions to science, technical and medical (STM) journals had risen by over 200 per cent in the period 1990–2000, at a time when inflation was in single figures (from Blackwell's Periodical Price Indexes 1990–2000, quoted in SQW, 2003). This, coupled with the knowledge that certain publishers were taking large profits out of the system (House of Commons, Science and Technology Committee, 2004a), suggested the market for publishing scientific research is, from our perspective, a failing market.

Second, researchers, as authors, give their research papers to publishers for free and are mostly unaware of the cost of reading the material – when they are readers – because subscriptions are dealt with through the library budgets. As such, there is no real link between the user of the journals and the cost of obtaining access to those journals and consequently, no downward pressure on prices (see Figure 10.1)

As journal costs were increasing at a far greater rate than library budgets, the total number of journal titles to which researchers had access actually fell. Data from the Association of Research Libraries

Figure 10.1 The economic cycle of scientific research publishing

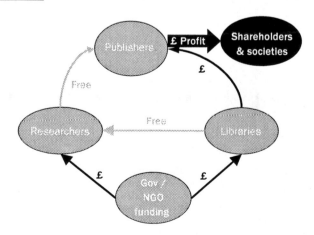

(ARL Statistics and Measurement Program) showed that in the last decade of the twentieth century the number of serials titles purchased by large academic research libraries fell by 5 per cent.

Against this background – often referred to as the 'serials crisis' – and fuelled by the Internet revolution, a new method of distributing peer-reviewed research papers was born: the open access model.

Defining open access

For the Wellcome Trust, an open access publication is one that meets two conditions, as defined by the Bethesda Statement (2003). The Bethesda statement, drafted in 2003 following a meeting organised by the Howard Hughes Medical Institute, is important as it marked the first occasion when funding bodies discussed the issues pertaining to open access with a number of publishers, learned societies and universities (see Bailey, Jr., this volume).

The Bethesda Statement (2003) defines access, reuse and archiving as important elements of an open access work:

(a) The author(s) and copyright holder(s) grant(s) to all users a free, irrevocable, worldwide, perpetual (for the lifetime of the applicable copyright) right of access to the work, and a licence to copy, use, distribute, perform and display the work publicly and to make and distribute derivative works in any digital medium for any reasonable purpose, subject to proper attribution of authorship, as well as the right to make printed copies for their personal use.

(b) A complete version of the work and all supplemental materials, including a copy of the permission as stated above, in a suitable standard electronic format, are deposited immediately upon initial publication in at least one online repository that is supported by an academic institution, scholarly society, government agency, or other well-established organisation that seeks to enable open access, unrestricted distribution, interoperability, and long-term archiving.

In practice this means that the Trust supports two routes to making the research it funds freely available. One is to publish the original research paper in an open access publication (such as journals published by the Public Library of Science, or BioMed Central); the complementary approach is to publish in any journal that allows deposition of a copy of the final manuscript into PubMed Central (PMC) or, once established, UK PubMed Central (UKPMC) – see below.

Wellcome Trust: realising the goals of open access

The Trust was the first – and to date, the only – research funder to introduce a grant condition that *requires* grantees to make their research papers freely available to all.

Specifically, Trust grantees are required to deposit in PMC, electronic copies of any research papers that have been accepted for publication in a peer-reviewed journal, and are supported in whole or in part by Wellcome Trust funding. All deposited papers must be available for free no later than six months after the official journal publication date (Wellcome Trust, 2005b). Recognising the significant change this introduced to research publishing, the Trust phased in this condition over a 12-month period. It applied to all new papers arising from grants awarded after 1 October 2005, but does not come into force for existing grants until 1 October 2006. In addition, the Trust has provided grant holders with additional funding to cover the costs of page processing charges, levied by publishers who support the open access model.

The Trust is also working with the National Center for Biotechnology Information (NCBI) to establish a UK version of PubMed Central (UKPMC). The aim is to create a stable, permanent, and freely accessible digital archive of the peer-reviewed biomedical research publications.

Initially this service will simply mirror the data held in PMC, but the long-term objective is to create an independent resource that can process new content, offer enhanced linking and searching capabilities and be configured to meet the specific requirements of both UK researchers and funders. We anticipate UKPMC to be available early in 2007.

The driver for open access: a funder's perspective

For a funder such as the Wellcome Trust, providing open access to the literature it has funded is attractive for a number of reasons.

First, it is a fundamental part of our charitable mission to ensure that the work we fund can be read and utilised by the widest possible audience. Unrestricted distribution, via the Internet, currently offers the best available method to do this. In contrast, the current 'reader pays' model significantly restricts access. For example, a survey undertaken by BioMed Central found that fewer than half of the articles resulting from NHS research grants are accessible online to NHS employees (Cockerill, 2004).

Second, providing open access to the research literature enables these outputs to be linked and integrated with other resources. Research papers that are tagged in a standard, uniform way – such as the NLM Journal Archiving and Interchange DTD – can be read and searched by computers (as well as people), thus enabling context-sensitive links to be made to other online sources, such as gene and chemical compound databases. Figure 10.2 shows how an article in PubMed Central is linked to a number of online resources, including PubChem and OMIM.

Over the next few years we will start to see new types of search facilities being developed – based on data-mining techniques – which will create new knowledge by linking research papers that previously had not been seen as being relevant to each other. The creation of this capability will be a hugely significant development in the life sciences as massive data sets, such as gene sequences are linked with environmental data sets and patient records in cohort studies. For the development of new drugs, compound databases can be searched and matched with

Figure 10.2 Context-sensitive linking from PubMed Central to other online resources

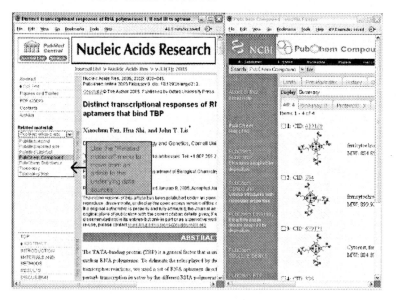

references in the published literature to help discover previously unrelated activity or side effects.

Making research outputs freely accessible also helps funding bodies evaluate the research they have funded. In a recent exercise conducted by the Trust it was found that only 10 per cent of papers in which the Trust was acknowledged as a funder were available online without a charge. This makes any systematic analysis of the value of the research we fund, using the Web, very difficult and costly. Once all Wellcome-funded research is available 'under one roof' (in PMC, or UKPMC) it will be possible to examine the effectiveness of our funding strategy and realign it as appropriate.

Finally, by mandating its grantees to make all research outputs accessible through PMC/UKPMC, the Trust is helping to ensure that the digital record of medicine can be preserved. All papers that are added to the PMC/UKPMC repository are marked-up to the NLM Journal Archiving and Interchange DTD. Mapping documents to this standard, non-proprietary format should ensure that future generations will be able to read these digital files, irrespective of developments to either hardware or software environments.

Cost of open access

The effect of the author (funder)-pays model is that it realigns the market, making publishing a research cost, rather than a library cost. In addition the volume of funds available to publish should remain in line with those research budgets. It will be a more transparent system enabling a clear comparison between the charge made to publish and the service offered by the publisher.

Although the open access model provides free access to the literature for the reader, there are costs associated with this approach. For example, managing the peer-review process, and copy-editing the final manuscripts are value-added services that incur expenses.

However, looking at the costs (see Table 10.1) levied by both open access publishers and those publishers that have introduced a hybrid model, these, from the perspective of the Wellcome Trust, are affordable.

In a typical year the Trust is acknowledged in approximately 4,000 original research papers. If every single one of those papers was published as an open access article, and taking the average cost

Table 10.1 Typical costs (January 2006) of publishing in an open access journal

Publisher	Example title	Cost per article (assumes no discount)
BioMed Central	Arthritis Research and Therapy	£750
Blackwell: Online Open	Journal of Physiology	£1,250
Oxford University Press: Oxford Open	Rheumatology	£1,500
Public Library of Science	PLoS Medicine	$1,500 (approx. £850)
Springer	Journal of Human Genetics	$3,000 (approx. £1,700)

Average cost per article (across these five publishers) £1,210

calculated above (£1,210 per article), the total cost to the Trust would be £4.84 million; just over 1 per cent of our annual research budget.

It is also worth noting that the Trust is rarely the sole funder of a research team, and more than 80 per cent of papers that acknowledge our support also acknowledge the support of one or more other funders. In time these costs will be spread throughout the research budget and fall below the 1 per cent figure estimated here.

Much of the debate around open access has focused on the traditional publisher and whether this model will bring about their decline. However, though the rhetoric has, at times, been apocalyptic in tone, what evidence there is suggests that open access publishing *can* provide a means by which publishers can continue to meet costs and turn a profit. Springer, for example, a traditional for-profit publisher, believes that it can generate a profit through open access; Jan Velterop, Director of Open Access Publishing at Springer, commented 'we are absolutely convinced that with open access we can have good profit margins' (quoted in Pincock, 2005).

Further, a study (Waltham, 2005) that looked at the viability of the open access model for learned societies concluded these publishers could *continue* to deliver the average surplus to their societies, by introducing an open access fee of £1,166 per article (2004 costs) (see also Waltham, this volume.)

In support of these arguments are the experiments by a number of established publishers with a hybrid model of publishing (author-pays open access articles) within a subscription journal. This appears to be a low risk way of exploring the viability of the open access model, both by journal title and subject discipline. The two models, subscription and author-pays, should be able to co-exist for as long as they are both needed.

Conclusion

Providing free and open access to all research outputs provides real benefits to both the research community, and the funding bodies. Over the next few months it is likely that the Research Councils UK (RCUK) will mandate its grant holders to make their research papers freely available – either through institutional or subject-based repositories.

In the USA, the National Institutes of Health (2005) Public Access Policy has – through the creation of PubMed Central and the supporting manuscript submission system (National Institutes of Health Manuscript Submission) – provided the infrastructure for improved public access. However, the supporting policy of encouraging (rather than requiring) NIH grantees to deposit research papers in PMC can be described as a failure. At a meeting in November 2005 of the NIH Public Access Working Group[2] (2005), it was reported that less than 3 per cent of unpublished manuscripts authored by NIH investigators were being deposited in PMC (see also Suber, this volume). It will be interesting to see whether this failure to make a critical mass of research available to the US taxpayer will encourage Congress to require the NIH to adopt a stronger, mandatory approach.

It should surprise no one that many funding bodies from around the world are making a commitment to increasing open access to the research they fund, for example by signing the Berlin Declaration (2003). Funding bodies have clear objectives, in the case of the Wellcome Trust to improve human and animal health, so they are obliged to explore and use the most efficient and modern practices to achieve those objectives. Making the research and data they fund accessible to as many people as possible, for free, via the Internet, offers a significant advance in the research process and should form a key aim for all research funders.

Notes

1. The Wellcome Trust is an independent charity funding research to improve human and animal health. Established in 1936, and with an endowment of around £11 billion (2005), it is the UK's largest non-governmental source of funds for biomedical research. See *http://www.wellcome.ac.uk/*.
2. The NIH Public Access Working Group is a subgroup of the National Library of Medicine's Board of Regents to review the impact of the NIH Public Access policy.

11

Business models in open access publishing
Matthew Cockerill

Introduction

The move towards open access in scholarly publishing is a curiously two-stranded affair. Theoretical debate about the feasibility and desirability of open access continues, as it has for years, with little sign of movement in entrenched positions on either side. Meanwhile, the 'facts on the ground' in scientific publishing have been changing rapidly, with sustained growth in the number of new open access journals, and with ever more existing journals introducing open access options or switching to a fully open access model.

This chapter provides an open access publisher's viewpoint on the economics of scholarly publishing, laying out the case for open access as a viable and clearly preferable alternative to the traditional model. While no arguments are likely to convince those who have a reason to defend the status quo, I hope to at least provide a useful perspective on the changes that are undeniably happening in the world of scholarly publishing.

What is an open access business model?

The defining characteristic of an open access business model for scholarly publishing is that it should not depend on restricting access to the published research in order to recoup the inherent costs associated with publication. As the subscription and pay-per-view models used by most traditional scholarly publications inherently depend on restricting access, other models are clearly needed.

The most well-known model for open access, often misleadingly referred to as 'author pays', is based an article processing charge (APC), generally paid by the author's funder or institution, which covers the cost of publication. Hundreds of journals now offer this type of open access, either for all articles, or as an option for the author. The APC model is simple and has the benefit of making authors aware of the cost of publication, something that is unfortunately opaque in a subscription-based system. Given that page charge and colour figure charges have long played a role in covering at least some of the publication costs for many traditional journals, APCs introduce no fundamentally new issues.

Are journals encouraged to publish any old rubbish by page charges or article processing fees? Open access opponents frequently imply that this is the case, but it is evidently not true. Journals only attract submissions if they can convince authors that they will achieve kudos and credibility from publication in the journal. If a journal cannot offer such credibility then it serves no purpose for an author to publish in it. As a result, all journals, including open access ones, are strongly motivated to ensure that they do not harm their reputation by publishing poor quality research. There is abundant evidence that open access journals offer every bit as high a standard of peer review as their toll access competitors. *BMC Bioinformatics*, *PLoS Biology*, and *Nucleic Acids Research* are just three examples of fully open access APC-funded journals that are at the forefront of their respective fields in terms of citation impact and quality.

Another increasingly common business model is for a journal to be directly funded, by a society, a foundation, or a research organisation, as part of the mission of that organisation. This results in the journal then being free at the point of use for both authors and readers. Examples of BioMed Central journals funded in this way include the *Beilstein Journal of Organic Chemistry* and *Chinese Medicine*.

It is sometimes inaccurately claimed that such journals are 'subsidised', in contrast to traditional journals that are 'commercially self-sustaining'. The distinction is illusory however. Profitable journals do not make their profits from thin air – the majority of revenue for scholarly journals comes from academic library budgets, and thus the scholarly community is 'subsidising' traditional journals too, even if those journals appear profitable. There is nothing inherently unsustainable about either form of subsidy. Scholarly publication is a service that must be paid for somehow and for the most part it is already the scholarly community that pays for it.

Having established what constitutes an open access business model, it is worth taking a step back to look at the fundamental objectives of scholarly publishing to see why open access publishing provides a model that is better suited to the needs of the research community. To do so, it is informative to contrast scholarly publishing with the other types of publicly funded material.

Open scholarship vs open government

If you are a UK citizen and you want to know what your elected representative has been doing in Parliament, it is impressively easy to find out. *Hansard*, the official record of parliamentary proceedings, is freely available via its official website. Furthermore, anyone can get permission to reuse and/or redistribute the material in *Hansard*, just by filling out a Click-Use form, to take out a 'Click-Use licence'.

What does this freedom of re-use mean in practice? TheyWorkForYou.com is an independent, volunteer-run website which reorganises parliamentary material by bringing all the latest speeches and written answers by an MP together on a single web page, organised by date and topic. It thereby makes the material vastly more informative and accessible for constituents. In this case, it is clear that freedom of reuse made possible innovation that has furthered the democratic goals that are the reason for publishing *Hansard* in the first place.

Similar possibilities exist for the re-use and enhancement of the scholarly literature. For example, Google Scholar mirrors TheyWorkForYou.com in that it too takes information available on the Web (in this case, scholarly articles), and provides navigational enhancements. Specifically, Google Scholar makes it possible to find articles that cite another article, and to search for the most highly cited articles on a given topic. Until recently, this kind of citation information was so labour-intensive to gather, and so complex to manage that it was only available through expensive services such as the Institute for Scientific Information's ISI Web of Science. In contrast, Google Scholar, by using modern technology to automatically extract this information from articles already available on the Web, is able to deliver a similar service that is free to all.

A major limitation of the service, however, is that much of the scholarly research literature is currently 'owned' by publishers, and Google Scholar can only index what publishers allow it to index. At the time of writing, for example, Elsevier, which controls more than 20 per cent of the scientific research publishing market, does not allow any of its articles to be indexed by Google Scholar. As a result, Google's Scholar's coverage is significantly incomplete and skewed.

It is not only commercial innovators such as Google who are held back by lack of access to the scientific literature – academics too are frustrated by restrictions as to which scholarly articles that they can access and reuse. For example, taxonomists and biodiversity researchers are keen to create a comprehensive database that would provide authoritative information about all the world's biological species. Unfortunately, however, most descriptions of new species are published in journals that claim exclusive rights to the articles concerned, As a result, species descriptions cannot be included in such a database without complicated negotiations for licensing rights (Agosti, 2006).

Scholarly publication: communication not cash

Like parliamentary publishing, scholarly publishing operated for hundreds of years on the basis of print economics – those who wished to have access to the material had to pay for a printed copy. However, in both cases the purpose of the publishing activity *from the point of view of the producer* was not, fundamentally, to maximise financial return, but to ensure that the material concerned should achieve wide visibility and readership at reasonable cost.

The arrival of the Web fundamentally changed the economics of distributing such information. The cost to distribute additional copies suddenly became negligible. As a result, when wide distribution and readership is the key objective, universal access suddenly becomes the most obvious and natural model *from the point of view of the producer*. Making content freely available via the Web reduces or eliminates both printing and subscription-management costs, while maximising access.

The alternative chosen by most traditional science publishers, however, was to charge for online subscriptions just as they did for print subscriptions. If we consider applying this model to parliamentary information, we can imagine that *Hansard* might be turned into a subscription-only website, charging for an annual subscription. This would certainly generate additional revenue, and it could be argued that anyone who truly wanted to know what had been going on in Parliament could subscribe to find out. But it seems clear that closing off free access to the parliamentary record in this way, and thereby obstructing both casual users and websites such as TheyWorkForYou.com, would be a retrograde step for open democracy. Similarly, the scholarly community currently loses out because access to scholarly literature is not as free and open as the Web allows it to be.

The UK government has no great reputation for technological innovation, but it is to be credited with recognising that the best model for information distribution in the age of the Web may not be simply to translate the print model into its online equivalent.

Scientific funders, such as the National Institutes of Health (NIH) in the USA and the Wellcome Trust in the UK, have made a similar realisation. They understand that their research budgets would be used more effectively if they could ensure that the published results of the research were universally accessible so that researchers could build on them. Both the National Institutes of Health (2005) and Wellcome (2005a) have introduced policy statements to that effect. However, although funders ultimately pay the bills, they do not directly control all aspects of the publishing process. Librarians, authors and publishers (both commercial and non-commercial) are involved in a complex web of relationships and dependencies. As a result, shifting towards a more open model of publishing is not something that will happen overnight – it will require coordination between the various players concerned.

Publication and dissemination: part of the research process

In 2007, the Large Hadron Collider (LHC) at CERN is expected to begin collecting experimental data. The LHC is probably the most ambitious and complex physics project ever brought to fruition. Vast public sums have been invested in the project over several decades. As such, it provides a very clear example of the unsatisfactory nature of conventional scientific publishing. After vast investment by publicly funded research agencies, the research articles which constitute the final payoff from that investment would traditionally end up owned and controlled by publishers whose contribution has been, in the grand scheme of things, quite miniscule.

CERN's Director General, Robert Aymar, is well aware of the undesirability of this situation, and is taking steps to address it. In his own words:

> The next phase of LHC experiments at CERN can be a catalyst for a rapid change in the particle physics communication system. CERN's articles are already freely available through its own website but this is only a partial solution. We wish for the publishing and archiving systems to converge for a more efficient solution which will benefit the global particle physics community'. (European Organization for Nuclear Research, 2005)

Several funding organisations (such as the Wellcome Trust) have similarly noted that seeing the publication and dissemination of research as the last part of the research process, and paying for it upfront, inherently makes more sense than surrendering control of research to publishers and then paying for access (Walport, 2004). By paying for the cost of publication, research funders not only ensure that their research is universally accessible, but also ensure that funding for journal publication naturally keeps pace with the amount of research that is being funded. The Wellcome Trust estimates that in biomedical research the cost of publication is typically only around 2 per cent of the cost of doing the research in the first place (SQW, 2004). Currently this cost of publishing is paid indirectly through library budget. Paying it directly from research funding is equally feasible and need not lead to any overall increase in expenditure, seen from the perspective of the system as a whole.

The myth of 'sustainability'

Of all the objections raised against the open access model, one of the most prevalent and yet misguided is the suggestion that it has not been proven whether open access publishing is 'sustainable'.

Questioning the 'sustainability' of open access journals misses the very basic point that in macroeconomic terms it is obvious that both an open access model and a toll access model are equally 'sustainable' (that is, affordable to the scholarly community). At most, an open access model has the same costs as a toll access model. Funders such as NIH and

Wellcome have recognised this point, for example, see Wellcome's report 'Costs and business models in scientific research publishing' (SQW, 2004). However, it is steadfastly ignored by those who oppose open access, who choose instead to speak ominously of the potentially 'disastrous consequences' (Royal Society, 2005) of switching to an open access model of unproven sustainability.

Traditional toll access scholarly publishing is 'sustainable' (that is, profitable) because the academic/research community funnels large amounts of money into it through library budgets. It is not 'self-supporting'. The fact that journals 'break even' (and in fact often make large profits) in an environment such as this simply indicates that the community is currently choosing to pay for these journals from library budgets. Looking at the system as a whole, the same funds can clearly cover the cost of open access publishing (as opening up access introduces no new costs). This is a choice that the community can make, but given the intertwined roles of authors, libraries, funders and publishers in the process, it will require coordinated action. Meanwhile, it is a particularly unhelpful form of circular for organisations to try to block the policy changes and budgetary shifts that are a necessary part of the process of funding open access, on the basis that open access has not been 'proven' to be sustainable.

In fact, the large publisher profits that are regarded as an indicator of the 'sustainability' of the traditional toll access publishing model are better seen as one of its greatest pathologies. Librarians are prepared (however reluctantly) to pay inflated sums in order to get access to the research literature for their users. This is entirely understandable, as their users *need* access to the latest research. The problem is that authors, through historical circumstances and inertia, have given away the rights to the research articles concerned and the research is now owned by publishers. Publishers (even so-called not-for-profit publishers) therefore have libraries over a barrel – and journal pricing inevitably reflects this. The willingness of libraries to pay whatever it takes to get access to research is not an indication of greater 'sustainability' for traditional publishing so much as it is an indication of a failure of the market mechanism. The problem is that you cannot have a truly effective market for access to research articles because you cannot substitute one research article for another. If you need to follow up a citation, you really do need *that* article – no other can serve as a substitute.

Under an open access model, on the other hand, there is a choice and therefore a genuine market. Journals can compete to offer authors the best quality of service and value. As open access evolves, market forces will naturally ensure that the open access publishers who are efficient and provide a good service will be able to recoup their costs and make a reasonable profit. Those that are inefficient or provide poor service will not. A move towards open access is therefore not likely to leave the scholarly publishing landscape unchanged, but rather it will be a positive force for change and improvement in the services offered by scholarly journals.

What can an open access publisher reasonably charge?

One of the great virtues of open access publishing is that it offers a far greater degree of pricing transparency than the traditional model.

When an author publishes in a traditional journal, the scientific community is paying the publisher for the service of publication and dissemination, just as with open access publication. In the case of traditional publishing, however, the service is paid for indirectly through large numbers of subscriptions, and so it is generally unclear how much is paid by the community for this service, per article published.

In a few cases, the figures are available for comparison, however. For example, the American Physical Society is considered by many to offer reasonably priced subscription-only journals. Figures presented by Martin Blume (2005) indicated that the society received US$30 million of annual revenue from its journal publishing activity, and published about 16,000 articles, meaning that their revenue per published article from the subscription model was around $1,900. This suggests that open access charges in the $1,000–$1,500 range, as charged by many open access journals such as those from BioMed Central and Public Library of Science, are certainly not excessive. These open access publishers are providing universal access, for a total cost per article published than is lower than even relatively inexpensive conventional journals.

The future for open access

Given the benefits of open access to the scientific community, it might be asked why open access has not already taken over completely from traditional publishing. One might point to the necessary and proper conservatism of science, which ensures that trusted paradigms are not discarded overnight. On the other hand, one might also note the recent survey by the Deutsche Forschungsgemeinschaft on attitudes to open access among its researchers, which found that younger researchers were consistently both more aware of open access, and more enthusiastic in their support for it, than their elder peers (Over, Maiworm and Schelewsky, 2005). Change is never easy, and no doubt many obstacles remain, but the enthusiasm of a new generation of researchers for open access, and the ongoing expansion of activity in this area by funders and policy-makers, together mean that open access to the results of scientific research could soon be the norm rather than the exception.

12

Learned society business models and open access

Mary Waltham

During the past two to three years (2003–2006) there has been much debate about the sustainability of an open access[1] (producer pays) business model for scholarly journals, with particular interest from the learned societies whose mission and purpose is aligned with the overarching goals of such a model. However, in the absence of factual data on publisher economics and the impact of long-term trends that are affecting journal publishing performance, it was not possible for learned society publishers or their boards to make well-informed decisions about the appropriate strategy with respect to open access for their journal. A study commissioned by JISC in March 2005 set out to contribute to the knowledge and understanding that then existed by providing detailed case studies of a sample of typical learned society publishers, by identifying trends through analysis of three years of precise financial and circulation data provided by the publishers for 2002, 2003 and 2004, noting landmarks and proposing best practice guidelines for publishers wishing to move to an open access model (Waltham, 2005).[2] The full report gives a practical, fact-based framework which the publishing leadership in learned societies can use to support and inform active engagement with the key and core business issues surrounding a move to an open access business model, and the steps involved in doing so.

Why change the business model?

The annual world production of research results as peer-reviewed published articles is increasing from the level estimated to be 1.2 million articles in 2003, driven by growth in global research funding and in certain disciplines the tendency to produce many more articles to describe one substantive research finding (the 'least publishable unit' problem). Individual journal pricing and annual price increases have been driven by a number of economic factors including the increasing numbers of articles and pages published. The costs associated with the selection and production of more edited content drives up the cost of both print and online versions of scholarly journals.

As the volume of the research literature grows, higher education is not in a position to provide all the injection of funds required to pay for increased print and online publishing costs expressed as rising subscription and site licence prices.

For these reasons alternative models for publishing peer-reviewed research are likely to be required because existing business models for the scholarly communications system which rely solely and most heavily on subscription fees paid by institutions may become unsustainable.

Overview of the publishers and the journals

Nine learned society publishers agreed to take part in the 2005 JISC study of business models and provided detailed profit and loss information about one or more journals based on the complete confidentiality of the information submitted. Eight of these publishers were based in the UK. One learned society publisher from the USA was invited to take part in the study to help provide further context to the particular issues facing the UK publishers. In total these nine publishers provided detailed circulation and profit and loss information about 13 journals. One journal was already fully open access (producer pays) and so no circulation figures could be provided. All of the publishers can be described as not-for-profit and all use the surplus generated by publishing to support other activities central to their mission as a learned society.

The nine study participants were active in the following areas of science, technical and medical (STM) publishing:

- clinical medicine: two publishers
- biomedicine: one publisher
- applied biology: two publishers
- science: one publisher
- technology: two publishers

Table 12.1 Print publishing frequency of journals included in the 2005 JISC study

Frequency per year	Number of journals
24	1
12	9
6	2
4	1

In addition, one publisher was active in both the life and physical sciences. The frequency of their publications is detailed in Table 12.1.

Although the sample size was small and each journal quite individual, the results show overall trends that are consistent within STM publishing. The type of research content published varied as would be expected across traditional STM areas, with some journals including extensive mathematical setting, numerous graphs and charts and very little colour, and others frequently including numerous illustrations such as half-tone photomicrographs or four-colour histopathology figures. Length of article also varied by broad discipline and, within the 'Information for Authors' for each journal, maximum and optimal article lengths were provided by the publishers.

Open access as a business model?

Open access business models have been widely promoted within the scholarly publishing community as the basis for transforming and resolving the funding problems of the communication of research. However, precise data on revenues and costs of publishing peer-reviewed journals in print and online have been difficult to access. Estimates of the cost per article for publication vary widely with sketchy or incomplete data to support figures proposed and poor definition of which elements of the publishing process are to be covered by open access author fees, for example. Although several of the participants in the JISC study were interested in experimenting with open access, the justified nervousness about the impact of such an experiment on overall business performance is likely to lead to more cautious experimentation with small and less critical journals.

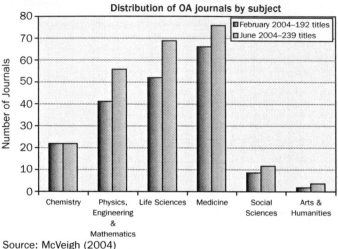

Figure 12.1 Change in coverage of open access journals within ISI JCR from February to June 2004

Source: McVeigh (2004)

Uptake of open access

Within certain disciplines there may be some resistance to shifting to a producer pays model because of enduring scholarly traditions and/or questions of quality. The uptake of open access by publishers and the research community by discipline can be mapped using Thomson ISI Journals Citation data and in particular work done by ISI to identify open access journals covered by the Journal Citation reports (JCR). In Figure 12.1, compare the number of new open access journals in chemistry in the ISI database with the numbers in physics, life sciences and medicine. Although the timescale over which this analysis took place is short, the trends are quite clear.

What do the learned society business models reveal?

Based on information provided by the nine learned society publishers participating in the 2005 JISC funded study, the surplus delivered by their journals is used to support any or all of the following within each publishing operation:

- new product development, for example, back issue digitisation;
- new journal launches, for example, in the emerging interdisciplinary research areas;
- other society activities, for example, research-based meetings and conferences;
- other activities, for example, travel scholarships for young scientists.

As a result, either the business model selected by the publishers needs to deliver cost recovery plus a modest surplus or the society will need to find funds from other sources to support investments and member service activities. The decision on this will doubtless need to be made at the individual society and publisher level but an active choice needs to be made in the event of falling journal revenues and surplus.

The open access model as currently construed is unlikely to meet the needs of learned societies although it is attractive in principle to many learned society publishers because it is aligned with their mission and provides increased visibility to their journal (or journals) and the authors and research they publish. Deep concern is expressed by the leadership of learned societies over the financial sustainability of a switch to this model across the board.

The costs of publishing each of the learned society journals included in the JISC study increased year on year throughout the period 2002–2004 (up 11 per cent over three years). If a journal relies on open access to support publication, then it is important that the per-article fees can be raised to take account of this. If not, then open access publishers will have to rely on subsidies and alternative revenue streams that will require new or additional resources to generate them. Costs have increased as a result of increased numbers of submissions – which take time and money to handle, increased numbers of articles and pages published, higher labour costs with the need for more technically qualified staff to work with the online version and the additional costs of publishing in dual versions. The fixed costs of publishing have been a primary source of the increased cost levels and these are costs that are not reduced by falling print runs.

Costs per article are driven by a number of factors irrespective of print or online version, which have not been addressed in much of the literature on the topic. These include:

- the overall rejection rate: the higher the rate, the higher the cost per published article;

- the length of article: long articles cost more to publish than short articles as the costs of creating journal content are driven by the volume of content processed;

- the number and complexity of figures and illustrations and the amount of colour: the more of any of these, in general, the more expensive the article;

- the first language of the author can also affect the extent of post-acceptance editing of an article that is required, for example, as research output grows in Asia, editing of articles from this region will be more costly for publishers.

There is heavy reliance by learned society publishers on institutional subscription revenue to support the journals, while the number of institutional subscriptions is falling. In contrast, the price charged to members for their society subscriptions is, in general, not covering the costs of providing the print journal. Online only member subscriptions would reduce the cost and some publishers are implementing this change. Net margin/surplus patterns are shown in Table 12.2.

Although average numbers mask the differences in the journals analysed, the average publishing cost per article in print and online was £1,447 (range £493–£2,232) and per page £144 (range £65–£203) in 2004. The average revenue per article was £1,918 (range £389–£3,380) and per page was £194 (range £21–£538) in 2004.

If all print costs are removed, the average publishing cost per page was £97 for an average article of 9.8 pages. Above this length, costs per article will increase and below them the variable costs will fall, but fixed costs will not. In determining open access fees to authors it is essential to factor in article length as this is a major cost driver irrespective of format.

Table 12.2 Net margin/surplus patterns – ten learned society journals

Year	Highest net surplus (%)	Average net surplus (%)	Lowest net surplus/loss
2002	60 (£240,000)	23	A loss of £220,000
2003	60 (£242,000)	19	A loss of £200,000
2004	62 (£268,000)	22	A loss of £161,000

Online only?

In order to cover the average online *only* costs for a ten-page article and deliver the average surplus, the open access fee per article for 2004 would need to be set at £1,166 for the society journals included in the 2005 JISC study. However, revenues from print deliver a considerable proportion of the surplus generated by the learned society journals included in this journal study.

Learned society publishers are not all separating print and online costs in a way that is helpful in predicting the impact of falling print circulation on the total cost of publishing the journal. In part this is due to the bundling of outsourced print and online services by third-party suppliers, and in part it is because there is a quite widespread view based on current trends that print cannot 'go away' until institutions stop wanting to buy it. As this transition proceeds it becomes essential for publishers to understand their distinctly print, distinctly online and shared print and online costs and revenues.

Although there would doubtless be savings and efficiencies within the publishing system from removing print, it will need to be removed entirely for those to be realised. In the meantime, statements that publishers should be charging open access author fees that are equal to the costs of online publication are somewhat difficult for many publishers to translate into a sum because many are not collecting the financial information required to do this.

Value Added Tax (VAT) is a barrier to making the transition from print to online in the UK and Europe because of the anomalous situation that protects print (and bundled print and online) subscriptions from VAT, but not online only. This is not the case in North America or Asia. It is possible that moving to online and abandoning print entirely would save more than the 17.5 per cent of VAT but, as noted above and described more fully in the report (Waltham, 2005), the move to online only is not necessarily to the advantage of all publishers because for some a considerable proportion of their current surplus comes from print subscriptions sold to institutions. Notice also that VAT is chargeable on individual open access author fees.

Acceptability of open access

None of the learned society publishers could see substantial savings from moving to an open access publishing model although most agreed that there should be some savings. Also noted were the additional costs that would be incurred for administering and collecting author publishing fees and the additional costs of marketing to authors versus institutions, that is many individuals versus a few institutions.

From the results reported by publishers experimenting with the open access business model across STM publishing including the exclusively open access publishers, there is not yet a strong and positive 'pull' from the author community for open access to their articles despite increased financial support from funding agencies. Such a change may take a long time. Nevertheless a market is emerging for the price of publishing an article open access within existing (and newly launched) journals with open access fees ranging from US$500 to US$3,000 per article.

Author acceptance of and interest in open access – the producer pays publishing model – is generally low but shows some variation by discipline. The landscape of this pattern of preference is becoming clearer as the various publisher experiments with a hybrid model proceed and exclusively open access journals, such as those from The Public Library of Science and BioMed Central, build a track record within their respective fields. As more results of the responses to open access opportunities become available, they should be carefully and independently documented and broadly disseminated to the scholarly communication communities for reference.

Two key features seem most likely to influence the uptake of open access by authors as customers and publishers as service providers. First, are articles that are open access from first publication cited, read and integrated into research more, and more rapidly than subscription-only access articles? (On this point, see Kurtz and Brody, this volume.) Second, does an open access journal receive more high-quality submissions than a competing subscription-based journal? The answers to these questions will take time and rigour to develop a clear understanding as there are important disciplinary differences to consider.

There is no universal answer to the issues faced in funding publication of the research literature but alternatives need to be explored collaboratively and based on sound information. Solutions are likely to emerge on a case by case, discipline by discipline and market by market basis.

Acknowledgments

Thanks are certainly due to the nine deliberately anonymous learned society publishers who took part in the 2005 JISC study for the generous and thoughtful way in which they provided highly confidential data and spent time and effort interacting with me so that their case study information included in the JISC report was as accurate and complete as possible.

Notes

1. Throughout this chapter open access is used to refer only to the situation where the author pays the publisher a fee on acceptance of an article to cover the costs of publication. There is no subscriber access control of the journal article and on publication the article is available free of charge online to anyone.
2. Readers not familiar with publisher terminology and publishing economics will find the account of each in this report especially helpful.

13

Open all hours? Institutional models for open access

Colin Steele

Open access and scholarly communication futures

It seems likely that scholarly publishing will evolve along two distinct paths in the near future: one in which large multinational commercial publishers increase their dominance of the global science, technology and medicine (STM) market, and the other in which a variety of open access initiatives emerge and become commonplace.

Open access is here taken in its widest sense of making scholarly research available to readers through the Internet free of charge, notably through the mechanisms of placing research outputs in institutional or subject repositories, the 'green' strategy, and the 'gold' route of meeting publisher article costs to ensure open access (see Bailey, Jr., this volume).

Institutional settings and open access

Initially, a wide perspective needs to be adopted in the context of institutional settings, for example, consideration of institutional budgets in terms of public good input and output information costs, before addressing the specifics of open access initiatives.

Major research universities spend hundreds of millions of dollars in each first-world country on acquiring information in acquisition programmes which are far from business-like in terms of cost-benefit analyses. Much of the material acquired, moreover, is often not used or is little used, as evidenced by various print collection use statistics in the twentieth century and by digital download analyses in the twenty-first. The UK NESLI analyses reveal the relative low use of material acquired under the JISC 'Big Deals' serial purchases, and that a comparatively small percentage of the titles generated high use (Woodward and Conyers, 2005).

Reed Elsevier publications cost the University of California Library half its budget in 2002 for online publications, yet Elsevier titles accounted for only a quarter of the journal use (Willinsky, 2005). Candee has noted that the University of California annual budget for licensed content by 2005 was US$27 million (Candee quoted in Poynder, 2005). One wonders in that context how many of the articles purchased are actually used/read/downloaded and how value for money was defined.

It is disingenuous for publishers to criticise universities for using free infrastructure for open access initiatives when they benefit from similar infrastructure for researcher's submissions. Much of the research from universities in the major STM journals is provided 'free' by the institution, through 'free' laboratories, offices, IT infrastructure, academic refereeing, and so on. Maybe institutions should 'dig up the pitch' in terms of resource allocations and start again?

University libraries employ a merchant model in dealing with publishers and a community model in dealing with staff and students. The institutional dysfunctionality of the scholarly communication system is heightened by the 'Jekyll and Hyde' syndrome of the academic researcher who adopts one set of values as a creator of knowledge and one markedly different as the reader of research publications (see Sale, this volume). The researcher in many cases bears little, or no, responsibility for the purchasing of the scholarly information that they have 'given away'.

Increasingly, the sentiment is being expressed globally that publicly funded research should be publicly and freely available. In Australia, Dr Mike Sargent, Chair of the national e-Research Coordinating Committee has stated that, 'the Government regards publicly-funded research as a public good' and that 'as a general statement of principle, researchers ought to be able to find out what research is going on and gain access to that research. Use of open access regimes and institutional repositories will be critical to both the development of the Accessibility Framework and the Research Quality Framework' (Sargent, 2005).

Institutional repositories and open access

Institutional repositories have potentially significant benefits for institutions if they are integrated holistically into university frameworks. Probets and Jenkins in their analysis of seven institutional repositories have reaffirmed the importance of collaborative activity in institutions by academics and relevant university departments (Probets and Jenkins, 2006). Establishing the place of the institutional repository within the university's mission and strategic plan is a crucial first step.

As Lynch has cogently stated: 'At the most basic and fundamental level, an institutional repository is a recognition that the intellectual life and scholarship of our universities will increasingly be represented, documented, and shared in digital form, and that a primary responsibility of our universities is to exercise stewardship over these riches: both to make them available and to preserve them' (Lynch, 2003).

While the open access debate has largely focused on the deposit in institutional repositories of peer-reviewed articles, particularly in the sciences, it should be noted that institutional repositories are often much wider in practice than just e-prints, for example, hosting institutional datasets and digital cultural objects. Open access carries also the responsibility for curation of digital material. A repository can also be an important element in collaborative learning environments and university marketing initiatives but these aspects are not the focus of this chapter.

A UK study (Mark Ware Consulting, 2004) indicated the following main uses of an institutional repository: scholarly communication, education, e-publishing, collection management, long-term preservation, institutional prestige, knowledge management and research assessment exercises. The 'gather once and use many times' concept provides administrative efficiency for institutions.

Jones, Andrew and MacColl (2006) note the advantage of institutional repositories in that they allow the free sharing of information and increase the visibility and impact of UK education and research. What distinguishes institutional repositories 'is the idea that an internal database can serve more than an administrative purpose, and can constitute a building block in a distributed international service' (Jones, Andrew and MacColl, 2006).

Institutional repositories can hold the intellectual record of the university's output, increase access to institutional research and thus its impact and provide input to national research outputs, as has been evidenced by the DARE initiatives in The Netherlands (Heijne, 2005). Kircz (2005a) believes an institutional repository can become 'a research tool in itself' and, for the institution, becomes 'the central metabolic organ for knowledge'.

Institutional repository cost settings

The value proposition in institutional repositories has been analysed by Blythe and Chachra (2005), who conclude that they will yield 'maximum value to institutions only if economies of scale and economies of scope are fully leveraged'.

The following cost figures are simply indicative as institutional repository costs will depend on the individual structure of the repository within a particular institution. Swan and Brown (2005) note that 'an average-sized research-based university can set up a functional archive for, say, 10,000 US dollars' and 'for all the benefits such an archive brings to an institution represents excellent value for money'. Kemp (2005) quotes costs from ten libraries from the USA, UK, Canada and Ireland revealing a range from circa US$7,000 to US$1 million for set-up costs.

Swan and her colleagues (Swan et al., 2005) have also reported the following costs for two institutional repositories. MIT DSpace, which is at the upper end of the complexities of repositories, was set up with a US$1.8 million grant, with annual staffing costs of US$225,000, US$35,000 for systems equipment and US$25,000 for operating costs. Queens University in Canada, with its Q-space incurred CA$50,000 for set-up programming and CA$50,000 annual staffing costs. Rankin (2005) in his New Zealand study has suggested that institutional repository staffing could require 1–3 full-time employees for set-up costs, with ongoing support thereafter requiring less than one full-time employee.

These are still relatively low-cost figures in a total institutional budgetary setting. Institutional repositories can also be relatively easily incorporated into library and information and communication technology (ICT) support programmes. Hong Kong University of Science and Technology (HKUST), for example, has indicated the benefits of spreading the workload among systems staff and reference/subject librarians who perform faculty liaison tasks, while collection development librarians resolve copyright issues and support staff become involved in data input (Chan, 2005).

Some institutions, usually smaller ones, have preferred not to get involved in the downloading and support of repository software.

ProQuest offer commercially their 'Digital Commons@', based on the University of California's bepress software. ProQuest apparently charges between US$19,000 to US$125,000 pa depending on university 'equivalent full-time student units', with database service, data entry and recruitment of content costs borne by the university. In the USA, where e-print institutional repositories were late developers, ProQuest has been the predominant force.

Institutional barriers to open access via repositories

Institutions certainly need effective open access leadership. The Australian Group of Eight Vice-Chancellors issued a significant statement on open access in 2004 (Group of Eight, 2004) but very little direct action ensued because no one was designated to take responsibility in the senior academic arena within those universities. Queensland University of Technology's success in increasing its rate of deposit (see Sale, this volume) is partly due to the leadership of the Deputy Vice-Chancellor in that university. Callan and Cleary (2005) have described the QUT policies in terms of 'soft' mandatory frameworks and how marketing and novel policies can bring reward in an institutional setting.

Many researchers are still unaware that most publishers give them the right to self-archive their work, or that their institutions house a repository for this purpose. Sparkes has noted that the majority of respondents in all groups that she surveyed did not know whether their university had a repository, although more had awareness of subject-based repositories (Rightscom, 2005). The highest proportion of respondents depositing was in the physical sciences and the lowest in arts and humanities.

The number of humanities documents in institutional repositories is currently far lower than that in STM disciplines (Allen, 2005). This result has been confirmed by the recent major German study, which in a survey of 1,000 researchers, found that more doubts were expressed about open access publications by researchers in the social sciences and the humanities compared with those in the sciences (Over, Maiworm and Schelewsky, 2005).

Yet it is arguable that institutional repositories and open archives have much greater potential for scholarly distribution and access for the social sciences and the humanities than for the sciences, which by and large have a well-defined distribution system for their research, albeit often at high prices.

'Faculty resist all attempts to force them to publish in different formats and venues unless they can see the advantages clearly indicated and incorporated in reward systems' (Peet, 2005). Institutional business plans are not the issue here but rather institutional and national reward systems. Copyright and plagiarism concerns are also a major issue for scholars, yet these concerns can easily be defused if researchers are contacted directly. Libraries have a major advocacy role to play with their academic communities.

Many North American University Councils and Faculty Boards have issued statements in recent years calling on scholars to change scholarly communication practice. However, few major practical changes seem to have resulted. The various white papers issued in December 2005 by the University of California Senate promise, however, to contain more 'teeth' for institutional action (University of California, 2005b).

Funding and institutional policies

There is less institutional activity in the context of open access article financial support than in repository activity. The issues in setting up an open access journal, or converting an established journal to open access, or providing institutional funding models for open access subsidies are significantly more complex than simply depositing articles in institutional repositories.

Open access journals are not free journals; they are only free to the reader. There are significant costs in publishing that have to be met, such as managing the peer-review process and distribution mechanisms. The term 'author pays' is, however, an extremely misleading one. The author is not intended to pay personally, but rather to have the costs of the publication of an article met through a variety of funding mechanisms such as research grant funding, foundations, institutional support or revenue generated from advertising or related services.

A number of commercial publishers allow for open access article provision in a variety of ways, for example, making the contents of their journals freely available after a period of time in open access mode, for example, after six or twelve months. Others charge a fee, which can range from US$500 to US$3,000 per article. Such funding derives from the various funding sources mentioned above.

Costs related to publishing in open access journals, perhaps should be considered as charges related to institutional access to scholarly information. In this context, there has been some initial activity. Some universities like Columbia University Library have offered to pay the Columbia author open access fees. Others have modelled scenarios whereby the average cost of open access article provision is projected against the library acquisition vote, and other models are likely to emerge.

Davis and his colleagues concluded at Cornell that this would not bring about savings, given an average cost of around $1,500 per article (Davis et al., 2004). A more likely initial path for institutions to tread is to lobby research funding bodies, both individually and collectively, to incorporate the cost of making research available in open access outlets, as has been the case with the Wellcome Trust in Britain.

Institutional benefits of open access

Open access publishing can increase early advantage and impact of articles (Hitchcock, 2005; see also Kurtz and Brody, this volume). Antelman has shown that open access articles receive more citations than non-open access articles but notes that care still needs to be taken in stating overall that open access status causes citation advantage (Antelman, 2004).

HKUST Library institutional repository saw its 2,000 papers downloaded 10,000 times in October 2005 – an impressive figure. Even more impressively, the University of California had 2,421,218 full-text downloads by late January 2006 from its eScholarship Repository, which offers faculty on the University of California campuses a central facility for the deposit of research or scholarly output in a variety of forms.

Open access, apart from the major considerations of increased access and impact, also allows for the provision of enhanced methods of citation analysis, which can also link into performance indicators, both of researchers and institutions. Day has outlined how repositories can support the UK Research Assessment Exercise (Day, 2004).

Harnad has proposed that institutions should mandate the self-archiving of all peer-reviewed research in order to maximise research effectiveness (Harnad 2003c; see also Harnad, this volume; Swan, this volume). A number of universities are working with their research offices to streamline the collection of data and its inclusion in institutional repositories, thereby providing a systematic collection of an institution's research output. Edinburgh and Southampton University's work to develop solutions for integrating DSpace and Eprints repositories and their workflows into institutional research assessment activities is relevant here (Institutional Repositories and Research Assessment).

Scholars, by making their work available globally, will undoubtedly gain broader distribution of their ideas through global harvesting by search engines (Getz, 2005). Professor J. J. Fox, Director of the Research School of Asian and Pacific Studies at the Australian National University (ANU), had significant and unexpected international responses to his article, 'Currents in contemporary Islam in Indonesia' after placement in ANU's e-prints repository, not least its translation into Italian and wide distribution in Italy.

While the brief of this chapter was open access articles, the benefit of open access for scholarly monographs, particularly in the social sciences and humanities, is equally if not more significant in the long term. It makes little sense for researchers to spend many years writing a monograph (still the 'gold standard' for tenure in US Ivy League universities), only to find either that there is no outlet for their publication or that their monograph is published in such a small edition that global or local penetration is extremely limited. The evidence of some of the new e-presses, such as the ANU E-Press and the University of California's eScholarship editions have shown that placing institutional monograph material free on the Web (with print on demand copies purchased as required) is an effective public good research open access output mechanism for an institution.

Conclusion

In H. G. Wells's 'Country of the Blind' the 'one-eyed man is king', while Canadian author Margaret Atwood has said, 'an eye for an eye only leads to more blindness'! Many in the academic community remain 'blind' to open access issues and are often constrained in taking action by historical practices and, more importantly, by reward systems, both perceived and real. They thus occupy the academic institutional 'country of the blind'.

Informed institutional leadership, combined with vibrant advocacy programmes and enhanced reward systems, is required for relevant eyes to be opened to the nature and benefits of open access. Institutions now have the chance to accelerate the open access scholarly communication process. Such 'action does not require total agreement with the open access movement's beliefs and proposals, but it requires an active engagement with them' (Bailey Jr, 2006). This engagement with individual researchers in institutions will be the key to scholarly communication change.

Part 4
The position around the world

The definition and rationale for open access have been laid out, as have perspectives from a range of participants in scholarly communication. What, then, is the position on the ground? Is open access really happening? And if so, how is it happening? What are its characteristics when implemented? The following chapters summarise the situation in The Netherlands, the USA, the UK, India and Australia. The chapters illustrate the point made by Jean Claude Guédon earlier in this book that 'strategies that will miss their target in one particular cultural and/or economic context may well succeed in another'.

14

DARE also means dare: institutional repository status in The Netherlands as of early 2006

Leo Waaijers

The context

Emotions are the catalyst, technology the enabler and SURF the stimulator of the Digital Academic Repositories (DARE) Programme in The Netherlands.

During the decades before the DARE Programme, the way in which publishers used their copyright-based monopoly caused emotions to run high, particularly among librarians. An annual price rise for subscriptions averaging 11 per cent, combined with strict limitations on how they were used, was a constant source of irritation. Even though price rises have been cut in half in the first years of this century, they are still a good deal higher than inflation. Moreover, this figure is conditional upon there being no cancellations. The restrictions on use are still in place.

The DARE Programme was a welcome answer to the frustrations. Efforts could be directed towards creating a new situation, one which would give back to the institutions control of their own intellectual products while also ensuring better access to them. The grumbling at publishers faded into the background, making room for an 'open access' motivation based on the idea that unrestricted use of academic knowledge is of the utmost importance for progress in teaching and research, and is absolutely indispensable in a knowledge-intensive society. This viewpoint is a prime source of inspiration for the DARE participants.

Without the Open Archives Initiative (OAI), DARE would have been inconceivable. The initiative, published in Santa Fe in October 1999, goes beyond the use of the Internet, Web and XML to practically reinvent academic communication. It makes a crucial distinction between an open data layer that can be harvested anywhere in the world and a services layer based upon it (see Awre, this volume). The data layer is in the public domain; the services can be developed in accordance with a variety of business models (see Figure 14.1).

After just over two years of testing and experimentation, version 2.0 of the Open Archives Initiative Protocol for Metadata Harvesting (OAI-PMH) was released on 14 June 2002. It is said that on the same day in The Netherlands, the Board of the SURF Foundation approved the DARE Action Plan, which is based on OAI-PMH technology, using Dublin Core as the metadata format. An application will seldom have been adopted more quickly. In the meantime, OAI-PMH 2.0 has shown itself to be very robust and is still in use all over the world.

A third crucial factor for the success of DARE is that selfsame SURF Foundation. SURF is an independent organisation founded in 1987 by the joint Dutch universities to give shape to their collaboration in academic computer centres. The organisation grew successfully and now also includes the major research institutes and all universities of applied sciences, giving a total of nearly 60 participants. Its work is no longer limited to networking and supercomputing, but now covers the entire field of information and communication technology in research, education and management. An organisation that closely resembles it, and one with which SURF has regular and intensive collaboration, is

Figure 14.1 Data and services layer in OAI-PMH

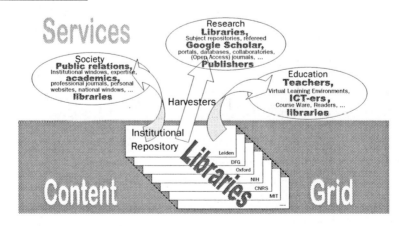

JISC in the UK; JISC is a committee of the Higher Education Funding Council for England (HEFCE).

Once SURF had given its support to the DARE Action Plan, additional financing was found fairly quickly, and the programme was launched on 1 January 2003. The DARE Programme will run for a period of four years; the budget is €5.9 million (€2.2 million from SURF, €2.0 million from the Ministry of Education and €1.7 million from Pica).

The DARE Programme has seven areas of responsibility. Alongside general management and communication, an important focal area was specifying the way in which Dublin Core would be used within DARE. But the largest portion of the funding was reserved to develop decentralised services, based on the requirement that these services would demonstrate the potential of the OAI model and would thus help to populate the repositories. Another area of work focused on constructing a link with the e-Depot of the National Library of The Netherlands, so that the material in the repositories could be assured of sustainable storage. Finally, some funds were reserved for applications used at repositories in education.

The first year

When DARE first started, a number of universities had e-archives; digital storage places for material such as dissertations or scanned documents from the university's mine of information. Some e-archives were left over from earlier projects, and they were not always properly maintained. None of the archives was OAI-compliant. Most universities had nothing, or at least no collection of digital documents that was publicly accessible.

The first step was to build the community. All universities were asked to appoint a representative ('anchorperson') who would be locally responsible for the implementation of the DARE Programme. The joint anchorpersons advised SURF at a strategic level. Other aspects of the consultative structure related to organisation, communication and technology. A community site was immediately set up at the outset and maintained well; as the programme progressed, it played a role of increasing importance as a platform for the exchange of practices, news and opinions.

An important early result was the document entitled 'DARE use of Dublin Core metadata' (Domingus and Feijen, 2004), in which the DARE partners reached an agreement on the use of Dublin Core format.

They decided to start with simple Dublin Core, but an optional DARE-qualified Dublin Core was also defined.

The collaboration became much more tangible when the participants took on a collective challenge: all partners would have an operational repository by 1 January 2004, one year after the start of the DARE Programme. Operational was to mean harvestable, and the proof would be furnished by a national site showing the joint result. A demonstration model was built for this purpose, although it would only harvest metadata that were linked to an openly accessible full-text document. And indeed, DAREnet was officially and festively opened on 27 January 2004. This remarkable result – The Netherlands was the first and for a long time the only country that could boast a nationwide network of repositories – came through genuine teamwork, in which the front-runners took pride and pleasure in helping their more 'needy' colleagues, who in their turn acknowledged that they would not have managed without this help.

The start-up phase of DARE has since been described in several articles (van der Vaart, 2004; van der Kuil and Feijen, 2005).

The second phase

Although some smaller-scale service projects were started while DAREnet was still being built, this process could only come to full fruition when the data infrastructure was operational. A broad call for tenders went out in early January 2004 (total amount €2.4 million) and 18 projects were awarded in April. The yield reflected creativity and enthusiasm, but not always experience. Opinions on the sustainability of the projects submitted were mixed. Nevertheless, new DARE services are emerging.

Alongside all these separate projects, the collective success of DAREnet held further promise. And so another ambitious joint project was started in September 2004. Each DARE participant would collect the complete works of ten top researchers of its institute, would digitise the material if necessary by means of scanning, and would place the complete result in the institutional repository. Within DAREnet, this special collection would be shown as a separate view under the name of 'Cream of Science'. In this case – exceptionally – DAREnet would also harvest metadata that were not linked to an open full-text document. This project was also a success and on 10 May 2005, during a two-day international leadership conference on 'Making the strategic case for institutional repositories' (Kircz, 2005b), the new site was opened by the president of the Royal Netherlands Academy of Arts and Sciences, Professor Frits van Oosterom (van Oosterom, 2005). During the conference five DARE participants signed the Berlin Declaration (2003), preceded earlier in the year by two and afterwards followed by two more.

This project taught us important lessons, the most interesting of which was undoubtedly the enthusiasm of the researchers. We were not at all sure of this before we started, and we used role-play to practise the counterarguments we would put forward against possible objections. It turned out not to be necessary. Not only were almost all the researchers who were invited happy to lend their cooperation, but spontaneous registrations also started to flow in. The target of 150 participants was easily surpassed with 207 plus a waiting list of around 30. Recently the University of Tilburg has decided to add 70 new authors and the University of Utrecht is adding 28 more of their top researchers.

Naturally, copyright was a tricky problem. An important mental breakthrough came when we adopted the standpoint – with the exception of one category – not to develop a central policy, but to rely on the most important party in this matter: the authors themselves. This choice was prompted by the insight that the transfer of copyright to publishers is currently undergoing rapid development. It is no longer necessary for open access journals, while for the traditional subscription journals, policy varies per publisher,[1] with many exceptions being made on an ad hoc basis. Springer even surprisingly gave permission for open access to all Springer articles within the Cream of Science. The only category for which we did define a central policy concerned material that had been obtained by scanning paper articles from before 1997. Before then, the copyright in the articles had been transferred exclusively for publication in a printed journal. The copyright in the digital version therefore still rested with the author. Many authors were not aware of this. This view was therefore given wide and fairly emphatic publicity by SURF, naturally among the authors, but also among the publishers (who have never disputed the standpoint) and the libraries. The final and remarkable outcome of this agile approach to copyright was that 60 per cent of the complete works of the Cream of Science could be presented as open full-text documents.

A third crucial lesson was about the need for optimisation, both locally and nationally. The OAI protocol, in combination with the agreement to use simple Dublin Core as the bibliographic format, was an inadequate foundation on which to build a robust, scalable and efficient service. Locally, a workflow had to be set up that was compatible with the institutional environment, so that documents 'automatically' find their way into the repository. An extra complication with Cream of Science was the separate workflow required to deal with the scanned material. In harvesting on a national scale, the variety of repository software used by the DARE partners (not only DSpace but also ARNO, i-Tor and a number of local solutions), differences in architecture (such as the use of sets) and the loose use of Dublin Core were the cause of much brain-cudgelling by the central DARE team (Feijen and van der Kuil 2005).

Nevertheless, the site turned out to be a huge success – so huge that the day after the opening, the large number of visitors (50,000) caused the site to give out. A review of the repository situation in 13 countries (11 European, USA and Australia) showed that by mid-2005, DARE was still in a forward position internationally (van Westrienen and Lynch, 2005).

The final phase

The final phase of the DARE Programme was defined in September 2005. Based on previous experience, it was decided to demonstrate that when the DARE Programme reached its conclusion, The Netherlands would have an operational production environment of well-filled institutional repositories. Concrete decisions taken for this included the adoption of the digital object identifier (DOI) as the identifier for the digital objects, and the proposed introduction of a national system of digital author identifiers (DAIs). In order to show specific sub-collections within DAREnet – such as Cream of Science – emphasis will be shifted from constructing dedicated sets within the local repositories to the use of generic OAI filters. This means formal uniform agreements must be made about the use of Dublin Core within the DARE community. For instance, dc:type will distinguish between 'bachelor thesis', 'masters thesis' and 'doctoral thesis'. Metis will play a central role in the entry of metadata at the universities. Metis is an application for bookkeeping in research projects. Its data are used to generate the annual report on scientific research and to record progress of projects or production figures in research. Developed at a single university, Metis has gradually come to be adopted by all universities in The Netherlands. Just as in DARE, in Metis the metadata of academic publications are an essential part of the system. For this reason a link from Metis to DARE was realised in 2005. In its final phase, the DARE Programme will further attune the two systems.

The final phase of DARE takes its name, HunDAREd Thousand, from a quantitative challenge: by the end of 2006 the number of accessible full-text publications in DAREnet will have risen by 100,000 to a total of 150,000. A related goal is for the number of doctoral theses to grow from 6,000 to 10,000. These doctoral theses will be shown as a separate view within DAREnet under the name of 'Promise of Science'. To contextualise these figures, the annual scientific production at Dutch universities is 51,000 publications, 2,500 of which are doctoral theses.

Future

When the DARE Programme is concluded, The Netherlands will have a robust but elementary infrastructure of institutional repositories. At that time, there will no longer be any organisational or technical obstacles to the inclusion of the complete annual academic production of The Netherlands in the repositories and thus to making them available to numerous services in the fields of research (journals, refereed portals) and education (learning environment) or for society (practitioners, the general public). Promising spin-offs of the programme are the network of educational repositories LOREnet and the European DRIVER project (see Vogel and Enserink, 2005).

A DARE follow-up programme will address the development of enhanced publishing: not only the article itself, containing the research

Figure 14.2 The research–publishing–funding cycle

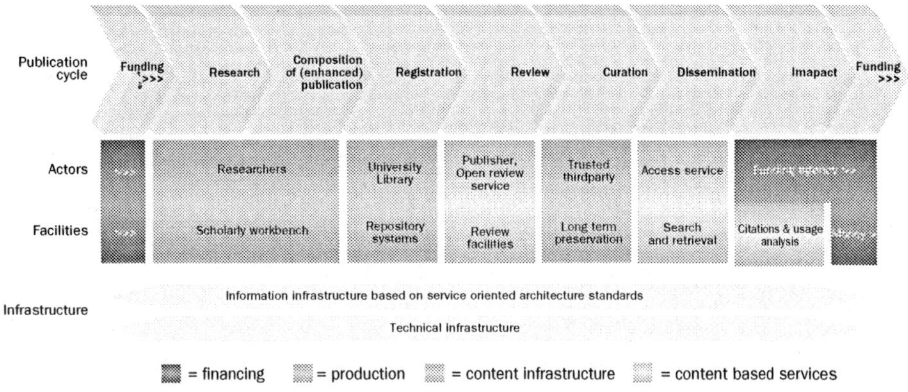

results, will be brought into circulation, but also the underlying research data, models and visual elements. The metadata needed for this are still being developed; not only will they relate to the contents, but also the structure, the rights and the technology of the digital objects. Thanks to the development of the repositories, researchers and management will be more able to live up to the responsibility of the institutions in respect to making accessible the results of scientific research (paid for by public money). The steps in this new publication process are shown in Figure 14.2, along with the possible actors, such as libraries (Waaijers, 2005), in each step.

Note

1. See the Sherpa/RoMEO list, available at: *http://www.sherpa.ac.uk/romeo.php*.

15

Open access in the USA

Peter Suber

The USA has a rich history of open access initiatives. In 1969 Americans built ARPANET, the direct ancestor to the Internet, for the purpose of sharing research without access barriers. In 1966, before ARPANET and well before the Internet and Web, Americans launched the Education Resources Information Center (ERIC) and MEDLINE, probably the first open access projects anywhere. ERIC and MEDLINE are still online and going strong – ERIC is hosted by the US Department of Education, and MEDLINE by the US National Library of Medicine in the Department of Health and Human Services. For other early open access initiatives, inside and outside the USA, see the Timeline of the Open Access Movement.[1]

To fit the large story of open access in the USA into my allotted space, I've decided to focus on the ten most important current open access initiatives. This means omitting important historical initiatives that are no longer current, such as David Shulenburger's National Electronic Article Repository (NEAR), Harold Varmus' E-BioMed (although this survives in the form of PubMed Central, discussed below), and Martin Sabo's Public Access to Science Act. It also means omitting many important current initiatives, such as ERIC and MEDLINE, the Astrophysics Data System, the Bethesda Statement (2003) on Open Access Publishing, Google, Highwire Press, the Information Access Alliance, Lots of Copies Keeps Stuff Safe, the National Academies Press, the National Science Digital Library, the Networked Computer Science Technical Reference Library, the Networked Digital Library of Theses and Dissertations, Ockham, the Open Archives Initiative (OAI), OAIster, Perseus, Project Gutenberg, Wikipedia, the US contributions to the international Human Genome Project and HapMap, and the many open access projects from the Library of Congress, the National Science Foundation, and branches of Government beyond the Department of Health and Human Services. Finally, it means I must apologise to the omitted and take responsibility for some necessary, regrettable, and ultimately subjective line-drawing.

Here are the ten initiatives are in roughly chronological order.

arXiv

Paul Ginsparg launched arXiv in August 1991, originally hosted by the Los Alamos National Laboratory and limited to high-energy physics. It now resides at Cornell University and has expanded its scope to nearly every branch of physics as well as mathematics, computer science, quantitative biology, and nonlinear sciences.

arXiv is the oldest open access e-print archive still in operation, and also one of the largest and most heavily used. It has earned a central place in physics research worldwide. As a result of arXiv, a larger percentage of physicists deposit their work in open access archives, and search open access archives for the work of others, than researchers in any other field. In some branches of physics the self-archiving rate approaches 100 per cent. While that is important for sharing knowledge and accelerating research in physics, it is also a valuable 'proof of concept' for other disciplines. ArXiv demonstrates that archiving technology can scale up to a whole discipline, that a disciplinary culture can adapt to (indeed, enthusiastically adopt) open access archiving, that open access archiving needn't be delayed in order to answer sceptical doubts (but can answer these doubts as it goes), and that high-volume open access archiving needn't undermine subscription journals.[2] Indeed, we are left to wonder how far the success of arXiv is transferable to other disciplines.[3]

Internet Archive

Brewster Kahle launched the Internet Archive in June 1996. From the start, the Internet Archive provided open access to its mirror of the historical Internet as well as to many special collections. The Internet Archive sponsors the Open Access Text Archive, Ourmedia, and the new

Open Education Resources project, and co-sponsors the open access Million Book Project with Carnegie Mellon University.

One of its most important open access projects is the Open Content Alliance (OCA), launched in October 2005. The OCA is a non-profit coalition of for-profit and non-profit organisations, led by the Internet Archive, dedicated to digitising print books for open access. Unlike the Google Library project, the OCA will limit itself to public domain books and copyrighted books for which the copyright holder has consented to participate. In addition, unlike Google, the OCA will offer full open access via the Open Library whenever it has permission to do so, while Google disables printing and downloading in the user's browser even for public domain books. Among the other members of the OCA are Yahoo, Microsoft, the Research Libraries Group, the European Archive, National Archives of the UK, and 19 major research universities (Suber, 2005a).

Finally, the Internet Archive has agreed to host a (forthcoming) universal open access repository that would mirror and preserve all the other, willing repositories in the world, and accept deposits from scholars who do not have repositories in their institutions or fields (Suber, 2005b).[4]

Public Library of Science

The Public Library of Science (PLoS) was launched by a letter to the editor in *Science Magazine* on 23 March 2001, quickly followed by an open letter,[5] eventually gathering over 30,000 signatures, calling on science journals to provide open access to their full contents by 1 September 2001, or the signatories would submit their work elsewhere. The deadline came and went without any significant publisher concessions and without any significant action by the signatories. The PLoS founders – Stanford biologist Patrick Brown, Berkeley biologist Michael Eisen, and Nobel laureate and former NIH Director Harold Varmus – decided that if existing publishers would not convert existing journals to open access, then they would have to become publishers themselves. PLoS launched its first journal, *PLoS Biology*, in October 2003, and its second, *PLoS Medicine*, in October 2005. PLoS currently publishes six open access journals and plans to add more. In 2005 *PLoS Biology* earned an impact factor of 13.9, the highest ranking in the category of general biology (Public Library of Science, 2005).

Repository software

There are over a dozen open source software packages for creating open access, OAI-compliant repositories. One of the two leaders, DSpace, is American. DSpace was developed by MIT and Hewlett-Packard, launched in November 2002, and is now used in over 100 open access repositories worldwide.

MIT has other important open access initiatives, most notably OpenCourseWare, a pioneering programme of open access courses now emulated by a growing number of other institutions around the world. MIT also sponsors the CWSpace (archiving open courseware files in DSpace), Open Knowledge Initiative (specifications for open components of learning software), SIMILE (Semantic Interoperability of Metadata and Information in unLike Environments), and TEK (Time Equals Knowledge, a bridge over the digital divide that distributes search engine results by e-mail).

Another of the other major open source packages for open access repositories is Fedora (Flexible Extensible Digital Object and Repository Architecture), developed by Cornell University and the University of Virginia and now used in about 30 repositories. Cornell has also collaborated with Pennsylvania State University on DPubS, an open source journal management package, and the University of Virginia is host to the major open access Electronic Text Center.

Creative commons

Until Lawrence Lessig launched Creative Commons on 16 May 2002, most open access initiatives gave no thought to appropriate open access licences. The Budapest Open Access Initiative (Open Society Institute, 2002), for example, said that 'the only role for copyright in this domain, should be to give authors control over the integrity of their work and the right to be properly acknowledged and cited'. But there were no licences at the time allowing copyright holders to retain these rights and waive the rest. Most open access providers simply put work online with no licence at all, leaving unclear which uses were permitted and which were not, and leaving users to choose between the delay of seeking permission and the risk of proceeding without it. Creative Commons licences solved this problem elegantly and were quickly adopted by open access-inclined authors (including scholarly authors), musicians, film-makers, and photographers. When the Public Library of Science and BioMed Central adopted Creative Commons licences for their journals, many open access journals followed suit. Both Google Advanced Search and Yahoo Creative Commons/Advanced Search now support filters that pick out content using Creative Commons machine-readable licences.

Creative Commons licences aren't the only licences to break with the 'all rights reserved' default (Liang, 2004) but, outside the special domain of open source software, they are by far the most widely used. Today over 50 million online objects carry Creative Commons licences.

Open access literature doesn't strictly need licences, which explains why many open access pages still don't use any. But licences can inform users that open access literature is really open access, assure users that permitted uses are really permitted, and help authors enforce any exceptions.

Creative Commons launched Science Commons[6] in early 2005. Under the leadership of John Wilbanks, Science Commons now has projects in open access publishing and archiving, open access data and databases, and licences optimised for scientific content.

University policies

A large number of US universities have adopted open access-friendly policies or resolutions, listed in university actions for open access or against high journal prices. These include Carleton College, Case Western Reserve University, Columbia University, Cornell University, Duke University, Gustavus Adolphus College, Harvard University, Indiana University at Bloomington, Indiana University – Purdue University at Indianapolis, Macalaster College, Massachusetts Institute of Technology, North Carolina State University, Oregon State University, St. Olaf College, Stanford University, University of California at Berkeley, University of California at San Francisco, University of California at Santa Cruz, University of Connecticut, University of Kansas, University of Maryland, University of North Carolina at Chapel Hill, and the University of Wisconsin.

Some of these university actions are policies to promote open access; some are resolutions by the faculty senate urging the adoption of such policies; and some are decisions to cancel expensive journals by the hundreds, accompanied by public statements on the unsustainability of the current subscription model and the need to explore alternatives.

Only five universities in the world today – none in the USA – mandate open access for research articles published by faculty. They are in Australia, Portugal, the UK, and two in Switzerland. Of the 18 universities with open access archiving policies sufficiently strong to sign the Eprints Registry of Open Access Repository Material Archiving Policies, only two are from the USA (Case Western Reserve and the University of Kansas). While the USA may lead in the number of universities taking active steps toward open access, it doesn't lead in the percentage of universities doing so.

Discussion forums

The two most widely read discussion forums devoted to open access issues are US-based: The American Scientist Open Access Forum, launched in August 1998 (American-hosted but moderated by Canadian Stevan Harnad) and the SPARC Open Access Forum, launched in July 2003 (moderated by myself). The AmSci Forum focuses on open access archiving and related issues like government open access policy, the effect of open access on citation impact, and strategies for spreading author self-archiving. The SPARC Open Access Forum deals with all open access issues, broadly construed. Several other US-based discussion lists often have open access-related threads: LibLicense from Yale University, OAI-Eprints from the Open Archives Initiative, ScholComm (for Scholarly Communication) from the American Library Association, SPARC-IR (on institutional repositories) and SPARC OpenData from SPARC, and SSP-L from the Society for Scholarly Publishing.

Advocacy organisations

The USA is fortunate to have several effective open access advocacy organisations: the Alliance for Taxpayer Access (ATA), Open Access Working Group (OAWG), Public Knowledge (PK), and the Scholarly Publishing and Academic Resources Coalition (SPARC).

SPARC is a coalition of more than 200 research institutions founded by Rick Johnson in 1998 and currently headed by Heather Joseph. Its early focus was on introducing competition into the journal marketplace and making journals more affordable. But since the Budapest Open Access Initiative in February 2002 (in which SPARC participated), it has worked actively for open access. SPARC has spearheaded a number of education and advocacy campaigns, including Create Change (grassroots advocacy tips for faculty and librarians), the Publisher Assistance Program (planning assistance for open access publishing), and the extensive Publisher Partner Program (supporting free and affordable journals). It has created an Authors Addendum (a contract supplement to help authors retain rights to their work), a directory of open access programmes (resources for librarians and administrators to help promote open access among faculty), an open access sponsorship guide (helping open access journals find sponsors), and a guide to open access business planning. To support these programs, it formed the SPARC Consulting Group, which provides business, financial, and strategic consulting services to universities, learned societies, and publishers. SPARC promotes community understanding of key issues through discussion forums on open access, open data, and institutional repositories, and by publishing the SPARC Open Access Newsletter (which I write). It also has a European arm called SPARC Europe, headed by David Prosser. Less visible to the public, SPARC has been an invaluable convenor and coalition-builder. It not only helped to form the ATA and OAWG, but continues to lead them as well.

Public Knowledge was founded in 2001 to speak for the public interest in information policy. Its primary policy interests under president and co-founder Gigi Sohn have been to protect the public domain, fair-use rights, and technological innovation, and to promote open access. PK's Open Access Project was launched in 2003 and works on all aspects of open access, both open access archives and journals, inside the USA and internationally, but especially on the open access policies of the federal government.[7]

While SPARC and PK were active in promoting open access before Congress asked the NIH to develop an open access policy in mid-2004, the OAWG and ATA sprang into existence in order to support open access policy in the federal government. The OAWG consists of the American Association of Law Libraries, the American Library Association, the Association of Academic Health Sciences Libraries, the Association of College & Research Libraries, the Association of Research Libraries, the Medical Library Association, Public Knowledge, Public Library of Science, and SPARC. The ATA is a coalition of US-based non-profit organisations working for open access to publicly-funded research. Among its dozens of members are universities, libraries, and patient and disease-advocacy organisations.

OAWG, PK and SPARC receive funding from the Open Society Institute.

One lesson from the USA for other countries is that governments that consider mandating open access to publicly-funded research will be lobbied intensively by publishers and will need well-organised, well-informed, and broad-based open access advocacy organisations to answer publisher objections and educate policy-makers about open access.

National Institutes of Health

The largest and most visible US initiative is the National Institutes of Health (NIH) Public Access Policy, which asks NIH grantees to deposit copies of any full-text, peer-reviewed articles resulting from NIH-funded research in PubMed Central (PMC), the open access repository maintained by the NIH.

In July 2004, Congress instructed the NIH to develop a policy requiring open access to the results of NIH-funded research and requiring it to be available online within six months of its publication in peer-reviewed journals. The final version of the policy fell short of the Congressional directive, substituting a request for the requirement and extending the permissible delay to 12 months after publication. The first weakness aggravated the second. Because there is no deposit requirement, the 12-month figure is just another request, not a firm deadline. The policy 'strongly encourages' grantees to deposit their work in PMC 'as soon as possible' after publication, but this is just an exhortation without sanction. Open access proponents criticised the weakness of the new policy, while open access opponents criticised its remaining strength (see Suber, 2005c, 2005d).[8]

I was among the critics of its weakness, and remain one, but a policy can fall short of high expectations and still be a major step forward. The NIH was the first research funding agency, public or private, to encourage open access archiving for the research it funds.[9] It was a good agency to go first: it funds medical research, which directly serves an urgent public need, and it is very large. In fact, the NIH is the world's largest funder of medical research, and its 2005 budget, at US$28 billion, was larger than the gross domestic product of 142 nations (World Bank, 2004). The NIH policy simply applies to more literature than any other single initiative is ever likely to cover – about 5,500 peer-reviewed journal articles per month. It rightly focuses on open access archiving rather than open access journals. It allows grantees use grant funds to pay the processing fees charged by open access journals. And it completely avoids the pitfalls of the June 2003 Sabo Bill, which would have put publicly-funded research into the public domain without actually providing open access. The NIH approach, by contrast, provides open access to publicly-funded research without putting any into the public domain.

Finally, as Elias Zerhouni, Director of the NIH, told the Washington Fax in January 2005, '[t]he fundamental breakthrough of this policy is ... the fact that we're creating for the first time the precedent and the right for a federal agency to have a venue or pathway for its scientists to ... give access to the public' (quoted in Coleman, 2005).

Because the policy doesn't require compliance, the compliance rate has been very low (Suber, 2005e). Because it allows embargoes of up to 12 months, most journals with a policy on NIH-funded authors require 12-month embargoes (Suber, 2005f, 2005g). However, there are three reasons to think that the NIH will soon strengthen the policy in both of the critical respects in which it fell short of the intent of Congress.

The first is that the agency's own Public Access Working Group (PAWG), appointed to advise it on implementing and improving the policy, recommended in November 2005 that the request become a requirement and the NIH impose a firm six-month deadline on public access. PAWG includes journal publishers and editors as well as researchers, librarians, and representatives of patient-advocacy groups and other medical non-profits. PAWG is advisory but its advice will carry weight with the NIH and Congress (Suber, 2005e).

The second and third reasons are two bills now pending before Congress: the CURES Act, which would be even better than the PAWG recommendation, and the Federal Research Public Access Act, which would be even better than the CURES Act. For details, see the next section.

Before leaving this section, we should note the NIH's other notable open access initiatives. The chief among them is PubMed Central (PMC), the OAI-compliant repository where the NIH asks its grantees to deposit their work. PMC and arXiv are the largest and most-used open access repositories in the world. The NIH also hosts important open access databases like ChemBank, ClinicalTrials, GenBank, Gene, GenSat, HomoloGene, Nucleotide, Protein, PubChem, and Taxonomy. An important aspect of the NIH public access policy is that the NIH enhances the author manuscripts it receives by linking them with these open access databases (Suber, 2005h, 2005i).

Federal legislation

Congress is currently considering two separate bills that would mandate open access to different bodies of publicly-funded research. Both would subsume the NIH.

The American Center for Cures Act (called the CURES Act) was introduced in the US Senate by Senator Joseph Lieberman on 14 December 2005. It would create a new agency within the NIH, the American Center for Cures, whose primary mission would be to translate fundamental research into therapies. In addition to creating and regulating the new Center, the Bill contains a notable provision on public access. The Act would mandate open access to NIH-funded research within six months of publication, and extend the same policy to all medical research funded by the larger Department of Health and Human Services, which embraces the NIH as well as the Centers for Disease Control and Prevention and the Agency for Healthcare Research. Over half of the non-classified research funded by the federal government is funded by the Department of Health and Human Services (Suber, 2006b).

The CURES Act would also fix a subtle but serious problem with the current NIH policy. The entire Department of Health and Human Services has a licence to disseminate the results of the research it has funded. When drafting its public access policy, the NIH acknowledged the existence of the licence but chose to rely instead on publisher consent, which had the effect of accommodating publisher resistance. The CURES Act would rely on the pre-existing licence and make publisher consent irrelevant.

The Federal Research Public Access Act (FRPAA) was introduced in the Senate by Senator John Cornyn in May 2006. It would mandate open access to nearly all federally-funded research within six months of publication. It would also rely on the government licence rather than publisher consent. The FRPAA directs all major federal agencies that fund research to adopt open access policies within a year and lays down strong guidelines for those policies. For this purpose, an agency is major if its research budget is US$100 million per year or more. Ten agencies fall into this category: the Environmental Protection Agency, National Aeronautics and Space Administration, National Science Foundation, and the cabinet-level Departments of Agriculture, Commerce, Defense, Education, Energy, Health and Human Services, and Transportation.

Both the CURES Act and FRPPA Act have bipartisan support in Congress, but as we go to press it is too early to assess their chances. If the PAWG recommendation is adopted, or if either one of these bills is passed, then the world's largest funder of medical research will have one of the world's strongest open access policies.

Concluding remarks

I am glad to celebrate the US contribution to open access. But science and scholarship are international, and open access initiatives worldwide are unusually collaborative. National boundaries matter much less than disciplinary differences, and open access activists in different countries are much more allies than rivals. If one country has an open access success, open access proponents in other countries will want to spread the success as quickly as possible; if one country suffers an open access setback, open access proponents elsewhere will want to see it overcome. If open access activists feel urgency, it is not the urgency of competition but the urgency to implement this beautiful solution to the serious problem of costly and limited access to research. We are all conscious that open access to one country's literature benefits researchers worldwide and setbacks to open access in one country are setbacks to researchers worldwide (Suber, 2005j).

Notes

1. See *http://www.earlham.edu/~peters/fos/timeline.htm*.
2. Swan (2005) reported in May 2005 that the American Physical Society (APS) and the Institute of Physics Publishing Ltd (IOPP) were unable to identify any subscriptions lost in the 14 years of arXiv's existence. The APS and IOPP both support open access archiving by accepting submissions directly from arXiv, which encourages authors to deposit their preprints there. In 1999, the APS went so far as to help launch an arXiv mirror at the Brookhaven National Laboratory and the IOPP is the process of launching an arXiv mirror of its own.
3. See the disciplinary differences relevant to open access at *http://www .earlham.edu/~peters/fos/lists.htm#disciplines*.
4. Disclosure: I am working with the Internet Archive on this project.
5. The Public Library of Science open letter, available at: *http://www.plos.org/ about/history.html*.

6. Disclosure: I am a member of the Science Commons Publishing Working Group.
7. Disclosure: I direct PK's Open Access Project.
8. See also the NIH Public-Access Policy: Frequently Asked Questions, available at: *http://publicaccess.nih.gov/*.
9. The first funding agency to let grantees use grant funds to pay processing fees at open access journals charging fees was the US-based Howard Hughes Medical Institute, *http://www.hhmi.org/*.

16

Towards open access to UK research

Frederick J. Friend

Progress towards open access to UK research reports is slow but steady. The growth in open access has been remarkable when the past ten years are set in the historical timescale of over 500 years of availability of print publications and over 300 years of scientific journal publishing. And yet so many more results from UK taxpayer-funded research could already have been made freely available if the UK government had the vision to see the opportunities in new forms of scholarly communication. The story of open access in the UK is one of initiatives by organisations and individuals to develop the opportunities provided by new technologies, while the benefits from those initiatives have not been realised by a hesitant government influenced by lobbying from vested interests.

Academic origins

The UK interest in open access to academic publications has roots in both the academic and the library communities. Although the origins of open access are perceived to be in the concerns of librarians about journal price rises, members of the academic community were the first to make preprints of research articles freely available on the Internet through the use of open websites. 'Self-archiving', as the practice came to be known, began on a large scale with the deposit of preprints by physics scholars in the arXiv database. Professor Stevan Harnad of Southampton University had the vision to see how self-archiving could be extended to all research reports, stimulating an e-mail discussion on his 'subversive proposal' in the summer of 1994 (Harnad, 1995). The vision at that time was of fast electronic publication of preprints for which there was no market, leaving publishers to continue to publish the peer-reviewed version of an article. Publishers quickly realised, however, that their own future lay in electronic publication and – rightly or wrongly – many of them perceive access to any version of a journal article to be part of the market from which they derive their profits. Publishers' concerns have increased as search engines have enabled easy access to the growing content in open repositories. Although Stevan Harnad sees self-archiving as no threat to conventional journal publication, it was inevitable that the 'subversive proposal' became a business issue as well as a technical issue.

The concerns of librarians

Independently from Stevan Harnad's work, some members of the UK library community in the 1990s were thinking that change was necessary in the way in which scientific and medical journals are made available to those who needed access to the research those journals contained. To librarians whose professional motivation was to provide access for the maximum number of readers to the maximum quantity of relevant content, it was frustrating to have to exclude readers outside publishers' licensing definitions and to have to cancel titles known to be of value to readers. Although librarians regularly asked for higher budgets, price rises continually outstripped the extra money made available, such as when the UK government made an extra £10 million available to academic libraries in 1987 (Standing Conference of National and University Libraries, 1988), and the inflationary effect led to a further rise in journal prices.

During the 1990s UK librarians were looking across the Atlantic for new publishing models. The Mellon-funded project JSTOR attracted a great deal of interest as an innovative collaboration, although the value of JSTOR was perceived to be in saving costs on the storage of low-use volumes rather than on the purchase of current journals. Of more general application was the formation of the Scholarly Publishing and Academic Resources Coalition (SPARC), (see Friend, 1998), which held out the promise of competition for high-priced journals from new low-priced journals and of alliances to support those new journals. One feature noticeable in visiting the USA at that time was the involvement of senior members of the academic community with scholarly communication issues, an involvement then – but not now – missing in the UK. The Tempe meeting in March 2000 (Tempe Principles, 2000) illustrated academic involvement, with the participation of a number of presidents, provosts and deans of US universities as well as leading members of learned societies. JSTOR and SPARC had a common way of working, encouraging collaboration between various stakeholders, the value of which was not lost upon the UK library community following US developments.

JISC and scholarly communication developments

The website of the Joint Information Systems Committee notes that JISC 'supports further and higher education by providing strategic guidance, advice and opportunities to use information and communications technology'. It was natural therefore that JISC should have been monitoring new initiatives like SPARC and the Budapest Open Access Initiative (Open Society Institute, 2002), and picked up feelings in the UK academic and library communities about the need for change in scholarly publishing. During the 1990s JISC had funded the eLib Programme (Rusbridge, 1998), having a major impact upon the development of electronic services to library users. This programme also prepared the way for later open access work, for example through the funding of the Eprints software developed at the School of Electronics and Computer Science at Southampton University. As the technical developments proceeded the need for change in the structure of scholarly communication came to be realised.

Accordingly, in 2001 JISC set up the JISC Scholarly Communications Group to advise on actions they might take. Much of the work of the group has been in fact-finding and investigation of key issues through commissioned reports. In 2002 JISC embarked upon a major new programme entitled 'Focus on Access to Institutional Resources', the FAIR Programme. This programme was designed to improve access to all types of content produced within UK universities and colleges by encouraging the development of institutional repositories. Whereas self-archiving advocates approached open access from an author's perspective, the FAIR Programme approached open access from the direction of institutional needs, but the two approaches coincided in meeting the needs of both authors and institutions. Out of the FAIR Programme came several services of value to UK universities and to academic institutions world-wide. For example, the Sherpa/RoMEO list has been invaluable in listing publishers' policies on repository content and the experience of the SHERPA consortium has helped other universities in setting up open repositories.

The success of the FAIR Programme has led to the funding of the Digital Repositories Programme to run from 2005 to 2008. Increasingly, projects under this programme link technical developments to cultural issues, as with the Institutional Repositories and Research Assessment project, which is developing technical solutions to the integration of repository content into the national Research Assessment Exercise. Meanwhile JISC has not neglected the second route to open access, the publication of open access journals or the conversion of existing journals from subscription to open access, and in particular JISC has wished to support publishers willing to undertake trials of the open access model. The JISC Journals Working Group has been as interested as the Scholarly Communication Group in the development of new models, and from 2003 to 2006 has provided funds to a variety of publishers in support of a transition from a subscription to an open access model. This funding has encouraged UK authors to submit papers to peer-reviewed open access journals. Alongside these initiatives, JISC has funded advocacy work to explain to authors, to institutions and to publishers the benefits to be gained from new ways of disseminating academic content.

The role of research funding agencies

The Wellcome Trust was the first major UK funding agency to commit to open access. Its reasons for making this commitment are made very clear in a 'position statement' on its website (Wellcome Trust, 2005a): 'The Wellcome Trust has a fundamental interest in ensuring that the availability and accessibility of this material [i.e. journal articles resulting from Trust-funded research] is not adversely affected by the copyright, marketing and distribution strategies used by publishers'. Before making this commitment, the Trust had commissioned two studies into scholarly publishing, ensuring that its policy is built upon a factual foundation. Most of the UK Research Councils are also supportive of open access, but – unlike the Wellcome Trust – they have to take into account the views of the UK government in determining their policies. A further complication has been the Research Councils' wish to agree policies in common, which can lead to a 'lowest common denominator' result. Yet more pressure was exerted upon Research Councils UK through lobbying by publishers against RCUK's wish to support open access. With all these factors to consider, RCUK has taken over one year to finalise its policy. Even so, it is to be hoped that the RCUK 'Position Statement on Access to Research Outputs' – currently only available in draft (RCUK, 2006) – will still mark a significant step forward in the progress towards open access to the results of UK publicly-funded research.

Parliamentary inquiry and government inaction

The announcement of an inquiry into scientific publishing by the UK Parliament's Science and Technology Committee came out of the academic experience of several Members of the Committee and also out of the realisation that scientific publishing was not keeping pace with technological change. Ian Gibson MP expressed this dual inspiration in a Westminster Hall debate on 15 December 2005:

> Some members of the Committee who had experience of the publishing of academic journals knew how the problems had grown over the years and how, as in most things scientific and technological, the science and technology had moved on faster than regulation and faster than the communication of some of the discoveries that had been made. (Gibson, 2005)

The inquiry was thorough and resulted in a report entitled 'Scientific Publications: Free for All?' (House of Commons, Science and Technology Committee, 2004a). The report gave strong support to the self-archiving route to open access in institutional repositories, but also recommended further development of open access journals. Unfortunately the UK government failed to appreciate the benefits to the UK from the Committee's recommendations and issued a response (House of Commons, Science and Technology Committee, 2004b), claiming to aim for a 'level-playing field' for conventional and for new forms of scientific publishing but in fact doing nothing to facilitate the creation of that 'level playing-field'. Intense lobbying by vested interests was a major influence upon the government's response.

UK publishers' reaction to open access developments

The failure of many publishers to realise the opportunities for their businesses in open access developments is disappointing. When the Sherpa/RoMEO list of publisher copyright policies was first established, most publishers willingly adopted 'green' status, allowing authors to deposit copies of journal articles in repositories. During 2004 publishers began to express concern that large-scale take-up of the permission they had given could result in the cancellation of subscriptions by libraries, despite the fact that no evidence exists of cancellations on the basis of repository content. While publishers were unwilling to lose their 'green' status, time embargoes on the deposit by authors began to be introduced and publishers hardened their attitude towards policy statements by funding agencies encouraging repository deposit. There may be business opportunities for publishers in new markets for journal content, in the same way as the popular music industry has adapted to the Internet age, but even if publisher concerns about losses due to use of repository content prove to be justified, in delaying policy statements by funding agencies publishers have also delayed access to the research grants that can fund open access publication charges. The downward trend in library subscriptions has been clear for several years. Funding publication as part of the research process on an open access model will relate publication costs closely to research budgets, a relationship not achieved under the library subscription model. Open access publishers such as BioMedCentral and the Public Library of Science have committed fully to this model, and increasingly traditional publishers such as Oxford University Press have been willing to embark upon small-scale trials. However, the negative attitude towards open access fed into government policy by the publishing industry has not as yet enabled the UK to seize the opportunities in the new information environment.

Can the UK seize the opportunities provided by open access?

The growth in interest in open access within the UK has as much to do with opportunities as it has to do with problems in the current scholarly communication model. The opportunities provided by the Internet age are more fundamental than digitisation of print and cannot be met as fully through the subscription and licensing model as through an open access model. This is evident in relation to the interaction between text and data. Research data are used in the preparation of a journal article, but a conventional journal cannot easily enable the reader to pass seamlessly from freely-accessible data to subscription-based text and vice versa. In a speech in April 2002, Prime Minister Tony Blair recognised the importance of the development of the e-Science Grid: 'It's significant that the UK is the first country to develop a national e-Science Grid, which intends to make access to computing power, scientific data repositories and experimental facilities as easy as the Web makes access to information.' The value of an open access business model to enable the benefits of these technological developments to be fully-realised has not been appreciated by the government.

Open access to research reports also benefits the research community in opening up possibilities of new collaborations between research groups who may not have had access to reports only available on subscription. The evidence is growing that open access leads to higher citations (see Kurtz and Brody, this volume), improving the visibility of a nation's research. Changes in the way research is communicated can therefore provide the UK taxpayer with greater value for money from public investment in research. In this environment commercial and learned society publishers have an important role if they are prepared to change as radically as the research community they serve. The long history of research publication is a tradition of which the UK can be proud, and it is to be hoped that publisher and government hesitation will not delay further the realisation of the benefits from open access to UK research.

The views expressed in this chapter are those of the author and not necessarily those of any organisation or institution for which the author works.

17

Open access in Australia

John Shipp

The Australian scholarly community has not embraced orthodox open access, in terms of free and unrestricted availability of peer-reviewed journal literature, with great alacrity so far. There is, however, considerable support for a broader interpretation which encompasses all research outputs not just publications. There has been strong support for open access (as the term has been used in this volume) from the library profession and some individual scholars, however, most academics generally remain either unaware or unconvinced of the concept, or they are unable or unwilling to participate.

Acceptance has been affected also by indifference on the part of key national funding authorities and scholarly associations. The most prestigious Australian academies do not have open access policies even though the National Academies Scholarly Communications Forum has promoted scholarly communication issues including open access. The Australian Vice-Chancellors' Committee and the major government research funding agencies (Australian Research Council and the National Health and Medical Research Council) likewise make no public show of support. Even those organisations which have developed open access statements tend to hide them in the deep, dark recesses of their websites (Council of Australian University Librarians, 2004; Department of Education, Science and Training, Australian Research Information Infrastructure Committee, 2004; Group of Eight, 2004).

Open access has yet to be regarded as a systemic priority by Australian policy and funding agencies. There has been a tendency to regard it as a 'library issue' due to an initial association with the escalating cost of journals. The continuing focus on journal articles reinforces that notion and may be inhibiting opportunities for more pervasive change in the way in which scholarly information and ideas are communicated.

Like their colleagues elsewhere, Australian academics are expected to disseminate their research through refereed international publications as a benchmark of quality and as an indicator of individual and institutional performance. This is unlikely to change in the short term and a proposed revision of the Australian research quality assessment process maintains the hegemony of traditional publishing formats. The Research Quality Framework proposal does not signal any intent to mandate open access to publicly-funded research outcomes. International rankings of universities, such as the World University Rankings published in the *Times Higher Education Supplement*, and the Academic Ranking of World Universities by Shanghai Jiao Tong University, also reinforce the role of traditional publication. Acceptance of open access would be enhanced if research assessment rankings included criteria recognising the contribution and impact of open access.

There are thirty-nine Australian universities of which two are private institutions. All of the universities, however, receive some government funding and the majority of their research funding originates from the public purse. There are four significant research agencies which are also publicly funded: the Commonwealth Scientific and Industrial Research Organisation (CSIRO); the Australian Institute of Marine Science; the Defence Science and Technology Organisation; and the Australian Nuclear Science and Technology Organisation. In addition, there is considerable applied research undertaken by government departments and agencies. The majority of scholarly publishing, however, is associated with the universities.

Australia does not have a large scholarly publishing industry. CSIRO has a commercial press which publishes monographs and a range of journals. A number of universities and societies also undertake publishing through a mix of formal imprints and more ad hoc arrangements. The bulk of refereed publication, however, occurs through international scholarly societies and commercial publishers.

Many Australian academics now have personal websites which often include details of their publications but few provide links to the full text. The time involved in providing full-text, especially of older publications, is not generally perceived to be worth the effort. The barriers are reduced where central support is provided for authors to use an institutional repository. Barriers are reduced further once repository statistics reveal the extent of use (see Sale, this volume).

Fourteen universities currently have publicly available repositories containing digital versions of journal articles authored by their staff. These repositories contained over 9,000 items in January 2006. The bulk of items (7,000+) were concentrated in three repositories where considerable author support has been provided to assist deposit. What is significant is that over 40 per cent of the repositories have been implemented within the last 12 months and that more are planned. To date, only the Queensland University of Technology has mandated open access to a range of published research outputs.

The establishment of institutional repositories and the implementation of open access have been delayed by a range of factors. These include the availability of staff expertise, access to appropriate technical infrastructure, acceptance by the academic community and uncertainty about the long-term sustainability of repositories. Some of these issues have been addressed by initiatives funded by the federal Department of Education, Science and Training. Others will be resolved as individual institutions reach a state of readiness or external pressures are applied through government requirements, such as the research quality assessment process.

There is growing support among academics and research funding bodies for the provision of facilities that apply the open access ethos to a wide range of scholarly outputs not just journal publications. This approach is perceived to meet national and individual needs more appropriately. It has the potential to provide an holistic view of research endeavour by providing access to the data supporting research as well as the outcome synopsis represented by the journal article or other publication.

In 2002, the Australian Federal Government adopted and funded an innovation programme related to excellence in research, science and technology: Backing Australia's Ability. Part of the programme funding was reserved to support the development of research information infrastructure components at a systemic level including:

- improved access by Australian researchers to the information needed to carry out research;
- facilities to make the results of Australian research widely available and easily accessible.

Funding has been made available to support a number of projects aimed at providing open access, in its broadest sense, to Australian research. Projects were chosen for their potential to:

- develop principles to increase the accessibility of research information;

- promote standards-based approaches to information discovery, storage and sharing;
- demonstrate practical integrated information management solutions;
- promote cross-institutional, cross-sectoral and trans-national cooperation in research information management;
- improve access to key information resources, including major research data sets and databases of research publications;
- advocate the advantages offered by an improved information infrastructure.

Projects were also assessed to determine their capacity to support the Open Access Statement developed by the Australian Research Information Infrastructure Committee (Department of Education, Science and Training, Australian Research Information Infrastructure Committee, 2004). Although criticised in some quarters for its lack of orthodoxy, the Statement reflected the need for a broad policy foundation to underpin investment in systemic infrastructure supporting the maintenance, dissemination and preservation of research information created by Australian scholars. It also reflected a perceived need to support more innovative approaches to scholarly communication if Australian research were to improve its level of international impact.

The universities and the two major research funding agencies support the storage and retention of relevant data for at least five years after the publication of research results. The agreed guidelines advocate:

> Wherever possible, original data must be retained in the department or research unit in which they were generated. Individual researchers should be able to hold copies of the data for their own use. Retention solely by the individual researcher provides little protection to the researcher or the institution in the event of an allegation of falsification of data. (National Health and Medical Research Council and Australian Vice-Chancellors' Committee, 1997)

Systematic adherence to the guidelines has rarely been enforced and there is increasing awareness that the non-availability of data relating to previous research can require unnecessary duplication of effort.

Of the projects supported by the Department of Education, Science and Training from systemic infrastructure funds, six are directly related to developing facilities which will enable universities to provide open access to their research outcomes:

- Australasian Digital Thesis Program (ADT);

- Australian Partnership for Sustainable Repositories (APSR);

- Australian Research Repositories Online to the World (ARROW);

- Dataset Acquisition, Accessibility and Annotation e-Research Technology (DART);

- Open Access to Knowledge Law Project (OAK);

- Regional Universities Building Research Infrastructure Collaboratively (RUBRIC).

Twenty-eight universities currently provide open access to research higher degree theses through ADT, which is a programme of the Council of the Australian University Librarians. A total of 5,391 full-text files were available in mid-January 2006 with bibliographic details provided to a further 11,687. By the end of 2006, access to the bibliographic records of more than 130,000 theses will be provided. Several universities are in the process of scanning microfilm copies of older theses which will increase the full-text corpus significantly. To date, ten institutions have mandated the inclusion of new theses but implementation of the mandate has been of varying success.

The ARROW and APSR projects have been focused on demonstrating the feasibility of using open source software to establish institutional repositories capable of providing open access to a broad spectrum of digital objects which are likely to be produced, or required, as part of the research process. The RUBRIC project has been funded to support smaller universities to establish institutional repositories using products tested or developed by ARROW and APSR.

All of the repository projects build on earlier initiatives and take advantage of, and contribute to, international activities. Not 're-inventing the wheel' is regarded as essential if optimal use is to be made of limited funding. Selection of projects has included consideration of the extent to which the outcomes of prior or concurrent projects are utilised. Funding is generally not granted for the development of new repository software but has been made available for contributing to software refinement as part of international collaborations.

The universities which have implemented institutional repositories have used a mix of software solutions.[1] The initial adopters used the Eprints software but there are now installations using FEZ-Fedora,

VTLS-Fedora, DSpace, and Digital Commons@ as well as other proprietary content management systems.

As part of the ARROW project, a national resource discovery service has been developed which is capable of searching across Australian institutional repositories irrespective of their operating software, providing they comply with OAI-PMH.

The OAK Law project will develop a set of legal protocols and generic licences that can be used across universities to facilitate and break down barriers to open access to copyright material. The project will also develop best practice guides for managing copyright issues and a rights expression language that can be used to enhance technologically open access to existing and proposed electronic stores of research and other data.

Complementary to the repository projects, is the Metadata Access Management System (MAMS), which aims to provide the integration of multiple solutions for managing authentication, authorisation and identities. The project also seeks to bring together common services for digital rights, search services and metadata management.

An interpretation of open access based on the content of institutional repositories is likely to dominate in Australia well into the future. Monash, Sydney and the Australian National Universities have already established e-presses to facilitate the publication of repository content. Swinburne and the University of Technology Sydney are among those universities using repository content to publish online open access journals.

The broader interpretation of open access is not without its difficulties. Establishing repositories of this kind requires skills and resources currently not available at every university. It is also significantly more costly than an e-print archive. The successful implementation of a national system of institutional repositories will require continued collaboration within and between institutions nationally and internationally. It will also require continued support from government to ensure the provision of a robust national information infrastructure and support for changes in institutional intellectual property policies.

Note

1. See the AuseAccess University Policies, available at: *http://leven.comp.utas .edu.au/AuseAccess/pmwiki.php?n=General.UniPolicies.*

18

Open access in India

D. K. Sahu and Ramesh C. Parmar

In the scholarly publishing world, India is exceptional in not having a high percentage of its scientific journals available online. Among the top 25 publishing countries, India ranks 12th for the overall number of journals, but drops to 18th for journals with online content (Haider, 2005). Surprisingly, however, its position in the list of open access journals is fifth, well ahead of countries such as The Netherlands, China, Germany, Australia, and so on, which are higher in the list of online journals. Among the non-high-income countries, India ranks second only to Brazil for the number of open access journals. Almost 50 per cent (48 out of 103) of the online journals from India are open access (see Haider, 2005). What makes India do so well in the list of open access journals? How can such a large percentage of electronic journals in India provide open access without even charging the author or authors' institution for publication of the articles?

In the Registry of Open Access Repositories, India ranks 11th in the list of countries with registered interoperable archives. Unfortunately, out of the 15 listed archives, only 11 were accessible and functional at the time of writing this piece. Eleven of these were institutional archives and only one institutional archive had more than 500 documents. Why does the country with the largest number of information technology professionals fail to build e-archives for their institutions? Why are the existing archives near empty and not filling up?

Open access journal publishing in India

A large number of the journals published in India belong to learned societies and associations, and are published by the association or the

---

editor themselves without the involvement of any commercial publisher. The members of these learned societies receive the print copies of the journals without paying an annual or recurring fee. For continuing their publication activities the associations depend on non-member subscriptions, which are limited in number and restricted by and large to the Indian universities and colleges, on advertisements in print editions, and on income generated from other sources, such as the annual conferences of the associations. Most of the Indian journals suffer from 'low circulation – low visibility – low impact factor' syndrome. With many fewer paid regional or international subscriptions, these journals have limited visibility, restricted mainly to the members of the association. With this limited visibility, these journals are cited less frequently than their western counterparts. The low impact factor inhibits authors from submitting their quality work to the Indian journals. Thus, it is expected that with open access, Indian journals will be able to reach to a wider audience. At the same time, loss, if any, of paid non-member subscriptions is less likely to have a major effect on the economics of these journals.

A number of biomedical journals have been online from late 1990s; *Neurology India*, *Current Science*, *Indian Pediatrics*, and the *Indian Journal of Critical Care Medicine* have been online since 1998–1999. These individual endeavours have now evolved into more organised and collaborative efforts, including those of the Indian Medlars Centre, the Indian Academy of Sciences, and the Indian National Science Academy in the not-for-profit sector, and Medknow Publications in the commercial sector. International players such as Bioline International have also helped many Indian journals to have web presence.

Indian Medlars Centre

The Indian Medlars Centre (IMC), set up jointly by the National Informatics Centre and the Indian Council of Medical Research, has taken the pioneering step of putting Indian biomedical journals accessible from a single platform. IMC's first bibliographic database IndMed, established in 1998, provides abstract level information from more than 70 journals. Each of the articles in the database is tagged with medical subject headings. In 2003, IMC launched its full-text database, MedInd, which now hosts the full-text version of 38 journals in PDF format. The understanding between the journals and the IMC ensures that the digitised work hosted by IMC will continue to be accessible even if the journal is discontinued.

Indian Academy of Sciences

The Indian Academy of Sciences (IAS), founded in 1934, publishes 11 journals with the basic philosophy that no journal published by the Academy is in competition with another journal published in the country. *Current Science*, published by the Current Science Association in collaboration with the IAS, has entire back volumes from 1932 online as PDF files and has been online since 1999. Many other journals including the *Journal of Biosciences*, *Sadhana*, and *Pramana* also have the entire back volumes online.

Indian National Science Academy

The Indian National Science Academy (INSA), established in 1935, publishes four journals including the *Proceedings of INSA*. Under the project 'Building digital resources: creating facilities at INSA for hosting S&T journals on online', INSA launched the open access version of these journals in December 2003.

Bioline International

Bioline International is a not-for-profit collaborative effort of the University of Toronto Libraries, Canada, the Reference Center on Environmental Information, Brazil, and Bioline, UK. It provides electronic publishing services to journals published in developing countries. Bioline provides access to 14 Indian journals on their primary site as well as archives these journals at the Bioline E-prints Archive.

Medknow Publications

Medknow Publications is a commercial publisher providing publishing services to over 30 biomedical journals. These journals provide immediate free access and do not charge the author or author's institution for publication of the articles. The journals also permit authors' self-archiving. Most of the journals published are archived at multiple places including interoperable repositories, Bioline International and MedInd, ensuring the long-term archiving and accessibility of the published content.

Impact of open access publishing

Open access has certainly helped Indian journals to reach an international audience, as can be seen by the number and distribution of article downloads. The *Journal of Postgraduate Medicine*, a quarterly journal with a print circulation of less than 1,000, attracts close to 100,000 visitors with more than 110,000 article downloads per month. The increased accessibility and visibility has also increased the citations received by this journal (Bavdekar and Sahu, 2005; Sahu, Gogtay and Bavdekar, 2005). The number of manuscripts submitted to the journals has increased manifold (see Figure 18.1), with increases in the number of articles coming from other countries ranging from 12 to 44 per cent for various journals (see Figure 18.2).

Interestingly, these open access journals have not lost the paid non-member subscriptions (see Figure 18.3) but, in fact, have benefited from increased subscriptions, including many international subscriptions (Rajashekar, 2004; Sahu, 2006). As the cost of Web dissemination is miniscule compared with the cost of sending printed copies free to hundreds of members, the online publication has not had any impact on the economics of these journals. In addition, helping hands from MedInd and Bioline have helped these journals to take care of the expenses for the open access version.

Figure 18.1 Number of articles submitted per year for select journals published by Medknow Publications, 2003–2005

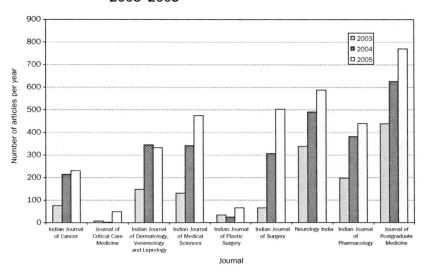

Figure 18.2 Percentage of articles from India and abroad for select journals published by Medknow Publications, 2005

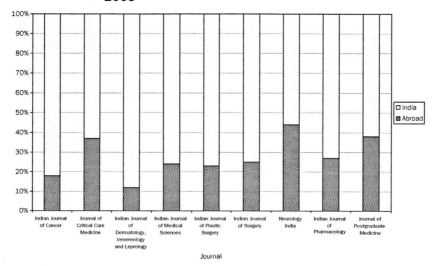

Figure 18.3 Subscriptions of select journals from Medknow Publications, 2003–2005

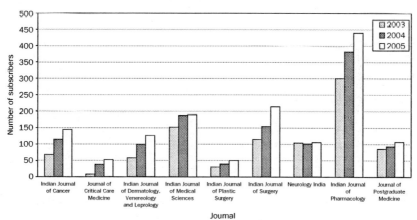

Open access archiving in India

Scientists have always preferred to publish their work in high-impact journals. Until recently, India had no journal with an impact factor of more than 1.0; consequently, the best science from India is rarely published in the Indian journals. There have been thoughts to mandate publication of government-funded research in the Indian journals and a 'publish in India' movement (John, 2004; Satyanarayana, 2004). In spite of calls for such movements, Indian research work continues to be published in high-impact overseas journals, not all of which are accessible even for the most affluent universities and colleges in India. Thus, open access publishing adopted by Indian journals will not help the Indian scientists to access the Indian science. Indian scientists need to make their work published in toll-based journals accessible to others through self-archiving. In the last couple of years, a number of institutional and subject-based repositories have been set up in India.

Open access repositories in India

The Indian Institute of Science was the first in the country to set up an interoperable institutional repository (ePrints@IISc), under the leadership of the late Dr T. B. Rajashekar. The archive now has more than 3,000 documents, with over 90 per cent having full text. The Institute has a separate Archives Unit and well-documented submission guidelines. The Archives Unit also helps the institution staff to submit papers by e-mail, which are then deposited by the Archives Unit. In spite of these efforts, the repository has less than 5 per cent of the published papers of the Institute. Most of the documents in the archive have been deposited by the Archive Unit and less than 5 per cent of the existing documents are actually self-archived by the authors. Other institutional repositories in India are less than a year old; many are in the testing phase, and none have more than 500 papers.

What could be the reasons for the dismal performance on this front? We sent a set of 20 questions to the contact persons of 11 institutional repositories in the country, which generated eight responses. The important factors which could have contributed to the non-filling of the repositories could be the lack of an institutional mandate (8 out of 8), no dedicated archive unit (7 out of 8), and an absence of active help for the staff (6 out of 8). Respondents considered motivating the staff to deposit their papers as their biggest challenge.

Efforts to popularise open access archives

Professor Subbiah Arunachalam, the greatest open access advocate in the country, organised a workshop on 'Open access and institutional repositories' under the aegis of the M. S. Swaminathan Research Foundation, Chennai, in May 2004. Forty-eight information scientists and decision-makers from various disciplines of science were trained for installing, maintaining, and promoting open access archives. The majority of the existing repositories in India have been established by the participants of this workshop. A number of training workshops have been conducted by Dr Rajashekar, Dr A. R. D. Prasad, Dr M. G. Sreekumar, and others.

A special session on open access was held at the 93rd Indian Science Congress in January 2006, which came up with the following recommendation for the 'Optimal national open access policy': The Indian government expects authors of research papers resulting from publicly-funded research to maximise the opportunities to make their results available for free. To this end, the government:

- requires electronic copies of any research paper that has been accepted for publication in a peer-reviewed journal, and is supported in whole or in part by government funding, to be deposited into an institutional open access repository immediately on acceptance for publication;

- encourages government grant holders to publish in a suitable open access journal where one exists; the government will cover the publication costs, if any;

- encourages government grant holders to retain ownership of the copyright of published papers, where possible.

Hindrance for promoting and propagating E-archives

We asked the participants of the Chennai workshop the reason(s) for not being able to set up an archive in the 20 months since the workshop. The main reason given was the lack of infrastructure. The institutions that have been able to set up an archive already had a dedicated server, the bandwidth or the technical staff; others lacked this technical support. Administrative apathy was the second commonest reason given for not able to start an archive. With respect to self-archiving, those who have already set up archives are experiencing inertia among institution staff.

Other open access projects in India

The Digital Library of India aims to include a free-to-read, searchable collection of one million books, predominantly in Indian languages. The project is hosted by the Indian Institute of Science, Carnegie Mellon

University, and ERNET, and has already completed the digitisation of more than 50,000 books.

Vidyanidhi, an initiative of the University of Mysore, is an archive of doctoral theses. It also maintains the archive using DSpace.

The Scientific Journal Publishing in India (SJPI) project aims to improve the accessibility of scientific literature published in Indian journals by introducing an indexing system.

Open J-Gate, recently launched, provides a search across over 2,500 open access journals and link to the full-text articles.

Richard Smith, the editor of the *British Medical Journal*, has said, 'If researchers do not publish their research then they distort the research record, potentially leading astray those who undertake the important work of systematically reviewing evidence' (Smith, 2002). A research paper published in an obscure, inaccessible or toll-based journal and not archived for the rest of the world to use it, is as good as not published. Indian journals often get neglected in international meta-analyses and Indian papers published in international journals are inaccessible for those Indian authors conducting research. The combined 'green' and 'gold' roads to open access could help break this jinx.

Acknowledgments

The authors thank Professor Subbiah Arunachalam for providing valuable suggestions on the draft of this paper, Ms Jutta Haider for providing data from her study and the respondents of the two questionnaires about institutional repositories in India.

Part 5
The future

Scholarly communication is undergoing profound changes, and almost everyone involved is experiencing discomfort of one kind or another as a result. For some, the change is technology-driven, and self-archiving is merely a rationale response to a new opportunity. For others, the scholarly information chain is being radically re-engineered, so that nothing should be taken for granted, and open access is merely one symptom of this deeper realignment. In the final chapters of this book I have given key writers in this field a relatively free rein to imagine a world where open access to research papers has been achieved. What would this world look like? How would it work? What can research become?

19

Open computation: beyond human reader-centric views of scholarly literatures

Clifford Lynch

Introduction

This chapter is probably the book's most speculative, in that it discusses broad-based computational access to scholarly literatures – a collection of developments that are likely to happen largely as a consequence of increasing open access. Traditional open access is, in my view, a probable (but not certain) prerequisite for the emergence of fully developed large-scale computational approaches to the scholarly literature. It may not be a sufficient prerequisite, particularly if the legal and systems architecture frameworks currently being developed and deployed to support traditional open access are not quickly adjusted to accommodate the needs of open computational access. Indeed, even if such accommodations are made, and if appropriate open access provisions were to be universally established for all scholarly works going forward, there is still an enormous, long-lasting problem with the established historical base of scholarly literature. While scholars tend to focus largely on new contributions to the literature, computational technologies value and demand scale and comprehensiveness in the literature base that they address; constraints on the use of the historical literature will continue to represent a massive barrier to such computational uses. A move to open access may not help much with this retrospective material.

I am confident that the other chapters of this volume have done a fine job of describing the various access models and practices that are being characterised by the term 'open access' in different settings, and the virtues and benefits that they share in terms of democratising access to varying degrees and in varying dimensions. Indeed, we are seeing some of these benefits today – for example, access by readers in developing countries – not just as a result of author and publisher choices about open access, but sometimes as a result of publisher practices that could only be termed 'open access' by the most imaginative and dedicated public relations functionary. Similarly, we are seeing some developments in computational access to literature – most prominently for indexing (think of Google and similar search engines, and their explicit arrangements with publishers, or their efforts to implicitly compromise with publishers within the framework of copyright law's fair use provisions through the indexing of copyrighted text but the presentation only of brief 'snippets' of copyrighted material) – outside of the open access framework. Some publishers are also making explicit provisions for experimental text mining, or allowing re-hosting under licence agreements which opens the door to arbitrary computational exploitation or representation of their material within closed organisational contexts.

The case for the benefits of open computational access to the scholarly literature is also much more complex than the arguments usually marshalled for traditional open access – in part because these benefits are indirect, and in part because they are still considered largely speculative and unproven. They are indirect in that they merely open the way for various players with good ideas to advance the progress of research and scholarship in perhaps new and perhaps more accelerated ways; presumably, in the long run, such research progress is of value to everyone. (Note that, paradoxically, computational access to a scholarly literature for the purposes of indexing may also make that literature more economically valuable in the non-open access case, in that it may increase demand: witness the interest of commercial journal publishers in having their material indexed in search engines.)

The benefits are speculative in the sense that we are just beginning to understand and demonstrate what we can accomplish, computationally, with large scholarly literature corpora. A number of interrelated technologies such as text mining and analysis are very active, vibrant and well-funded research areas, attracting extensive participation and investment from government and industry as well as academia. And, more recently, we are seeing experiments not only in computing on literatures to derive insights, but in the actual *re-hosting* of literatures within new analysis, usage and curation environments: here a scholarly literature is actually imported into a new usage environment that adds value through computation and perhaps also through social interaction – leading examples of this might include the work of the US National Center for Biotechnology Information at the National Library of Medicine for the molecular biology literature, or the fascinating experiments carried out by Greg Crane and his colleagues at Tufts University in the Perseus Project. But it is important to recognise that while researchers focusing specifically on computational manipulation of scholarly literatures are reporting great advances in their work, I think that the broad community of working scholars remain to be convinced of the critical future contributions of such technologies.

This brief chapter begins an exploration of both the technical and the legal issues involved in enabling widespread application of computational techniques and technologies to the research literature. There are many more questions than answers at this stage.

Technological opportunities

Let's perform a thought experiment. Let us suppose, for the moment, that the only copyright encumbrance on the scholarly literature was that of attribution; articles could be freely replicated, and arbitrary computations could be performed upon these articles. The results of these computations could be freely and widely employed and shared. In such a world, what do current technology trends suggest might be done with the collection of articles that constitute the vast majority of the scholarly literature in so many fields?

Clearly we would see the widespread creation of copies of the scholarly literature, or very sizeable subsets of this literature; these copies would reside in a great range of personal, workgroup and disciplinary settings for convenience of access and searching. Storage is getting very cheap, and students and researchers cannot always count on the ubiquitous availability of very inexpensive broadband connectivity. We would see these copies of the published literature federated in various ways with unpublished, preliminary and proprietary materials forming knowledge bases that were unique to specific researchers, research groups, corporations and other entities. These federations would be facilitated by the ability to computationally re-arrange and re-structure the literature.

We would also see an explosion in services that provided access to this literature in new and creative ways. Such services would also incorporate specialised vocabulary databases, gazetteers, factual databases, ontologies, and other auxiliary tools to enhance indexing and retrieval. They would rapidly transcend access to address navigation and analysis. One path here leads towards more customised re-hosting of scholarly literatures and underlying evidence into new usage and analysis environments attuned to the specific scholarly practices of various disciplines.

We would also see a move beyond federation and indexing to actual text mining and analysis, to the extraction of hypotheses and correlations that would help to drive ongoing scholarly inquiry. Indeed, the literature would be embedded in a computational context that reorganised and re-evaluated the existing body of knowledge as new literature became available. Initially, we would likely see a series of leap-frog breakthroughs as these technologies rapidly advanced, but, over time, I think it is likely that the state of the art in text mining and analysis would stabilise or converge to a point where new computations over the common literature base using the best state-of-the-art tools would only produce, at best, modest incremental advances. At this point the key leverage for wringing new discoveries from the literature would pivot on two points of competitive advantage. The first would be early access to and rapid integration of new contributions – including, most likely, preprints that had not, at least yet, been peer reviewed, and perhaps segments of the historical literature base newly entering the digital domain. The second would be the ability to quickly and successfully integrate and exploit unreleased or non-public information – not just unreleased preprints, but data, including negative data that had never seen publication, in conjunction with the common shared public literature base and ancillary public data and knowledge bases.

It is near certain that these innovations would not apply to all scholarly disciplines uniformly. Areas such as biomedicine or chemistry, where much of the literature is relatively well-structured and where a base of investment in the development of auxiliary knowledge structures, such as factual databases, ontologies, specialised vocabularies and vocabulary mappings and similar tools, has been extensive, would likely be fertile ground for early advances. Indeed, in these fields we are already seeing the beginning of a re-evaluation of authorial practices that propose the incorporation of markup to facilitate exactly such computational processing of the literature – consider the work of scholars such as Peter Murray-Rust in chemistry, or the various proposals for specialised markup languages in areas as diverse as history and molecular biology. (In other web settings, these efforts are being characterised as 'micro-formats'.) Other 'hard' sciences, and certainly many branches of the social sciences, would yield results more slowly. Many of the humanities would remain recondite. And, of course, changes in disciplinary practices of scholarly authoring would have a great influence: to the extent that new articles in the public literature base are routinely structured to facilitate computational verification, integration or correlation, these disciplines would presumably see greater payoffs for the applications of textual mining and analysis. One can even imagine, in certain highly competitive and commercially significant fields, deliberate release of what is in effect *disinformation* to divert the attention of research driven by text mining and literature analysis in deliberately unproductive directions.

Finally, in an environment largely unencumbered by intellectual property issues, it is likely that the tension between distributed and centralised computation will be resolved primarily according to the mandates of technical simplicity and universality rather than being shaped by the contortions enforced by licensing agreements and the services that individual publishers choose to make available. While, in theory, there is a performance trade-off between the choice of moving an interoperable, transportable network-based representation of the computation to the servers where the data resides, and doing remote execution of procedural computational code on this remote database – the concepts implicit in the seminal work of Kahn and Cerf (1988) in their classic report 'The world of knowbots' for example – and the infinitely simpler model that just *copies* all relevant data to a local store upon which computation occurs, it seems to me most probable that in the absence of intellectual property concerns and licensing constraints that the obvious and universally understood framework of creating local copies will triumph. The practical will dominate the theoretically optimal. The local replication model is so much simpler and more reliable and predictable than the alternatives, where it seems likely that every remote execution environment will have its local idiosyncrasies and constraints, and where large-scale literature analysis will have to adapt to the variety of interfaces offered by different publishers. These interfaces will inevitably incorporate a series of trade-offs that publishers design to prevent computational access from allowing actual copying of the literature base (consider, for example, the as yet nebulous Open Text Mining Interface proposal – see Hannay, 2006).

Thus, without proprietary content ownership constraints, the dominant paradigm will be to accumulate a local representation of the relevant literature, and perform ongoing computations on that literature locally. This will be the fastest path to the payoffs of textual mining and analysing the application of new digital library technologies designed to import and host literatures in ways that add value to that literature.

Real-world conundrums

Let's move on from our idealised thought experiment.

We are very unclear today about whether even the systems that claim to offer 'open access' to collections of scholarly literature are being – or should be – designed to permit simple, large-scale replication of these collections in order to facilitate the creation of local resources that can be computed upon. This is both a technical question (is it easy to make a copy of the full collection?) and a legal one (concerning what uses are allowed under the implicit or explicit licences). Thus, a prime question is whether we will provide the enabling technical infrastructure and legal permission to facilitate computational access to scholarly literatures even in the context of the various definitions of open access.

For the proprietary scholarly literature, today's licence agreements generally preclude the creation of large literature subsets external to the publisher's site, and, indeed, user attempts to perform large-scale downloading have raised alarms and led to difficult and awkward discussions involving publishers or aggregators, licensing institutions (universities) and end users about the appropriateness and legality of creating such local mirror databases. At least in theory, if the creation of local copies of literature databases derived from large-scale downloads from various publishers becomes a standard and accepted practice for faculty at licensing universities, one might presume – or at least hope – that most publishers (though there would undoubtedly be holdouts) would revise and adapt their licence agreements to recognise and permit such practice.

For open access materials, the creation of large-scale collections of copies is often ambiguous in the absence of specific permissions; we are moving towards a legal understanding that suggests public access content is available for reading, but the ability to re-host long-lived copies is less clear. Open access content offered under terms such as the Creative Commons licence agreements reduces the uncertainty here – but not necessarily for downstream use, as I will shortly discuss.

Clear legal rights to make large-scale copies of the literature are just the beginning of the legal conundrums that will create barriers to open literature computation. What is the legal status of the results of computations upon such copies? What is the legal status of a re-hosting of these materials within a new computational context that facilitates linkages, re-presentation, exploration and analysis of a literature corpus? As far as I can determine, these questions are largely unexplored and unresolved in law – both case law and legislation. We have the well-established concept of a derivative work – for example, a translation of a work; creating a derivative work requires permission from the rights holder of the original work. At least when the process of creating the derivative incorporates substantial new human intellectual effort, new rights are overlaid upon those of the original author in the ownership of the derivative. It is completely unclear whether an algorithmic computation produces a true derivative work or whether it is just considered a re-presentation of the original, but in either case, rights in the algorithmic product certainly seem to include claims from the source work. In cases where the computation process takes as input an entire literature base, consisting of perhaps hundreds of thousands of individual works, the authors of *each and every one* of these input works might have a claim on the output. It is not at all clear that we can make the case that only a small and selected subset of the input works made a material contribution to the output and thus have claims upon that output. For example, if we run the algorithm on a copy of the literature base and get the same result whether or not we include a certain article, then could we not argue that this proves the result was independent of the source article in question? The sheer volume of rights that need to be cleared may effectively preclude the application of computational technologies to large literature bases. If the literature base is offered by a publisher operating within a framework where authors transfer copyright to the publisher, then presumably the publisher could grant the necessary rights to allow meaningful text mining of the corpus, or the importation of the corpus into a new analysis and presentation environment. (Whether publishers will actually be willing to do so is another, and doubtful, proposition.) In cases where the corpus is produced through open access type arrangements, unless the transfer of (most likely non-exclusive) permissions to the host of the corpus are crafted with great care and specific focus on the computational opportunities, text miners and those wanting to import materials into new use environments will have to engage in completely impractical and unrealistic author-by-author clearing of permissions.

The Creative Commons licence is a good case study here. It is a very valuable tool in reducing ambiguity about the permitted uses of scholarly works, but it also illustrates how little thought has been given to computational applications. The Creative Commons licence offers authors options about whether to permit the creation of derivative works, and also options about whether they can insist on author attribution in downstream uses of their works. Permission to create derivative works seems to be a clear prerequisite for computational use of articles; yet this is rather different than the way that this choice is presented to authors creating a Creative Commons licence to their works today. Even the attribution requirement may be a source of problems – will we have to list author attributions for every work in a literature corpus as part of the attribution for any computational result from this literature corpus? And, if so, how will we practically meet this mandate? Is there a need for a new Creative Commons provision that specifically deals with authorising and enabling the potential to text-mine, re-host or otherwise compute upon works offered under Creative Commons licences?

Creative Commons is beginning to examine some of these issues through its NeuroCommons initiative within the Science Commons programme.

Preliminary conclusions

As the scholarly literature moves to digital form, what is actually needed to move beyond a system that just replicates all of our assumptions that this literature is only read, and read only by human beings, one article at a time? What is needed to permit the creation of digital libraries hosting these materials that moves beyond the 'incunabular' view of the literature, to use Greg Crane's very provocative recent characterisation (Crane, 2006)? What is needed to allow the application of computational technologies to extract new knowledge, correlations and hypotheses from collections of scholarly literature?

Part of the answer is legal. Clearly we need freedom to copy, re-host, repurpose and compute upon the components of this literature. (Note that while I have not explicitly discussed large-scale retrospective digitisation projects here, this is equally applicable to these efforts, not just to new contributions to the scholarly literature.) We need licence terms that minimise or render moot the uncertainties surrounding the creation of derivative works and possibly even the requirements of attribution for source materials that have contributed to the production of these derivative works. The Creative Commons licensing framework offers a particularly urgent and compelling environment for exploring these requirements.

The other part of the requirement is technical. We need to see provisions in hosting systems for large-scale replication as well as item-by-item downloads of occasional copies of parts of the scholarly literature. While in theory this need might be mitigated by the availability of interfaces that allow us to export computations to repositories, I suspect that these will not fully satisfy the needs for literature analysis and for new content analysis and synthesis environments that assume the ability to re-host materials.

The opportunities are truly stunning. They point towards entirely new ways to think about the scholarly literature (and the underlying evidence that supports scholarship) as an active, computationally-enabled representation of knowledge that lives, grows and interacts with its contributors rather than as a passive archive or record. They suggest ways in which information technology can accelerate the rate of scientific discovery and the growth of scholarship. It would be a disgrace if we allowed the inertia of historic scholarly publishing practices and the intellectual property arrangements that underlie these patterns to foreclose such opportunities. Open access offers an important simplification and reduction of the barriers if its development is shaped in a way that is responsive to these opportunities, although it is certainly not a panacea in its current form.

What is ultimately at stake here is a fundamental reconceptualisation of the roles and uses of scholarly literatures and the evidence that supports scholarship. The traditional intellectual property framework of scholarly publishing is not hospitable to this reconceptualisation. The implications of resolving this incompatibility will ultimately have far more extensive ramifications than what we might today characterise as the 'traditional' open access movement; but they will be crucial to the future of science and scholarship.

20

The Open Research Web

Nigel Shadbolt, Tim Brody, Les Carr and Stevan Harnad

Most of this book has been about the past and the present of open access. Let's now take a brief glimpse at its future, for it is already within reach and almost within sight. Imagine a world in which the optimal outcome for the research literature has become actual, with all 2.5 million of the annual articles in the planet's 24,000 peer-reviewed research journals freely accessible online to all would-be users (Odlyzko, 1995; Okerson and O'Donnell, 1995; Berners-Lee et al., 2005; DeRoure et al., 2005):

- All their OAI metadata and full-texts will be harvested, inverted and indexed by services such as Google, OAIster and still newer open access/OAI services, making it possible to search all and only the research literature in all disciplines using Boolean full-text search (and, or, not, etc.).

- Boolean full-text search will be augmented by artificial intelligence based text-analysis and classification techniques superior to human pre-classification, infinitely less time-consuming, and applied automatically to the entire open access full-text corpus.

- Articles and portions of articles will also be classified, tagged and annotated in terms of 'ontologies' (lists of the kinds of things of interest in a subject domain, their characteristics, and their relations to other things, see Figure 20.1) as provided by authors, users, other authorities, or automatic artificial intelligence techniques, creating the open access research subset of the 'Semantic Web' (Berners-Lee et al., 2001).

- The open access corpus will be fully citation interlinked – every article forward-linked to every article it cites and backward-linked to every article that cites it – making it possible to navigate all and only the

---

Figure 20.1 Various visualisations of an ontology

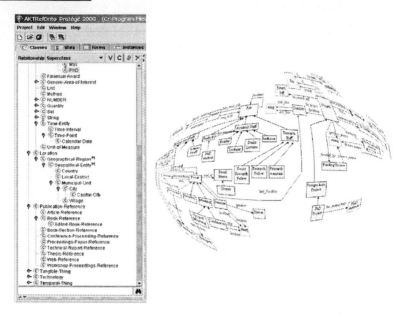

research journal literature in all disciplines via citation-surfing instead of just ordinary link-surfing.

- A CiteRank analogue of Google's PageRank algorithm will allow hits to be rank-ordered by weighted citation counts instead of just ordinary links (not all citations are equal: a citation by a much-cited author/article weighs more than a citation by a little-cited author/article; Page et al., 1999).

- In addition to ranking hits by author/article/topic citation counts, it will also be possible to rank them by author/article/topic download counts (consolidated from multiple sites, caches, mirrors, versions; Adams 2005; Bollen et al., 2005; Moed, 2005b).

- Ranking and download/citation counts will not just be usable for searching but also (by individuals and institutions) for prediction, evaluation and other forms of analysis, online and offline (Moed, 2005a).

- Correlations between earlier download counts and later citation counts will be available online (see Figure 20.2), and usable for extrapolation, prediction and eventually even evaluation (Brody et al., 2006).

Figure 20.2 An earlier window of downloads (pale line) may predict a later window of citations (dark line)

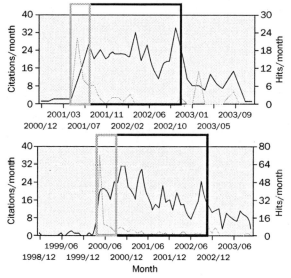

Source: Brody et al. (2006)

- Searching, analysis, prediction and evaluation will also be augmented by co-citation analysis (who/what co-cited or was co-cited by whom/what?), co-authorship analysis (Figure 20.3), and eventually also co-download analysis (who/what co-downloaded or was co-downloaded by whom/what? [user identification will of course require user permission]).

- Co-text analysis (with artificial intelligence techniques, including latent semantic analysis [what text and text-patterns co-occur with what? Landauer et al., 1998], Semantic Web analysis, and other forms of 'semiometrics'; McRae-Spencer and Shadbolt, 2006) will complement online and offline citation, co-citation, download and co-download analysis (what texts have similar or related content or topics or users?).

- Time-based (chronometric) analyses will be used to extrapolate early download, citation, co-download and co-citation trends, as well as correlations between downloads and citations, to predict research impact, research direction and research influences (Figure 20.4).

- Authors, articles, journals, institutions and topics will also have 'endogamy/exogamy' scores: how much do they cite themselves?

Figure 20.3 A small co-authorship graph depicting collaborations between scientists across topic and subject boundaries

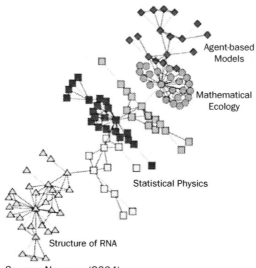

Source: Newman (2004)

Figure 20.4 Results of a simple chronometric analysis, showing collaboration via endogamy/exogamy scores

Collaboration over time

View: ● by year ● by area

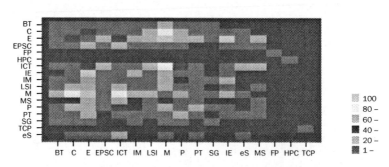

Source: Alani et al. (2005)

In-cite within the same 'family' cluster? Out-cite across an entire field? Across multiple fields? Across disciplines?

- Authors, articles, journals, institutions and topics will also have latency and longevity scores for both downloads and citations: how quickly do citations/downloads grow? How long before they peak? How long-lived are they (Figure 20.5)?

- 'Hub/authority' analysis (Kleinberg, 1999) will make it easier to perform literature reviews, identifying review articles citing many articles ('hubs') or key articles/authors ('authorities') cited by many articles.

- 'Silent' or 'unsung' authors or articles, uncited but important influences, will be identified (and credited) by co-citation and co-text analysis and through interpolation and extrapolation of semantic lines of influence.

- Similarly, generic terms that are implicit in ontologies (but so basic that they are not explicitly tagged by anyone) – as well as other 'silent' influences, intermediating effects, trends and turning points – can be discovered, extracted, interpolated and extrapolated from the patterns

Figure 20.5 Time course of downloads and citations

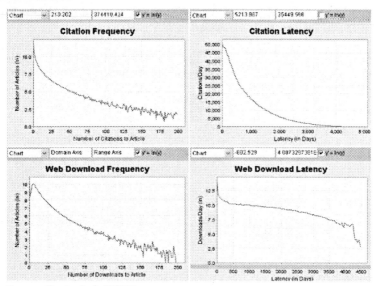

Source: Brody et al. (2006)

among the explicit properties such as citations and co-authorships, explicitly tagged features and relationships, and latent semantics.

- Author names, institutions, projects, URLs, addresses and e-mail addresses will also be linked and disambiguated by this kind or triangulation (Figure 20.6).

- Resource Description Framework (RDF) graphs (who is related to what, how?) will link objects in domain 'ontologies'. For example, social network analyses (Figure 20.7) on co-authors will be extended to other important relations and influences (projects directed, PhD students supervised etc.).

- Co-text and semantic analysis will identify plagiarism as well as unnoticed parallelism and potential convergence.

- A 'degree-of-content-overlap' metric will be calculable between any two articles, authors, groups or topics.

- Co-authorship, co-citation/co-download, co-text and chronometric path analyses will allow a composite 'heritability' analysis of individual articles, indexing the amount and source of their inherited

Figure 20.6 Linked map of research entities

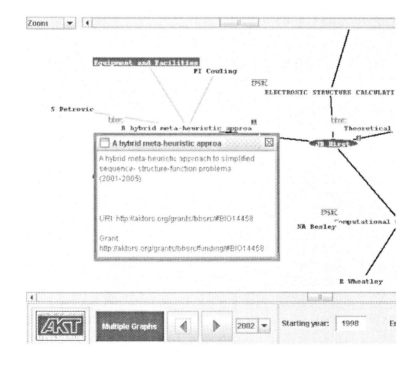

Figure 20.7   A social network analysis tool rendering an RDF graph

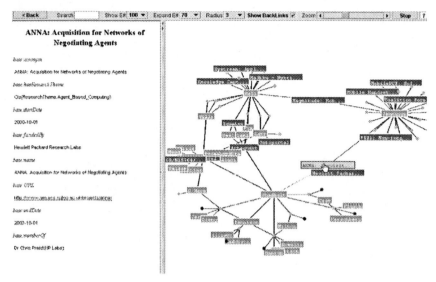

Source: Alani et al. (2003)

content, their original contribution, their lineage, and their likely future direction.

- Cluster analyses and chronograms will allow connections and trajectories to be visualised, analysed and navigated iconically (Figure 20.8).

- User-generated tagging services such as Connotea (allowing users to both classify and evaluate articles they have used by adding tags anarchically) will complement systematic citation-based ranking and evaluation and author-based, artificial intelligence-based, or authority-based Semantic Web tagging, both at the article/author level and at the level of specific points in the text.

- Commentaries – peer-reviewed, moderated, and unmoderated – will be linked to and from their target articles, forming a special, amplified class of annotated tags (Harnad, 1979; 1990).

- Referee selection (for the peer reviewing of both articles and research proposals) will be greatly facilitated by the availability of the full citation-interlinked, semantically-tagged corpus.

- Deposit date-stamping will allow priority to be established.

Figure 20.8 A self-organising map supporting navigable visualisation of a research domain

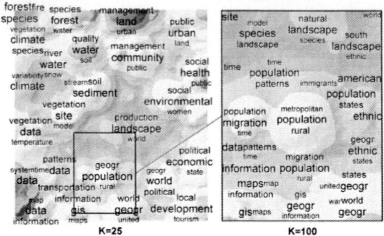

K=25   K=100

Source: Skupin (2004)

- Research articles will be linked to tagged research data, allowing independent re-analysis and replication.
- The Research Web will facilitate much richer and more diverse and distributed collaborations, across institutions, nations, languages and disciplines (e-science, collaboratories).

Many of these future powers of the Open Access Research Web revolve around *research impact*: predicting it, measuring it, tracing it, navigating it, evaluating it, enhancing it. What is research impact?

Research impact

The reason the employers and funders of scholarly and scientific researchers mandate that they should publish their findings ('publish or perish') is that if research findings arc kept in a desk drawer instead of being published then the research may as well not have been done at all. The *impact* of a piece of research is the degree to which it has been useful to other researchers and users in generating further research and applications: how much the work has been read, used, built-upon, applied and cited in other research as well as in educational, technological, cultural, social and practical applications (Moed, 2005a).

The first approximation to a metric of research impact is the publication itself. Research that has not yielded any publishable findings has no impact. A second approximation metric of research impact is where it is published: To be accepted for publication, a research report must first be peer-reviewed, that is, evaluated by qualified specialists who advise a journal editor on whether or not the paper can potentially meet that journal's quality standards, and what revision needs to be done to make it do so. There is a hierarchy of journals in most fields, the top ones exercising the greatest selectivity, with the highest quality standards. So the second approximation impact metric for a research paper is the level in the journal quality hierarchy of the journal that accepts it. But even if published in a high-quality journal, a paper that no one goes on to read has no impact. So a third approximation impact metric comes from a paper's usage level. This was hard to calculate in print days, but in the online era, downloads can be counted (Harnad and Brody, 2004; Kurtz et al., 2004; Bollen et al., 2005; Moed, 2005b; Brody et al., 2006). Yet even if a paper is downloaded and read, it may not be used – not taken up, applied and built upon in further research and applications. The fourth metric and currently the closest approximation to a paper's research impact is accordingly whether it is not only published and read, but *cited*, which indicates that it has been used (by users other than the original author), as an acknowledged building block in further published work.

Being cited does not guarantee that a piece of work was important, influential and useful, and some papers are no doubt cited only to discredit them; but, on average, the more a work is cited, the more likely that it has indeed been used and useful (Garfield, 1955, 1973; Wolfram, 2003). Other estimates of the importance and productivity of research have proved to be correlated with its citation frequency. For example, about every six years for two decades now, the UK Research Assessment Exercise (RAE) has been evaluating the research output of every department of every UK university, assigning each a rank along a five-point scale on the basis of many different performance indicators, some consisting of peer judgments of the quality of published work, some consisting of objective metrics (such as prior research grant income or number of research students). A panel decides each department's rank and then each is funded proportionately. In many fields the ranking turns out to be most highly correlated with prior grant income, but it is almost as highly correlated with another metric: the total citation counts of each department's research output (Smith and Eysenck, 2002; Harnad et al., 2003) even though citations – unlike grant income – are not counted explicitly in the RAE evaluation. Because of the high correlation of the overall RAE outcome with metrics, two decades after the inception of the RAE:

> the Government has a firm presumption that after the 2008 RAE the system for assessing research quality and allocating 'quality-related' (QR) research funding to universities from the Department for Education and Skills will be mainly metrics-based. (UK Office of Science and Technology, 2006)

Measuring and monitoring research impact

ISI first provided the means of counting citations for articles, authors or groups (see Garfield, 1955, 1973). We have used the same method – of linking citing articles to cited articles via their reference lists – to create Citebase Search (Brody, 2003, 2004), a search engine like Google, but based on citation links rather than arbitrary hyperlinks, and derived from the open access database instead of the ISI database. Citebase already embodies a number of the futuristic features listed earlier. It currently ranks articles and authors by citation impact, co-citation impact or download impact and can be extended to incorporate multiple online measures (metrics) of research impact.

With only 15 per cent of journal articles being spontaneously self-archived overall today, this is still too sparse a database to test and analyse the power of a scientometric engine like Citebase. However, with nearly 100 per cent open access in a few areas of physics that use arXiv, this is where Citebase has been focused. Boolean search query results (using content words plus 'and', 'or', 'not' and so on) can currently be quantified by Citebase and ranked in terms of article or author download counts, article/author citation counts, article/author co-citedness counts (how often is a sample of articles co-cited with – or by – a given article or author?), hub/authority counts (an article is an 'authority' the more it is cited by other authorities; this is similar to Google's PageRank algorithm, which does not count web links as equal, but weights them by the number of links to the linking page; an article is a 'hub' the more it cites authorities; Page et al., 1999). Citebase also has a Citebase download/citation correlator, which correlates downloads and citations across an adjustable time window. Natural future extensions of these metrics include download growth-rate, latency-to-peak and longevity indices, and citation growth-rate, latency-to-peak and longevity indices.

So far, these metrics are only being used to rank-order the results of Citebase searches, as Google is used. But they have the power to do a great deal more, and will gain still more power as open access approaches 100 per cent. The citation and download counts can be used to compare research impact, ranking articles, authors or groups; they can also be used to compare an individual's own research impact with itself across time. The download and citation counts have also been found to be positively correlated with one another, so that early downloads, within six months of publication, can predict citations after 18 months or more (Brody et al., 2006). This opens up the possibility of time-series analyses, not only on articles', authors' or groups' impact trajectories over time, but the impact trajectories of entire lines of research, when the citation/download analysis is augmented by similarity/relatedness scores derived from semantic analysis of text, for example, word and pattern co-occurrence, as in latent semantic analysis (Landauer et al., 1998).

Benefits

The natural objective is to develop a scientometric multiple regression equation for analysing research performance and predicting research direction based on an open access database, beginning with the existing metrics. Such an equation of course needs to be validated against other metrics. The 14 candidate predictors so far ([1–4] article/author citation counts, growth rates, peak latencies, longevity; [5–8] the same metrics for downloads; [9] download/citation correlation-based predicted citations; [10–12] hub/authority scores; [12–13] co-citation (with and by) scores; [14] co-text scores) can be made available open-endedly via tools like Citebase, so that apart from users using them to rank search query results for navigation, individuals and institutions can begin using them to rank articles, authors or groups, validating them against whatever metrics they are currently using, or simply testing them open-endedly.

The method is essentially the same for navigation as well as analysis and evaluation. A search output – or an otherwise selected set of candidates for ranking and analysis – could each have the potential regression scores, with weights that could be set to zero or a range from minimum to maximum, with an adjustable weight scale for each, normalising to one across all the non-zero weights used. Students and researchers could use such an experimental battery of metrics as different ways of ranking literature search results; editors could use them for ranking potential referees; peer-reviewers could use them to rank the relevance of references; research assessors could use them to rank institutions, departments or research groups; institutional performance evaluators could use them to rank staff for annual review; hiring committees could use them to rank candidates; and authors could use them to rank themselves against their competition.

It is important to stress that at this point all of this would not only be an unvalidated regression equation, to be used only experimentally, but that even after being validated against an external criterion or criteria, it would still need to be used in conjunction with human evaluation and judgment, and the regression weights would no doubt have to be set differently for different purposes, and always open for tweaking and updating. But it will begin ushering in the era of online, interactive scientometrics based on an open access corpus and in the hands of all users.

The software we have already developed and will develop, together with the growing Webwide database of open access articles, and the data we will collect and analyse from it, will allow us to do several things: (1) motivate more researchers to provide open access by self-archiving; (2) map the growth of open access across disciplines, countries and languages; (3) navigate the open access literature using citation linking and impact ranking; (4) measure, extrapolate and predict the research impact of individuals, groups, institutions, disciplines, languages and countries; (5) measure research performance and productivity; (6) assess candidates for research funding; (7) assess the outcome of research funding; (8) map the course of prior research lines, in terms of individuals, institutions, journals, fields, nations; (9) analyse and predict the direction of current and future research trajectories; (10) provide teaching and learning resources that guide students (via impact navigation) through the large and growing open access research literature in a way that navigating the Web via Google alone cannot come close to doing.

At the forefront in the critical developments in open access across the past decade, our research team at Southampton University, UK:

- hosts one of the first open access journals, *Psycoloquy* (since 1994);
- hosts the first journal open access preprint archive, BBSPrints (since 1994);

- formulated the first open access self-archiving proposal (Okerson and O'Donnell 1995);

- founded one of the first central open access archives, Cogprints (1997);

- founded the American Scientist Open Access Forum (1998);

- created the first (and now the most widely used) institutional OAI-compliant archive-creating software, Eprints (Sponsler and Van de Velde, 2001), adopted by over 150 universities worldwide;

- co-drafted the Budapest Open Access Initiative, BOAI self-archiving FAQ (2001);

- created the first citation impact-measuring search engine, Citebase Search (Hitchcock et al., 2003);

- created the first citation-seeking tool (to trawl the Web for the full text of a cited reference), Paracite (2002);

- designed the first OAI standardised CV, Template for UK Standardized CV for Research Assessment (2002);

- designed the first demonstration tool for predicting later citation impact from earlier download impact, the Citebase download/citation correlator (Brody et al. 2006);

- compiled the Budapest Open Access Initiative, BOAI Eprints Software Handbook (2003);

- formulated the model self-archiving policy for departments and institutions, Actions for Departments to Achieve Open Access (2003);

- created and maintain ROAR, the Registry of Open Access Repositories worldwide (2003);

- collaborated in the creation and maintenance of the ROMEO directory of journals' self-archiving policies, Eprints Journal Policies (2004: of the top 9,000 journals across all fields, 92 per cent already endorse author self-archiving);

- created and maintain ROARMAP, the Registry of Open Access Repository Material Archiving Policies (2004);

- piloted the paradigm of collecting, analysing and disseminating data on the magnitude of the open access impact advantage and the growth of open access across all disciplines worldwide (Brody, 2004).

The multiple online research impact metrics we are developing will allow the rich new database, the 'Research Web', to be navigated, analysed, mined and evaluated in powerful new ways that were not even conceivable in the paper era – nor even in the online era, until the database and the tools became openly accessible for online use by all: by researchers, research institutions, research funders, teachers, students, and even by the general public that funds the research and for whose benefit it is being conducted: Which research is being used most? By whom? Which research is growing most quickly? In what direction? Under whose influence? Which research is showing immediate short-term usefulness, which shows delayed, longer-term usefulness, and which has sustained long-lasting impact? Is there work whose value is only discovered or rediscovered after a substantial period of disinterest? Can we identify the frequency and nature of such 'slow burners'? Which research and researchers are the most authoritative? Whose research is most using this authoritative research, and whose research is the authoritative research using? Which are the best pointers ('hubs') to the authoritative research? Is there any way to predict what research will have later citation impact (based on its earlier download impact), so junior researchers can be given resources before their work has had a chance to make itself felt through citations? Can research trends and directions be predicted from the online database? Can text content be used to find and compare related research, for influence, overlap, direction? Can a layman, unfamiliar with the specialised content of a field, be guided to the most relevant and important work? These are just a sample of the new online-age questions that the Open Research Web will begin to answer.

Links

Academic Ranking of World Universities: *http://ed.sjtu.edu.cn/rank/ 2005/ARWU2005_Top100.htm*

Accessibility Framework: *http://www.dest.gov.au/sectors/research_ sector/policies_issues_reviews/key_issues/accessibility_framework/*

Actions for Departments to Achieve Open Access: *http:// www.eprints.org/documentation/handbook/departments.php*

Alliance for Taxpayer Access: *http://www.taxpayeraccess.org*

American Center for Cures Act: *http://www.govtrack.us/congress/ bill.xpd?bill=s109-2104*

American Scientist Open Access Forum: *http://amsci-forum .amsci.org/archives/American-Scientist-Open-Access-Forum.html*

ANU E-Press: *http://epress.anu.edu.au/*

Arc: *http://arc.cs.odu.edu/*

ARL Statistics and Measurement Program: *http://www.arl.org/stats/*

ARL Statistics interactive edition: *http://fisher.lib.virginia.edu/arl/ index.html*

ARNO: *http://www.uba.uva.nl/arno*

ARPANET: *http://en.wikipedia.org/wiki/ARPANET*

ARROW Discovery Service: *http://search.arrow.edu.au/apps/ArrowUI/*

ArXiv: *http://xxx.lanl.gov/*

Astrophysics Data System: *http://adswww.harvard.edu/*

AuseAccess University Policies: *http://leven.comp.utas.edu.au/AuseAccess/ pmwiki.php?n=General.UniPolicies*

Australasian Digital Thesis Program: *http://adt.caul.edu.au/*

Australian Partnership for Sustainable Repositories: *http:// www.apsr.edu.au/*

Australian Research Repositories Online to the World: *http:// arrow.edu.au/*

Backing Australia's Ability: *http://backingaus.innovation.gov.au/ default2001.htm*

BBSPrints: *http://www.bbsonline.org/*

Beilstein Journal of Organic Chemistry: *http://bjoc.beilstein-journals.org/*

bepress: *http://www.bepress.com/*

Bioline Eprints Archive: *http://bioline.utsc.utoronto.ca/*

Bioline International: *http://www.bioline.org.br/*

BioMed Central: *http://www.biomedcentral.com/home/*

BOAI Eprints Software Handbook: *http://software.eprints.org/handbook/*

BOAI Self-Archiving FAQ: *http://www.eprints.org/self-faq/*

CERN: *http://www.cern.ch/*

ChemBank: *http://chembank.broad.harvard.edu/*

Chinese Medicine: *http://www.cmjournal.org/*

Citebase download/citation correlator: *http://www.citebase.org/analysis/correlation.php*

Citebase Search: *http://www.citebase.org/cgi-bin/search*

Citeseer: *http://citeseer.ist.psu.edu/*

Click-Use form: *http://www.opsi.gov.uk/click-use/system/online/pLogin.asp*

Click-Use licence: *http://www.opsi.gov.uk/click-use/system/licenceterms/ParliamentaryLicence_01-00.pdf*

ClinicalTrials: *http://www.clinicaltrials.gov/*

Coalition for Networked Information: *http://www.cni.org/*

Cogprints: *http://cogprints.org/*

Connotea: *http://www.connotea.org/about*

Cream of Science: *http://www.creamofscience.org/*

Create Change: *http://www.createchange.org/home.html*

Creative Commons: *www.creativecommons.org*

Creative Commons, Attribution 2.5: *http://creativecommons.org/licenses/by/2.5/*

Creative Commons, Attribution Non-commercial 2.5: *http://creativecommons.org/licenses/by-nc/2.5/*

CWSpace: *http://cwspace.mit.edu/*

DARE/DAREnet: *http://www.darenet.nl/*

DARE services: *http://www.darenet.nl/en/page/language.view/diensten.diensten*

Dataset Acquisition, Accessibility and Annotation e-Research Technology: *http://dart.edu.au/*

Demoprints: *http://demoprints.eprints.org/*

Digital Commons@: *http://umi.com/umi/digitalcommons*

Digital Library of India: *http://www.dli.ernet.in/*

Digital Object Identifier: *http://www.doi.org/*

Digital Repositories Programme: *http://www.jisc.ac.uk/index.cfm?name=programme_digital_repositories*

Directory of Open Access Journals: *http://www.doaj.org/*

Directory of Open Access Repositories: *http://www.opendoar.org/*

Disciplinary differences relevant to open access: *http://www.earlham.edu/ ~peters/fos/lists.htm#disciplines*

D-Lib Magazine: *http://www.dlib.org/*

DP9: *http://dlib.cs.odu.edu/dp9/*

DPubS: *http://dpubs.org/*

DSpace: *http://www.dspace.org/*

Dublin Core: *http://dublincore.org/*

E-BioMed: *http://www.nih.gov/about/director/pubmedcentral/ebiomedarch .htm*

e-Depot: *http://www.kb.nl/dnp/e-depot/e-depot-en.html*

Electronic Text Center: *http://etext.virginia.edu/*

E-LIS: *http://eprints.rclis.org/*

Eprints: *http://www.eprints.org/software/*

Eprints Journal Policies: *http://romeo.eprints.org/*

Eprints Journal Policies statistics: *http://romeo.eprints.org/stats.php*

ePrints UK: *http://www.rdn.ac.uk/projects/eprints-uk/*

ePrints@IISc: *http://eprints.iisc.ernet.in/*

ERIC: *http://www.eric.ed.gov/*

ERNET: *http://www.eis.ernet.in/*

eScholarship Repository: *http://repositories.cdlib.org*

FAIR Programme: *http://www.jisc.ac.uk/index.cfm?name=programme_fair*

Fedora: *http://www.fedora.info/*

GenBank: *http://www.ncbi.nlm.nih.gov/Genbank/index.html*

Gene: *http://www.ncbi.nlm.nih.gov/entrez/query.fcgi?db=gene*

GenSat: *http://www.ncbi.nlm.nih.gov/projects/gensat/*

Google Advanced Search: *http://www.google.com/advanced_search*

Google Books Library Project: *http://books.google.com/googlebooks/ library.html*

Google Scholar: *http://scholar.google.com/*

Hansard: *http://www.parliament.the-stationery-office.co.uk/pa/cm/ cmhansrd.htm*

HapMap Project: *http://www.hapmap.org/*

HarvestRoad: *http://www.harvestroad.com/*

HEFCE: *http://www.hefce.ac.uk/*

Highwire Press: *http://highwire.stanford.edu/*

HKUST Library institutional repository: *http://repository.ust.hk/dspace/*

HomoloGene: *http://www.ncbi.nlm.nih.gov/entrez/query.fcgi?db=homologene*

Human Genome Project: *http://www.ornl.gov/sci/techresources/ Human_Genome/home.shtml*

IMesh: *http://www.imesh.org/*

Indian Academy of Sciences: *http://www.ias.ac.in/*

Indian Council of Medical Research: *http://icmr.nic.in/*

Indian Medlars Centre: *http://indmed.nic.in/*

Indian National Science Academy: *http://www.insa.ac.in/*

IndMed: *http://indmed.nic.in*

Information Access Alliance: *http://www.informationaccess.org/*

Institutional Repositories and Research Assessment: *http://irra.eprints.org/*

Internet Archive: *http://www.archive.org/*

ISI: *http://www.isinet.com/*

ISI Web of Knowledge: *http://www.isiwebofknowledge.com/*

ISI Web of Science: *http://scientific.thomson.com/products/wos/*

i-Tor: *http://www.i-tor.org/en/*

JISC: *http://www.jisc.ac.uk/*

JISC Scholarly Communications Group: *http://www.jisc.ac.uk/index.cfm?name=jcie_scg*

Journal of Postgraduate Medicine: *http://www.jpgmonline.com*

JSTOR: *http://www.jstor.org/*

Kepler: *http://kepler.cs.odu.edu/*

LibLicense: *http://www.library.yale.edu/~llicense/index.shtml*

Library of Congress: *http://www.loc.gov/*

Lots of Copies Keeps Stuff Safe: *http://lockss.stanford.edu/*

LOREnet: *http://www.lorenet.nl/*

MARC: *http://www.loc.gov/marc/*

MedInd: *http://medind.nic.in*

Medknow Publications: *http://www.medknow.com/*

MEDLINE: *http://www.nlm.nih.gov/databases/databases_medline.html*

Metadata Access Management System: *http://www.melcoe.mq.edu.au/projects/MAMS/*

Million Book Project: *http://www.archive.org/details/millionbooks*

MIT DSpace: *https://dspace.mit.edu/*

MPEG-21 DIDL: *http://www.chiariglione.org/mpeg/standards/mpeg-21/mpeg-21.htm*

National Academies Press: *http://www.nap.edu/*

National Academies Scholarly Communications Forum: *http://www.humanities.org.au/Events/NSCF/Overview.htm*

National Center for Biotechnology Information: *http://www.ncbi.nlm.nih.gov/*

National Electronic Article Repository: *http://www.arl.org/newsltr/202/shulenburger.html*

National Informatics Centre: *http://home.nic.in/*

National Institutes of Health: *http://www.nih.gov/*

National Institutes of Health Manuscript Submission: *http://nihms.nih.gov/*

National Institutes of Health Public Access Policy: *http://publicaccess.nih.gov/*

National Library of Medicine: *http://www.nlm.nih.gov/*

National Science Digital Library: *http://nsdl.org/*

National Science Foundation: *http://www.nsf.gov/*

Nature: *http://www.nature.com/*

NESLI: *http://www.nesli2.ac.uk/*

Networked Computer Science Technical Reference Library: *http://www.ncstrl.org/*

Networked Digital Library of Theses and Dissertations: *http://www.ndltd.org/*

NIH Public-Access Policy: Frequently Asked Questions: *http://www.earlham.edu/~peters/fos/nihfaq.htm*

NLM Journal Archiving and Interchange DTD: *http://dtd.nlm.nih.gov/*

Nucleotide: *http://www.ncbi.nlm.nih.gov/entrez/query.fcgi?db=Nucleotide*

OAI /OAI-PMH: *http://www.openarchives.org/*

OAI-Eprints: *http://lists.openlib.org/mailman/listinfo/oai-eprints*

OAI Static Repositories: *http://www.openarchives.org/OAI/2.0/guidelines-static-repository.htm*

OAIster: *http://oaister.umdl.umich.edu/o/oaister/*

Ockham: *http://www.ockham.org/*

OMIM: *http://www.ncbi.nlm.nih.gov/entrez/query.fcgi?db=OMIM*

Open-Access Text Archive: *http://www.archive.org/details/texts*

Open Access to Knowledge Law Project: *http://www.oaklaw.qut.edu.au/*

Open Access Working Group: *http://www.arl.org/sparc/oa/oawg.html*

Open Citation Project: *http://opcit.eprints.org/*

Open Content Alliance: *http://www.opencontentalliance.org/*

Open Educational Resources: *http://www.archive.org/details/education*

Open J-Gate: *http://www.openj-gate.com*

Open Journal Systems: *http://pkp.sfu.ca/ojs/*

Open Knowledge Initiative: *http://www.okiproject.org/*

Open Library: *http://www.openlibrary.org/*

Open Repository: *http://www.openrepository.com/*

Open Society Institute: *http://www.soros.org/*

OpenCourseWare: *http://ocw.mit.edu/*

Ourmedia: *http://ourmedia.org/*

Oxford University Press: *http://www.oup.co.uk/*

Paracite: *http://paracite.eprints.org/*
Perseus: *http://www.perseus.tufts.edu/*
Pica: *http://oclcpica.nl/*
PLoS Biology: *http://biology.plosjournals.org/*
PLoS Medicine: *http://medicine.plosjournals.org/*
Project Euclid: *http://projecteuclid.org/*
Project Gutenberg: *http://www.gutenberg.net/*
Project Muse: *http://muse.jhu.edu/*
Protein: *http://www.ncbi.nlm.nih.gov/entrez/query.fcgi?db=Protein*
Psycoloquy: *http://psycprints.ecs.soton.ac.uk/*
Public Access To Science Act: *http://thomas.loc.gov/cgi-bin/query/z?c108:H.R.2613:*
Public Knowledge: *http://www.publicknowledge.org/*
Public Library of Science: *http://www.plos.org/*
Public Library of Science open letter: *http://www.plos.org/about/letter.html*
PubChem: *http://pubchem.ncbi.nlm.nih.gov/*
Publisher Partner Program: *http://www.arl.org/sparc/partner/ppp.html*
PubMed Central: *http://www.pubmedcentral.nih.gov/*
RCUK Position Statement on Access to Research Outputs: *http://www.rcuk.ac.uk/access/index.asp*
Regional Universities Building Research Infrastructure Collaboratively: *http://rubric.edu.au/*
Registry of Open Access Repositories: *http://archives.eprints.org/*
Registry of Open Access Repository Material Archiving Policies: *http://www.eprints.org/openaccess/policysignup/*
RePEc: *http://repec.org/*
Research Quality Framework: *http://www.dest.gov.au/sectors/research_sector/policies_issues_reviews/key_issues/research_quality_framework/default.htm*
Resource Description Framework: *http://www.w3.org/RDF/*
RSS: *http://www.w3.org/2002/01/rss/rss1_namespace*
ScholComm: *http://lp-web.ala.org:8000/*
SciELO: *http://www.scielo.org/*
Science Citation Index: *http://scientific.thomson.com/products/sci/*
Science Commons: *http://sciencecommons.org/*
Scientific Journal Publishing in India: *http://144.16.72.144/*
Scirus: *http://www.scirus.com/*
Scopus: *http://www.info.scopus.com/*
Sherpa: *http://www.sherpa.ac.uk/about.html*
Sherpa/RoMEO list: *http://www.sherpa.ac.uk/romeo.php*

SIMILE: *http://simile.mit.edu/*

SPARC: *http://www.arl.org/sparc/*

SPARC-IR: *https://mx2.arl.org/Lists/SPARC-IR/List.html*

SPARC Open Access Forum: *http://www.arl.org/sparc/soa/index.html#forum*

SPARC OpenData: *http://www.arl.org/sparc/opendata/index.html*

Springer Open Choice Program: *http://www.springer.com/sgw/cda/frontpage/0,11855,1-40359-0-0-0,00.html*

SpringerLink: *http://www.springerlink.com/*

SRW/U: *http://www.loc.gov/standards/sru/srw/*

SSP-L: *http://www.sspnet.org/i4a/pages/index.cfm?pageid=3625*

SURF Foundation: *http://www.surf.nl/*

Symposia: *http://www.iii.com/mill/digital.shtml#sym*

Taxonomy: *http://www.ncbi.nlm.nih.gov/entrez/query.fcgi?db=Taxonomy*

TEK: *http://tek.sourceforge.net/*

Template for UK Standardized CV for Research Assessment: *http://paracite.eprints.org/cgi-bin/rae_front.cgi*

The effect of open access and downloads ('hits') on citation impact: *http://opcit.eprints.org/oacitation-biblio.html*

TheyWorkForYou.com: *http://www.theyworkforyou.com/*

Timeline of the Open Access Movement: *http://www.earlham.edu/~peters/fos/timeline.htm*

University actions for open access or against high journal prices: *http://www.earlham.edu/~peters/fos/lists.htm#actions*

University of California's eScholarship editions: *http://texts.cdlib.org/ucpress/*

University of Tasmania repository: *http://eprints.comp.utas.edu.au:81/*

Vidyanidhi: *http://www.vidyanidhi.org.in*

VTLS-Fedora: *http://www.vtls.com/*

Web Citation Index: *http://scientific.thomson.com/press/2005/8298416/*

Web services: *http://en.wikipedia.org/wiki/Web_services*

Wellcome Library: *http://library.wellcome.ac.uk/*

Wellcome Trust: *http://www.wellcome.ac.uk/*

Wikipedia: *http://www.wikipedia.org/*

World University Rankings: *http://www.thes.co.uk/worldrankings/*

Yahoo Advanced Search: *http://search.yahoo.com/search/options?fr=fp-top&p=*

Yahoo Creative Commons Search: *http://search.yahoo.com/cc*

Zeno's paralysis: *http://www.eprints.org/openaccess/self-faq/#32-worries*

Bibliography

Adams, J. (2005) 'Early citation counts correlate with accumulated impact', *Scientometrics* 63(3): 567–81.

Agosti, D. (2006) 'Biodiversity data are out of local taxonomists' reach', *Nature* 439: 392: doi:10.1038/439392a.

Alani, H., Dasmahapatra, S., O'Hara, K. and Shadbolt, N. (2003) 'Identifying communities of practice through ontology network analysis', *IEEE IS* 18(2): 18–25.

Alani, H., Nicholas, G., Glaser, H., Harris, S. and Shadbolt, N. (2005) 'Monitoring research collaborations using Semantic Web technologies', 2nd European Semantic Web Conference (ESWC) 29 May – 1 June, Heraklion; available at: *http://eprints.ecs.soton.ac.uk/10736/*.

Allen, J. (2005) 'Interdisciplinary differences in attitudes towards deposit in institutional repositories', Masters thesis, Department of Information and Communications. Manchester: Manchester Metropolitan University; available at: *http://eprints.rclis.org/archive/00005180/*.

Amiran, E. and Unsworth, J. (1991) 'Postmodern culture: publishing in the electronic medium', *The Public-Access Computer Systems Review* 2(1): 67–76; available at: *http://info.lib.uh.edu/pr/v2/n1/amiran.2n1*.

Antelman, K. (2004) 'Do open-access articles have a greater research impact?', *College and Research Libraries* 65(5): 372–82; available at: *http://eprints.rclis.org/archive/00002309/*.

Association of Research Libraries (2003) 'Monograph and serials costs in ARL libraries 1986 to 2002'; available at: *http://www.arl.org/stats/arlstat/graphs/2002/2002t2.html*.

Australian Research Information Infrastructure Committee (2004) 'Australian Research Information Infrastructure Committee Open Access Statement, 17 December 2004'; available at: *http://www.caul.edu.au/scholcomm/OpenAccessARIICstatement.doc*.

Bailey, Jr., C. W. (1991) 'Electronic (online) publishing in action ... The Public-Access Computer Systems Review and other electronic serials, *ONLINE* 15(January): 28–35.

Bailey, Jr., C. W. (2005) *Open Access Bibliography: Liberating Scholarly Literature with E-Prints and Open Access Journals.* Washington, DC: Association of Research Libraries; available at: *http://www.digital-scholarship.com/oab/oab.htm.*

Bailey, Jr., C. W. (2006) 'Open access and libraries, in Mark Jacobs (ed). *Electronic Resources Librarians: The Human Element of the Digital Information Age.* Binghamton, NY: Haworth Press, forthcoming; available at: *http://www.digital-scholarship.com/cwb/OALibraries2.pdf.*

Barton, J., Currier, S. and Hey, J. (2003) 'Building quality assurance into metadata creation: an analysis based on the learning objects and e-prints communities of practice', *DC-2003 (2003 Dublin Core Conference): Supporting Communities of Discourse and Practice – Metadata Research and Applications)*, Seattle, Washington, 28 September to 2 October; available at: *http://www.siderean.com/dc2003/201_paper60.pdf.*

Bavdekar, S. B. and Sahu D. R. (2005) 'Path of progress: report of an eventful year for the *Journal of Postgraduate Medicine'*, *Journal of Postgraduate Medicine* 51(1): 5–8; available at: *http://www.jpgmonline.com/article.asp?issn=0022-859;year=2005;volume=51;issue=1;spage=5;epage=8;aulast=Bavdekar.*

BBC (2000) 'Call to publish all gene data praised', 15 March; available at: *http://news.bbc.co.uk/1/hi/sci/tech/677815.stm.*

Berlin Declaration (2003) 'Berlin declaration on open access to knowledge in the sciences and humanities', 22 October; available at: *http://www.zim.mpg.de/openaccess-berlin/berlindeclaration.html.*

Berlin 3 Open Access (2005) 'Berlin 3 open access: progress in implementing the Berlin declaration on open access to knowledge in the sciences and humanities', 1 March; available at: *http://www.eprints.org/events/berlin3/.*

Berners-Lee, T. (1989, 1990) 'Information management: a proposal'; available at: *http://preprints.cern.ch/cgi-bin/setlink?base=preprint&categ=cern&id=dd-89-001.* Revised version at: *http://www.w3.org/History/1989/proposal.html.*

Berners-Lee, T., Hendler, J. and Lassila, O. (2001) 'The Semantic Web', *Scientific American* 284(5): 34–43; available at: *http://www.scientificamerican.com/article.cfm?articleID=00048144-10D2-1C70-84A9809EC588EF21&catID=2.*

Berners-Lee, T., De Roure, D., Harnad, S. and Shadbolt, N. (2005) 'Journal publishing and author self-archiving: Peaceful co-existence and fruitful collaboration'; available at: *http://eprints.ecs.soton.ac.uk/11160/.*

Bethesda Statement (2003) 'Bethesda statement on open access publishing', 20 June; available at: *http://www.earlham.edu/~peters/fos/bethesda.htm*.

Bird, S. and Simons, G. (2003) 'Building an open language archives community on the OAI foundation', *Library Hi Tech* 21(2): 210–18.

Blair, T. (2002) 'Science matters'; available at: *http://www.pm.gov.uk/output/Page1715.asp*.

Blume, M. (2005) 'Open access: what is it and can we get there from here?', presented at the Colloquium on Open Access Publishing in Particle Physics, CERN, 7–8 December; available at: *http://open-access.web.cern.ch/Open-Access/docs/20051207_BLUME.pdf*.

Blythe, E, and Chachra, V. (2005) 'The value proposition in institutional repositories', *Educause Review* 40(5): 76–7; available at: *http://www.educause.edu/ir/library/pdf/erm0559.pdf*.

Bollen, J., Van de Sompel, H., Smith, J. and Luce, R. (2005) 'Toward alternative metrics of journal impact: A comparison of download and citation data', *Information Processing and Management* 41(6): 1419–40; available at: *http://Arxiv.org/cs.DL/0503007*.

Bowman, C. M., Danzig, P. B., Hardy, D. R., Manber, U. and Schwartz, M. F. (1995) 'The Harvest Information Discovery and Access System', *Computer Networks and ISDN Systems* 28(1/2): 119–25.

Brody, T. (2003) 'Citebase Search: autonomous citation database for e-print archives; available at: *http://eprints.ecs.soton.ac.uk/10677/*.

Brody, T. (2004) 'Citation analysis in the open access world', *Interactive Media International* (September); available at: *http://eprints.ecs.soton.ac.uk/10000/*.

Brody, T. and Harnad, S. (2004) 'Using web statistics as a predictor of citation impact'; available at: *http://www.ecs.soton.ac.uk/~harnad/Temp/timcorr.doc*.

Brody, T., Harnad, S. and Carr, L. (2006) 'Earlier web usage statistics as predictors of later citation impact', *Journal of the American Association for Information Science and Technology* (in press).

Callan, P. and Cleary, C. (2005) 'Digital repositories at Queensland University of Technology'; available at: *http://eprints.qut.edu.au/archive/00000516/01/callan_latn_04.PDF*.

Carr, L. and Harnad S (2005) 'Keystroke economy: a study of the time and effort involved in self-archiving'; available at: *http://eprints.ecs.soton.ac.uk/10688/*.

Chan, D. (2005) 'IR preserves HKUST's research output', *Access* 55: 1–2.

Cockerill, M. (2004) 'How accessible is NHS-funded research to the general public and the NHS's own researchers?' available at: *http://www.biomedcentral.com/openaccess/inquiry/refersubmission.PDF*.

Coleman, J. (2005) 'NIH public access policy gives authors posting discretion up to 12 months', *Washington Fax*, 21 January. Now published as 'Research Policy Alert', at: *http://www.researchpolicyalert.com/*.

Crow, R. (2002) 'The case for institutional repositories: a SPARC position paper'; available at: *http://www.arl.org/sparc/IR/ir.html*.

Crow, R. (2004) *A Guide to Institutional Repository Software* (3rd edn); available at: *http://www.soros.org/openaccess//software/*.

Council of Australian University Librarians (2004) 'Statement on open access'; available at: *http://www.caul.edu.au/scholcomm/OpenAccess2004.doc*.

Crane, G. (2006) 'What do you do with a million books? *D-Lib Magazine* 12 (3); available at: *http://www.dlib.org/dlib/march06/crane/03crane.html*.

Davis, P. M., Ehling, T., Habicht, O., How, S., Saylor, J. M. and Walker, K. (2004) 'Report of the CUL Taskforce on Open Access Publishing'; available at: *http://dspace.library.cornell.edu/handle/1813/193*.

Day, M. (2004) 'Institutional repositories and research assessment'; available at: *http://www.rdn.ac.uk/projects/eprints-uk/docs/studies/rae/rae-study.pdf*.

Department of Education, Science and Training, Australian Research Information Infrastructure Committee (2004) 'Open access statement'; available at: *http://www.dest.gov.au/sectors/research_sector/policies_issues_reviews/key_issues/australian_research_information_infrastructure_committee/documents/open_access_pdf.htm*.

De Roure, D., Jennings, N. R. and Shadbolt, N. R. (2005) 'The semantic grid: past, present and future', *Proceedings of the IEEE*, 93(3): 669–81.

Diamond, Jr., A. M. (1986) 'What is a citation worth?' *Journal of Human Resources* 21: 200–15; available at: *http://www.garfield.library.upenn.edu/essays/v11p354y1988.pdf*.

Domingus, M. and Feijen, M. (2004) 'DARE use of Dublin Core metadata', Utrecht: Stichting SURF; available at: *http://www.surf.nl/download/DARE%20use%20of%20DC%20v.%202.0.pdf*.

Duke, M. (2003) 'Delivering OAI records as RSS: an IMesh toolkit module for facilitating sharing', *Ariadne* 37 (October); available at: *http://www.ariadne.ac.uk/issue37/duke/*.

Ehling, T. (2005) 'DPubS: the development of an open source publishing system', *Publishing Research Quarterly*, 20(4): 41–3.

Ensor, P. and Wilson, T. (1997) 'Public-access computer systems review: testing the promise', *The Journal of Electronic Publishing* 3(1); available at: *http://www.press.umich.edu/jep/03-01/pacs.html*.

European Organization for Nuclear Research (2005) 'A step forward for open access publishing'; available at: *http://press.web.cern.ch/press/PressReleases/Releases2005/PR18.05E.html*.

Feijen, M. and van der Kuil, A. (2005) 'A recipe for Cream of Science: special content recruitment for Dutch institutional repositories', *Ariadne* 45 (October); available at: *http://www.ariadne.ac.uk/issue45/vanderkuil/*.

Friend, F. J. (1998) 'Alternatives to commercial publishing for scholarly communication', *Serials* 11(2): 163.

Garfield, E. (1955) 'Citation indexes for science: a new dimension in documentation through association of ideas', *Science* 122 (3159): 108–11.

Garfield, E. (1973) 'Citation frequency as a measure of research activity and performance', *Current Contents* 5: 406–8; available at: *http://www.garfield.library.upenn.edu/essays/V1p406y1962–73.pdf*.

Garfield, E. (1988) 'Can researchers bank on citation analysis?' *Current Comments* 44: 354–63; available at: *http://www.garfield.library.upenn.edu/essays/v11p354y1988.pdf*.

Getz, M. (2005) *Open Scholarship and Research*; available at: *http://dspace.library.cornell.edu/bitstream/1813/1344/1/GetzOpenScholarship18May05.pdf*.

Gibson, I. (2005) Contribution to Westminster Hall debate, 15 December; available at: *http://www.publications.parliament.uk/pa/cm200506/cmhansrd/cm051215/hallindx/51215-x.htm*.

Grieg, M. and Nixon, W. (2005) 'DAEDALUS: delivering the Glasgow ePrints service', *Ariadne* 45 (October); available at: *http://www.ariadne.ac.uk/issue45/greig-nixon/*.

Group of Eight (2004) 'Statement on open access to scholarly information, 25 May'; available at: *http://www.go8.edu.au/news/2004/Go8%20Statement%20on%20open%20access%20to%20scholarly%20information%20May%20%85.pdf*.

Haider, J. (2005) 'The geographic distribution of open access journals'; available at: *http://dlist.sir.arizona.edu/939/*.

Hajjem, C., Harnad, S. and Gingras, Y. (2005) 'Ten-year cross-disciplinary comparison of the growth of open access and how it increases research citation impact', *IEEE Data Engineering Bulletin* 28(4): 39–47; available at: *http://eprints.ecs.soton.ac.uk/11688/*.

Hammond, T., Hannay, T. and Lund, B. (2004) 'The role of RSS in science publishing: syndication and annotation on the Web. *D-Lib Magazine* 10(12); available at: *http://www.dlib.org/dlib/december04/hammond/12hammond.html*.

Hannay, T. (2006) 'Open text mining interface'; available at: *http://blogs.nature.com/wp/nascent/2006/04/open_text_mining_interface_1.html*.

Harnad, S. (1979) 'Creative disagreement', *The Sciences* 19: 18–20; available at: *http://www.ecs.soton.ac.uk/~harnad/Temp/Kata/creative.disagreement.html*.

Harnad, S. (1990) 'Scholarly skywriting and the prepublication continuum of scientific inquiry', *Psychological Science* 1: 342–3. Reprinted in 1991: *Current Contents* 45 (November): 9–13.

Harnad, S. (1995) 'Universal FTP archives for esoteric science and scholarship: a subversive proposal', in: Okerson, A. and O'Donnell, J. (eds) *Scholarly Journals at the Crossroads: A Subversive Proposal for Electronic Publishing*. Washington, DC: Association of Research Libraries; available at: *http://www.arl.org/scomm/subversive/toc.html*.

Harnad, S. (1996) 'Implementing peer review on the Net: scientific quality control in scholarly electronic journals', in Peek, R. and Newby, G. (eds) *Scholarly Publishing: The Electronic Frontier*. Cambridge, MA: MIT Press, pp. 103–18; available at: *http://eprints.ecs.soton.ac.uk/2900/*.

Harnad, S. (1997) 'How to fast-forward serials to the inevitable and the optimal for scholars and scientists', *Serials Librarian* 30: 73–81; available at: *http://cogprints.org/1695/*.

Harnad, S. (2000) 'Zeno's paradox and the road to the optimal/inevitable'; available at: *http://www.ecs.soton.ac.uk/~harnad/Hypermail/Amsci/0820.html*.

Harnad, S. (2003a) 'Re: free access vs. open access'; *SPARC-IR*, 15 December; available at: *https://mx2.arl.org/Lists/SPARC-IR/Message/167.html*.

Harnad, S. (2003b) 'For whom the gate tolls?', in Law, D. and Andrews, J., (eds) *Digital Libraries: Policy Planning and Practice*. Aldershot: Ashgate *http://eprints.ecs.soton.ac.uk/8705/*.

Harnad, S. (2003c) 'Open access to peer-reviewed research through author/institution self archiving: maximising research impact by maximising online access', *Journal of Postgraduate Medicine* 49(4): 337–42; available at: *http://www.jpgmonline.com*.

Harnad, S. (2005a) 'Impact analysis in the open access era'; available at: h*ttp://openaccess.eprints.org/index.php?/archives/2005/10/10.html*.

Harnad, S. (2005b) 'Fast-forward on the green road to open access: the case against mixing up green and gold', *Ariadne* 42; available at: *http://www.ariadne.ac.uk/issue42/harnad/*.

Harnad, S. (2006) 'Publish or perish? Self-archive to flourish: the green route to open access', *ERCIM News* 64; available at: *http://eprints.ecs.soton.ac.uk/11715/*.

Harnad, S. and Brody, T. (2004) 'Comparing the impact of open access (OA) vs. non-OA articles in the same journals', *D-Lib Magazine* 10(6); available at: *www.dlib.org/dlib/june04/harnad/06harnad.html*.

Harnad, S., Carr, L., Brody, T. and Oppenheim, C. (2003) 'Mandated online RAE CVs linked to university eprint archives', *Ariadne* 35; available at: *http://eprints.ecs.soton.ac.uk/7725/*.

Harnad, S., Brody, T., Vallieres, F., Carr, L., Hitchcock, S., Yves, G., Charles, O., Stamerjohanns, H. and Hilf, E. (2004) 'The access/impact problem and the green and gold roads to open access', *Serials Review* 30(4): 310–14; Available at: *http://dx.doi.org/10.1016/j.serrev.2004.09.013*.

Heijne, M. (2005) 'DARE: digital academic repositories'; available at: *http://www.iatul.org/conference/wkshp_semnr/dublin/docs/PRE_CO NUL_IATUL_Heijne1_Nov05.pdf*.

Henneken, E. A., Kurtz, M. J., Eichhorn, G., Accomazzi, A., Grant, C., Thompson, D., and Murray, S. S. (2006) 'Effect of e-printing on citation rates', *Journal of Electronic Publishing* (submitted).

Hitchcock, S. (2005) 'The effect of open access and downloads ('hits') on citation impact: a bibliography of studies'; available at: *http://opcit.eprints.org/oacitation-biblio.html*.

Hitchcock, S., Bergmark, D., Brody, T., Gutteridge, C., Carr, L., Hall, W., Lagoze, C. and Harnad, S. (2002) 'Open citation linking: the way forward', *D-Lib Magazine* 8(10); available at: *http://www.dlib.org/dlib/october02/hitchcock/10hitchcock.html*.

Hitchcock, S., Woukeu, A., Brody, T., Carr, L., Hall, W. and Harnad, S. (2003) 'Evaluating Citebase, an open access Web-based citation-ranked research and impact discovery service', Technical Report ECSTR-IAM03-005, School of Electronics and Computer Science, University of Southampton; available at: http://eprints.ecs.soton.ac.uk/8204/.

Ho, A. K. and Bailey Jr, C. W. (2005) 'Open access webliography', *Reference Services Review* 33(3): 346–64; available at: *http://www.digital-scholarship.com/cwb/oaw.htm*.

House of Commons, Science and Technology Committee (2004a) 'Scientific Publications: Free for all? Tenth Report of Session 2003–04

Volume I: Report'; available at: *http://www.publications.parliament.uk/pa/cm200304/cmselect/cmsctech/399/39902.htm.*

House of Commons, Science and Technology Committee (2004b) 'Responses to the Committee's Tenth Report, Session 2003–4, Scientific Publications: Free for all?'; available at: *http://www.publications.parliament.uk/pa/cm200304/cmselect/cmsctech/1200/1200.pdf.*

International Federation of Library Associations (2004) 'IFLA statement on open access to scholarly literature and research documentation', 24 February; available at: *http://www.ifla.org/V/cdoc/open-access04.html.*

Jeevan, V. K. J. and Nair, S. S. (2004) 'A brief overview of metadata formats', *DESIDOC Bulletin of Information Technology* 24(4): 3–11.

Jennings, E. M. (1991) 'EJournal: An account of the first two years', *The Public-Access Computer Systems Review* 2(1): 91–110; available at: *http://info.lib.uh.edu/pr/v2/n1/jennings.2n1.*

John, T. J. (2004) 'How often do ICMR scientists publish in IJMR?' *Indian Journal of Medical Research* 119: 208.

Jones, R., Andrew, T., and MacColl, J. (2006) *The Institutional Repository*, Stanton Harcourt: Chandos.

Kahn, R. E. and Cerf, V. G. (1988) 'The digital library project – Volume 1: The world of knowbots'. Technical Report. Reston, VA: Corporation for National Research Initiatives.

Kean, G. (2005) *17th Annual Study on Journal Prices for Scientific and Medical Society Journals: 2004 Pricing Trends for US Society Journals and Ten Recommendations for Pricing 2005 Volumes.* Lawrence, KS: Allen Press; available at: *http://www.allenpress.com/static/newsletters/pdf/JP-2004-01.pdf.*

Kemp, R. (2005) 'Costs of running open source institutional repositories'; available at: *http://library.uncwil.edu/Faculty/kempr/listserv-summary-IR-open-source-costs.xls.*

Keystone Principles (1999) Available at: *http://www.arl.org/training/keystone.html.*

Kircz, J. (2005a) *Institutional Repositories, a New Platform in Higher Education and Research.* Amsterdam: KRA Publishing Research; available at: *http://www.surf.nl/en/publicaties/index2.php?oid=47.*

Kircz, J. (2005b) *'Making the Strategic Case for Institutional Repositories: a conference Report.* Amsterdam: KRA Publishing Research; available at: *http://www.surf.nl/en/download/report%20cni-jisc-surf-conference.pdf.*

Kleinberg, J. M. (1999) 'Hubs, authorities, and communities', *ACM Computing Surveys,* 31(4); available at: *http://www.cs.brown.edu/memex/ACM_HypertextTestbed/papers/10.html.*

Kurtz, M. J. (2004) 'Restrictive access policies cut readership of electronic research journal articles by a factor of two', presented at: National Policies on Open Access (OA) Provision for University Research Output: an International Meeting. Southampton, 19 February; available at: *http://opcit.eprints.org/feb19oa/kurtz.pdf*.

Kurtz, M. J., Eichhorn, G., Accomazzi, A., Grant, C. S., Demleitner, M. and Murray, S. S. (2004) 'Worldwide use and impact of the NASA Astrophysics Data System digital library', *Journal of the American Society for Information Science and Technology* 56(1): 36–45; available at: *http://cfa-www.harvard.edu/~kurtz/jasist1-abstract.html*.

Kurtz, M. J., Eichhorn, G., Accomazzi, A., Grant, C. S., Demleitner, M., Murray, S. S. (2005) 'The effect of use and access on citations', *Information Processing and Management* 41(6): 1395–402: doi:10.1016/j.ipm.2005.03.010; available at: *http://cfa-www.harvard.edu/~kurtz/kurtz-effect.pdf*.

Kyrillidou, M. and Young, M. (2005) 'ARL Statistics 2003–04; available at: *http://www.arl.org/stats/pubpdf/arlstat04.pdf*.

Lagoze, C. and Van de Sompel, H. (2003) 'The making of the Open Archives Initiative Protocol for Metadata Harvesting', *Library Hi Tech* 21(2): 118–128.

Landauer, T. K., Foltz, P. W., and Laham, D. (1998) 'Introduction to Latent Semantic Analysis', *Discourse Processes* 25: 259–84.

Lawrence, S. (2001a) 'Online or invisible?' *Nature* 411(6837): 521.

Lawrence, S. (2001b) 'Free online availability substantially increases a paper's impact' *Nature*, 31 May; available at: *http://www.nature.com/nature/debates/e-access/Articles/lawrence.html*.

Leiner, B. M., Cerf, V. G., Clark, D. D., Kahn, R. E., Kleinrock, L., Lynch, D. C., Postel, J., Roberts, L. G. and Wolff, S. (2003) 'A brief history of the Internet'; available at: *http://www.isoc.org/internet/history/brief.shtml*.

Liang, L. (2004) 'A guide to open content licences'; available at: *http://pzwart.wdka.hro.nl/mdr/research/lliang/open_content_guide*.

LISU (2004) 'Annual library statistics 2004'; available at: *http://www.lboro.ac.uk/departments/dils/lisu/pages/publications/als04.html*.

Liu, X., Maly, K., Zubair, M. and Nelson, M. L. (2001) 'Arc – An OAI service provider for Digital Library Federation', *D-Lib Magazine* 7(4); available at: *http://www.dlib.org/dlib/april01/liu/04liu.html*.

Liu, X., Maly, K., Nelson, M. L. and Zubair, M. (2005) 'Lessons learned with Arc, an OAI-PMH service provider', *Library Trends* 53(4): 590–603.

Lynch, C. (2003) 'Institutional repositories: essential infrastructure for scholarship in a digital age', *ARL Bimonthly Report* 226(2); available at: *http://www.arl.org/newsltr/226/ir.html*.

McRae-Spencer, D. M. and Shadbolt, N. R. (2006) 'Semiometrics: producing a compositional view of influence' (preprint available from the authors).

McVeigh, M. E. (2004) 'Open access journals in the ISI databases: analysis of impact factors and citation patterns'; available at: *http://scientific.thomson.com/media/presentrep/essayspdf/openaccesscitations2.pdf*.

Maly, K., Zubair, M. and Liu, X. (2001) 'Kepler: an OAI data/service provider for the individual', *D-Lib Magazine* 7(4); available at: *http://www.dlib.org/dlib/april01/maly/04maly.html*.

Mark Ware Consulting (2004) *Publishing and Library Learning Solutions (PALS): Pathfinder Research on Web-based Repositories.* Bristol: PALS; pp. 20–21; available at: *http://www.palsgroup.org.uk/*.

Martin, R. (2003) 'ePrints UK: developing a national e-prints archive', *Ariadne* 35; available at: *http://www.ariadne.ac.uk/issue35/martin/*.

Medeiros, N. (2004) 'A repository of our own: the E-LIS e-prints archive', *OCLC Systems and Services* 20(2): 58–60.

Messina (2004) 'Messina declaration', 5 November; available at: *http://www.aepic.it/conf/viewappendix.php?id=49&ap=1&cf=1*.

Moed, H. F. (2005a) *Citation Analysis in Research Evaluation.* NY: Springer.

Moed, H. F. (2005b) 'Statistical relationships between downloads and citations at the level of individual documents within a single journal', *Journal of the American Society for Information Science and Technology* 56(10): 1088–97: doi.wiley.com/10.1002/asi.20200.

National Health and Medical Research Council and Australian Vice Chancellors' Committee (1997) 'Statement and guidelines on research practice'; available at: *http://www.nhmrc.gov.au/funding/policy/researchprac.htm*.

National Institutes of Health (2005) 'Policy on enhancing public access to archived publications resulting from NIH-funded research'; available at: *http://publicaccess.nih.gov/*.

National Institutes of Health Public Access Working Group (2005) 'Minutes of meeting', 15 November; available at: *http://www.nlm.nih.gov/od/bor/PublicAccessWG-11-15-05.pdf*.

National Science Foundation (2006) 'US R&D continues to rebound in 2004', *US National Science Foundation InfoBrief*, January; available at: *http://www.nsf.gov/statistics/infbrief/nsf06306/*.

Newman, M. E. J. (2004) 'Coauthorship networks and patterns of scientific collaboration', *Proceedings of the National Academy of Sciences* 101 (suppl): 5200–5.

Nixon, W., Drysdale, L. and Gallacher, S. (2005) 'Search services at the University of Glasgow: PKP Harvester and Google'; available at: *https://dspace.gla.ac.uk/handle/1905/425*.

Odlyzko, A. M. (1995) 'Tragic loss or good riddance? The impending demise of traditional scholarly journals', *International Journal of Human-Computer Studies* 42: 71–122, and electronic *Journal of University Computer Science* pilot issue (1994); available at: *http://www.dtc.umn.edu/~odlyzko/doc/tragic.loss.long.pdf*.

Odlyzko, A. M. (1997a) 'The economics of electronic journals', *First Monday* 2(8); available at: *http://firstmonday.org/issues/issue2_8/odlyzko/*.

Odlyzko, A. M. (1997b) 'The slow evolution of electronic publishing', in Meadows, A. J. and Rowland, F. (eds) *Electronic Publishing '97: New Models and Opportunities*. Washington: ICCC Press; pp. 4–18; available at: *http://www.dtc.umn.edu/~odlyzko/doc/slow.evolution.pdf*.

Odlyzko, A. M. (1997c) 'Silicon dreams and silicon bricks: The continuing evolution of libraries', *Library Trends* 46(1): 152–67; available at: *http://www.dtc.umn.edu/~odlyzko/doc/silicon.dreams.pdf*. Revised version in Ekman, R. and Quandt, R. E. (eds) *Technology and Scholarly Communication*, University of California Press; pp. 380–93.

Odlyzko, A. M. (2002) 'The rapid evolution of scholarly communication', *Learned Publishing* 15(1): 7–19. Presented at the 2000 PEAK Conference, Ann Arbor, MI, 23–24 March; available at: *http://www.dtc.umn.edu/~odlyzko/doc/rapid.evolution.pdf*.

OECD (2004) 'Science, technology and innovation for the 21st century'. Meeting of the OECD Committee for Scientific and Technological Policy at Ministerial Level, Final Communiqué, 29–30 January; available at: *http://www.oecd.org/document/0,2340,en_2649_34487_25998799_1_1_1_1,00.html*.

Okerson, A. and O'Donnell, J. (eds) (1995) *Scholarly Journals at the Crossroads; A Subversive Proposal for Electronic Publishing*. Washington, DC: Association of Research Libraries.

Open Society Institute (2002) 'Budapest Open Access Initiative'; available at: *http://www.soros.org/openaccess/read.shtml*.

O'Reilly, T. (2005) 'What Is Web 2.0: Design patterns and business models for the next generation of software'; available at: *http://*

www.oreillynet.com/pub/a/oreilly/tim/news/2005/09/30/what-is-web-20.html.

Over, A., Maiworm, F. and Schelewsky, A. (2005) 'Publishing strategies in transformation?' Bonn: Deutsche Forschungsgemeinschaft; available at: *http://www.dfg.de/en/dfg_profile/facts_and_figures/statistical_reporting/open_access/*.

Page, L., Brin, S., Motwani, R., Winograd, T. (1999) 'The PageRank citation ranking: bringing order to the Web'; available at: *http://dbpubs.stanford.edu:8090/pub/1999–66*.

Perneger, T. V. (2004) 'Relation between online "hit counts" and subsequent citations: prospective study of research papers in the BMJ', *British Medical Journal* 329: 546–7; available at: *http://bmj.bmjjournals.com/cgi/content/full/329/7465/546*.

Peet, R. K. (2005) 'Crises and opportunities: A scientist's view of scholarly communication', presented at Scholarly Communications in a Digital World, A Convocation, 27–28 January, University of North Carolina; available at: *http://www.unc.edu/scholcomdig/whitepapers/peet.pdf*.

Pincock, S. (2005) 'Will open access work?' *The Scientist* 6(1); available at: *http://www.the-scientist.com/news/20051011/02*.

Pinfield, S., Gardner, M. and MacColl, J. (2002) 'Setting up an institutional e-print archive', *Ariadne* 31; available at: *http://www.ariadne.ac.uk/issue31/eprint-archives/intro.html*.

Powell, A., Day, M. and Cliff, P. (2003) 'Using simple Dublin Core to describe eprints', ePrints UK report; available at: *http://www.rdn.ac.uk/projects/eprints-uk/docs/simpledc-guidelines/*.

Poynder, R. (2005) 'Changing the paradigm'; available at: *http://poynder.blogspot.com/2006/01/changing-paradigm.html*.

Price, D. de Solla (1970) 'Citation measures of hard science, soft science, technology and non-science', in Nelson, C. E. and Pollack, D. K. (eds) *Communication among Scientists and Engineers*. Lexington, MA: Heath; pp. 1–12.

Pringle, J. (2004) 'Do open access journals have impact?' *Nature (Web Focus)*; available at: *http://www.nature.com/nature/focus/accessdebate/19.html*.

Probets, S. and Jenkins, C. (2006) 'Documentation for institutional repositories', *Learned Publishing* 19, 57–71.

Public Library of Science (2005) 'The first impact factor for *PloS Biology* – 13.9', press release; available at: *http://www.plos.org/news/announce_pbioif.html*.

Queensland University of Technology (2004) 'OA self-archiving policy'; available at: *http://www.eprints.org/openaccess/policysignup/fullinfo.php?inst=Queensland%20University%20of%20Technology*.

Rajashekar, T. B. (2004) 'Open-access initiatives in India', in Esanu, J. M. and Uhlir, P. F. (eds) *Proceedings of Open Access and the Public Domain in Digital Data and Information for Science*; Paris, 10–11 March. Washington, DC: The National Academies Press, pp. 154–7; available at: *ttp://darwin.nap.edu/books/0309091454/html/154.html.*

Rankin, J. (2005) 'Institutional repositories for the research sector: feasibility study'. Wellington: National Library of New Zealand; available at: *http://wiki.tertiary.govt.nz/~InstitutionalRepositories/Main/ReportOfFindings.*

RCUK (2006) 'Position statement on access to research outputs'; available at: *http://www.rcuk.ac.uk/access/index.asp.*

Richardson, S. and Powell, P. (2003) 'Exposing information resources for e-learning – harvesting and searching IMS metadata using the OAI Protocol for Metadata Harvesting and Z39.50', *Ariadne* 34; available at: *http://www.ariadne.ac.uk/issue34/powell/.*

Rightscom Ltd. (2005) 'JISC disciplinary differences report'; available at: *http://www.jisc.ac.uk/index.cfm?name=jcie_scg.*

Rowlands, I. and Nicholas, D. (2005) 'New journal publishing models: an international survey of senior authors'. London: Publishers Association and International Association of STM Publishers; pp. 1–75.

Royal Society (2005) 'Royal Society warns hasty "open access" moves may damage science'; available at: *http://www.royalsoc.ac.uk/news.asp?id=3881.*

Rusbridge, C. (1998) 'Towards the hybrid library', *D-Lib Magazine* 4(7); available at: *http://www.dlib.org/dlib/july98/rusbridge/07rusbridge.html.*

Sahu D. K. (2006) 'Open Access: boon for journals from India', in: *93rd Indian Science Congress*, Hyderabad, 3–7 January; available at: *http://openmed.nic.in/1255/.*

Sahu D. K., Gogtay, N. J. and Bavdekar, S. B. (2005) 'Effect of open access on citation rates for a small biomedical journal', in: *Fifth International Congress on Peer Review and Biomedical Publication*, Chicago, 16–18 September; available at: *http://openmed.nic.in/1174/.*

Sale, A. (1975) 'Pythagorean triads', Technical Report R75-2, School of Computing, University of Tasmania; available at: *http://eprints.comp.utas.edu.au:81/archive/00000144/.*

Sale, A. (2006a) 'The impact of mandatory policies on ETD acquisition. *D-Lib Magazine* 12(4); available at: *http://eprints.comp.utas.edu.au:81/archive/00000222/.*

Sale, A. (2006b) 'Comparison of IR content policies in Australia'. Preprint; available at: *http://eprints.comp.utas.edu.au:81/archive/00000264/.*

Sanderson, R., Young, J. and LeVan, R. (2005) 'SRW/U with OAI: expected and unexpected synergies', *D-Lib Magazine* 11(2); available at: *http://www.dlib.org/dlib/february05/sanderson/02 sanderson.html*.

Sargent, M. (2005) 'Ubiquitous open access', presented at Open Access, Open Archives and Open Source, 2005 NSCF Roundtable Forum, Sydney, 27 September; available at: *http://www.humanities.org.au/ Events/NSCF/NSCFRT19/NSCFRT19.htm*.

Satyanarayana, K. (2004) 'Time for "Publish in India" movement', *Indian Journal of Medical Research* 119: vii–ix.

Scottish Science Information Strategy Working Group (2004) 'Scottish declaration of open access', 11 October; available at: *http://scurl.ac.uk/WG/OATS/declaration.htm*.

Skupin, A. (2004) 'The world of geography: Visualizing a knowledge domain with cartographic means', *Proceedings of the National Academy of Sciences*, 101 (suppl. 1): 5274–8.

Smith, A. and Eysenck, M. (2002) 'The correlation between RAE ratings and citation counts in psychology', Technical Report, Psychology, Royal Holloway College, University of London, June; available at: *http://psyserver.pc.rhbnc.ac.uk/citations.pdf*.

Smith, J. W. T. (2003) 'The deconstructed journal revisited – a review of developments', *ICCC/IFIP Electronic Publishing Conference (ElPub03) – From Information to Knowledge*, Universidade do Minho, Guimarães, 25–28 June; available at: *http://library.kent.ac.uk/ library/papers/jwts/d-jrevisited.htm*.

Smith, R. (2002) 'Publishing research from developing countries', *Stat Med* 21: 2869–77.

Sponsler, E. and Van de Velde E. F. (2001) 'Eprints.org software: a review', *SPARC E-News*, August-September; available at: *http://www.arl.org/ sparc/pubs/enews/aug01.html#6*.

SQW (2003) 'Economic analysis of scientific research publishing'; available at: *http://www.wellcome.ac.uk/assets/wtd003182.pdf*.

SQW (2004) 'Costs and business models in scientific research publishing'; available at: *http://www.wellcome.ac.uk/assets/wtd003184.pdf*.

Standing Conference of National and University Libraries (1988) 'Annual Report 1987', SCONUL, pp. 7–8; 29–30.

Suber, P. (2004a) 'Praising progress, preserving precision', *SPARC Open Access Newsletter* 77; available at: *http://www.earlham.edu/~peters/ fos/newsletter/09-02-04.htm*.

Suber, P. (2004b) 'Creating an intellectual commons through open access'; available at: *http://dlc.dlib.indiana.edu/archive/00001246/ 01/suberrev052804.pdf*.

Suber, P. (2005a) 'The Open Content Alliance', *SPARC Open Access Newsletter* 91; available at: *http://www.earlham.edu/~peters/fos/newsletter/11-02-05.htm#oca.*

Suber, P. (2005b) 'Getting to 100%', *SPARC Open Access Newsletter* 84 available at: *http://www.earlham.edu/~peters/fos/newsletter/04-02-05.htm#oara.*

Suber, P. (2005c) 'Comments on the weakening of the NIH public-access policy', *SPARC Open Access Newsletter* 82; available at: *http://www.earlham.edu/~peters/fos/newsletter/02-02-05 htm#nih.*

Suber, P. (2005d) 'The final version of the NIH public-access policy', *SPARC Open Access Newsletter* 83; available at: *http://www.earlham.edu/~peters/fos/newsletter/03-02-05.htm#nih.*

Suber, P. (2005e) 'Strengthening the NIH policy', *SPARC Open Access Newsletter* 92; available at: *http://www.earlham.edu/~peters/fos/newsletter/12-02-05.htm#nih.*

Suber, P. (2005f) 'Publisher policies on NIH-funded authors, *SPARC Open Access Newsletter* 86; available at: *http://www.earlham.edu/~peters/fos/newsletter/06-02-05.htm#nih.*

Suber, P. (2005g) 'Update on publisher policies on NIH-funded authors', *SPARC Open Access Newsletter* 87; available at: *http://www.earlham.edu/~peters/fos/newsletter/07-02-05.htm#nih.*

Suber, P. (2005h) 'First fruits of the NIH public-access policy', *SPARC Open Access Newsletter* 88; available at: *http://www.earlham.edu/~peters/fos/newsletter/08-02-05.htm.*

Suber, P. (2005i) 'Update on first fruits of NIH policy', *SPARC Open Access Newsletter* 89; available at: *http://www.earlham.edu/~peters/fos/newsletter/09-02-05.htm.*

Suber, P. (2005j) 'OA is not just a technical question about how to finance journals or launch repositories', *Libre Accès à l'Information Scientifique et Technique,* 20 April; available at: *http://www.inist.fr/openaccess/article.php3?id_article=80.*

Suber, P. (2006a) 'Open access overview: focusing on open access to peer-reviewed research articles and their preprints'; available at: *http://www.earlham.edu/~peters/fos/overview.htm.*

Suber, P. (2006b) 'The US CURES Act would mandate OA', *SPARC Open Access Newsletter* 93; available at: *http://www.earlham.edu/~peters/fos/newsletter/01-02-06.htm#cures.*

Swan, A. (2005) 'Open access self-archiving: an introduction'; available at: *http://eprints.ecs.soton.ac.uk/11006/.*

Swan, A and Brown, S. (2004) 'Report of the JISC/OSI open access journal authors survey'; available at: *http://www.jisc.ac.uk/uploaded_documents/JISCOAreport1.pdf.*

Swan, A. and Brown, S. (2005) 'Open access self-archiving: an author study'; available at: *http://eprints.ecs.soton.ac.uk/10999/*.

Swan, A., Needham, P., Probets, S., Muir, A., O'Brien, A., Oppenheim, C., Hardy, R. and Rowland, F. (2005) 'Delivery, management and access model for e-prints and open access journals within further and higher education'. Bristol: JISC; pp. 39–40; available at: *http://cogprints.org/4122/*.

Tempe Principles (2000) available at: *http://www.arl.org/scomm/tempe.html*.

Tenopir, C. and King, D. W. (2000) *Towards Electronic Journals: Realities for Scientists, Librarians and Publishers*. Washington DC: Special Libraries Assoc.

UK Office of Science and Technology (2006) 'Science and innovation investment framework 2004–2014: next steps'; available at: *http://www.hm-treasury.gov.uk/media/1E1/5E/bud06_science_332.pdf*.

Universidade do Minho (2004) 'OA self-archiving policy'; available at: *http://www.eprints.org/openaccess/policysignup/fullinfo.php?inst=Universidade%20do%20Minho%2C%20Portugal*.

Universities UK (2005) 'Access to research publications: Universities UK position statement', 8 September; available at: *http://www.universitiesuk.ac.uk/mediareleases/show.asp?MR=431*.

University of California (2005a) 'Statement of principles on scholarly publishing'; available at: *http://academic-senate.berkeley.edu/news/statement_of_prin_for_web.pdf*.

University of California (2005b) 'Academic Council Special Committee on Scholarly Communication draft white papers'; available at: *http://www.universityofcalifornia.edu/senate/committees/scsc/reports.html*.

US Government House Appropriations Bill (2004) 'HR 5006 recommendations'; available at: *http://thomas.loc.gov/cgi-bin/cpquery/?&db_id=cp108&r_n=hr636.108&sel=TOC_338641&*.

van der Kuil, A. and Feijen, M. (2005) 'The dawning of the Dutch Network of Digital Academic Repositories (DARE): a shared experience', *Ariadne* 41; available at: *http://www.ariadne.ac.uk/issue41/vanderkuil/*.

Van de Sompel, H. and Lagoze, C. (2000) 'The Santa Fe Convention of the Open Archives Initiative', *D-Lib Magazine* 6(2); available at: *http://www.dlib.org/dlib/february00/vandesompel-oai/02vandesompel-oai.html*.

Van de Sompel, H., Nelson, M. L., Lagoze, C. and Warner, S. (2004) 'Resource harvesting within the OAI-PMH framework', *D-Lib*

Magazine 10(12); available at: *http://www.dlib.org/dlib/december04/vandesompel/12vandesompel.html.*

Van de Sompel, H., Bekaert, J., Liu, X., Balakireva, L. and Schwander, T. (2005) 'aDORe: a modular, standards-based digital object repository', *The Computer Journal* 48(5): 514–35. Preprint available at: *http://arxiv.org/ftp/cs/papers/0502/0502028.pdf.*

van der Vaart, L. (2004) 'DARE, the voyage begun, Eleftheria'; available at: *http://www.surf.nl/publicaties/index2.php?oid=152.*

van Oosterom, F. (2005) 'Vooruitzien door terug te kijken', *SURF Web Cahier* 47; available at: *http://www.surf.nl/cahier/Pages/47/47focus.html.*

van Westrienen, G. and Lynch, C. (2005) 'Academic institutional repositories. Deployment status in 13 nations as of mid 2005', *D-Lib Magazine* 11(9); available at: *http://www.dlib.org/dlib/september05/westrienen/09westrienen.html.*

Vogel, G. and Enserink, M. (2005) 'Europe steps into the open with plans for electronic archives', *Science* 308(5722): 623.

Waaijers, L. (2005) 'From libraries to "libratories"', *First Monday* 10(12); available at: *http://www.firstmonday.org/issues/issue10_12/waaijers/.*

Walport, M. (2004) 'Open access: a funder's perspective', presented to The Foundation for Science and Technology, 23 June; available at: *http://www.foundation.org.uk/801/230604_Walport.pdf.*

Waltham, M. (2005) 'Learned society open access business models'; available at: *http://www.marywaltham.com/JISCReport.pdf* or *http://www.jisc.ac.uk/uploaded_documents/Learned%20Society%20Open%20Access%20Business%20Models.doc.*

Warner, S. (2004) 'Overlay journals breakout session', 3rd CERN Workshop on Innovations in Scholarly Communication (OAI3) – Implementing the Benefits of OAI, CERN, Geneva, 12–14 February; available at: *http://indico.cern.ch/getFile.py/access?resId=1&materialId=0&contribId=s19t1&sessionId=8&subContId=0&confId=a035925.*

Warner, S. (2005) 'The arXiv: 14 years of open access scientific communication', Symposium on Free Culture and the Digital Library, Emory University, Atlanta, 14 October; available at: *http://www.cs.cornell.edu/people/simeon/talks/Emory_2005-10-14/arXiv_history_talk.pdf.*

Washington DC (2004) 'Washington DC principles for free access to science', 16 March; available at: *http://www.dcprinciples.org/statement.htm.*

Wellcome Trust (2005a) 'Wellcome Trust position statement in support of open and unrestricted access to published research'; available at: *http://www.wellcome.ac.uk/doc_WTD002766.html.*

Wellcome Trust (2005b) 'Conditions under which a grant is awarded'; available at: *http://www.wellcome.ac.uk/assets/wtx026668.pdf*.

Willinsky, J. (2005) *The Access Principle: The Case for Open Access to Research and Scholarship*. Cambridge: MIT Publishing.

Wolfram, D. (2003) *Applied Informetrics for Information Retrieval Research*. Westport, CT: Libraries Unlimited.

Woodward, H. and Conyers, A. (2005) 'Analysis of UK academic library journal usage', presented to the XXIV Annual Charleston Conference on Book and Serial Acquisition, Charleston, SC, 2–5 November; available at: *http://www.katina.info/conference/2005%20Presentations.htm*.

World Bank (2004) 'Total GDP 2004'; available at: *http://siteresources.worldbank.org/DATASTATISTICS/Resources/GDP.pdf*.

World Summit on the Information Society (2003a) 'Declaration of principles', 12 December; available at: *http://www.itu.int/wsis/documents/doc_single-en-1161.asp*.

World Summit on the Information Society (2003b) 'Plan of action', 12 December; available at: *http://www.itu.int/wsis/documents/doc_single-en-1160.asp*.

Xiang, X. and Lease Morgan, E. (2005) 'Exploiting 'light-weight' protocols and open source tools to implement digital library collections and services', *D-Lib Magazine* 11(10); available at: *http://www.dlib.org/dlib/october05/morgan/10morgan.html*.

Index

Printed in the United Kingdom
by Lightning Source UK Ltd.
117887UK00001B/175-183